Refactoring Directions

CW00539213

Pattern	To	Towards	Away
Adapter	Extract Adapter (258), Unify Interfaces with Adapter (247)	Unify Interfaces with Adapter (247)	
Builder	Encapsulate Composite with Builder (96)		
Collecting Parameter	Move Accumulation to Collecting Parameter (313)		
Command	Replace Conditional Dispatcher with Command (191)	Replace Conditional Dispatcher with Command (191)	
Composed Method	Compose Method (123)		
Composite	Replace One/Many Distinctions with Composite (224), Extract Composite (214), Replace Implicit Tree with Composite (178)		Encapsulate Composite with Builder (96)
Creation Method	Replace Constructors with Creation Methods (57)		
Decorator	Move Embellishment to Decorator (144)	Move Embellishment to Decorator (144)	
Factory	Move Creation Knowledge to Factory (68), Encapsulate Classes with Factory (80)		
Factory Method	Introduce Polymorphic Creation with Factory Method (88)		
Interpreter	Replace Implicit Language with Interpreter (269)		
Iterator			Move Accumulation to Visitor (320)
Null Object	Introduce Null Object (301)		
Observer	Replace Hard-Coded Notifications with Observer (236)	Replace Hard-Coded Notifications with Observer (236)	
Singleton	Limit Instantiation with Singleton (296)		Inline Singleton (114)
State	Replace State-Altering Conditionals with State (166)	Replace State-Altering Conditionals with State (166)	
Strategy	Replace Conditional Logic with Strategy (129)	Replace Conditional Logic with Strategy (129)	
Template Method	Form Template Method (205)		
Visitor	Move Accumulation to Visitor (320)	Move Accumulation to Visitor (320)	

Advance Praise for *Refactoring to Patterns*

"For refactoring to be valuable it must be going somewhere, not just an abstract intellectual exercise. Patterns document program structures with known good properties. Put the two together and you have *Refactoring to Patterns*. If you want your refactorings to go somewhere, I suggest you read and apply *Refactoring to Patterns*."
—Kent Beck, Director, Three Rivers Institute

"In the GoF book we claimed that design patterns are targets for refactorings. This book finally shows that we didn't lie. By doing so, Joshua's book will deepen your understanding of both refactoring and design patterns."
—Erich Gamma, Eclipse Java Development Tools lead, IBM

"Now the connection between software patterns and agile development is finally told."
—Ward Cunningham

"Refactoring to patterns is a revolutionary approach to applying patterns that combines the top-down utility of design patterns with the bottom-up discovery of iterative development and continuous refactoring. Any serious software developer should be using this approach to discover new opportunities to use patterns to improve their code."
—Bobby Woolf, Consulting I/T Specialist, IBM Software Services for WebSphere, and coauthor of *Enterprise Integration Patterns* (Addison-Wesley) and *The Design Patterns Smalltalk Companion* (Addison-Wesley).

"With this unique catalog of design-level refactorings Joshua Kerievsky has given refactoring an entirely new dimension. *Refactoring to Patterns* shows developers how to make design-level improvements that simplify everyday work. This book is an invaluable reference for the refactoring practitioner."
—Sven Gorts

"This book refactors and restructures GoF, and much more. *Refactoring to Patterns* takes a subject that has been presented as static and rigid and makes it dynamic and flexible, converting it into a human process with experiments, mistakes, and corrections so you understand that good designs do not occur by turning some series of cranks—they evolve through struggle and reflection.

"Kerievsky has also restructured the presentation to make it far clearer and easier to assimilate. Indeed, he has solved a number of the organization problems that I have struggled with in *Thinking in Patterns*. This book is a clear introduction and combination of the disciplines of testing, refactoring, and patterns, and it is filled with easy reading, good sense, and great insights."

—Bruce Eckel, President of Mindview, Inc., and author of *Thinking in Java/Thinking in* C++ (Prentice Hall)

"The first time I met Joshua, I was struck by the depth of his passion for understanding, applying, and teaching design patterns. Great teachers care deeply about their subject and how to share it. I think Joshua is a great teacher—and developer—and that we can all benefit from his insight.

—Craig Larman, Chief Scientist, Valtech, and author of *Applying UML and Patterns, Second Edition* (Prentice Hall) and *Agile and Iterative Development* (Addison-Wesley)

"*Refactoring to Patterns* is important not only because it provides step-by-step instructions on how to improve your code through the methodical introduction of appropriate patterns, but more so because it teaches the principles that underlie the design patterns implemented. This book should be useful for novice and expert designers alike. This is a great book."

—Kyle Brown, IBM Software Services for WebSphere, and author of *Enterprise Java™ Programming with IBM® WebSphere®, Second Edition* (Addison-Wesley)

"Mastering a trade means more than just having the right tools—you also need to use them effectively. *Refactoring to Patterns* explains how to wield industrial-strength design tools with the skills of an artist."

—Russ Rufer, Silicon Valley Patterns Group

"Josh uses patterns to guide the small steps of refactoring toward larger goals and uses refactoring to introduce patterns into your code as it evolves. You'll learn how to make large improvements to existing code incrementally, rather than trying to force-fit a prefabricated solution. As the code changes you'll go beyond seeing better designs—you'll experience them."

—Phil Goodwin, Silicon Valley Patterns Group

Refactoring to Patterns

The Addison-Wesley Signature Series

The Addison-Wesley Signature Series provides readers with practical and authoritative information on the latest trends in modern technology for computer professionals. The series is based on one simple premise: great books come from great authors. Books in the series are personally chosen by expert advisors, world-class authors in their own right. These experts are proud to put their signatures on the covers, and their signatures ensure that these thought leaders have worked closely with authors to define topic coverage, book scope, critical content, and overall uniqueness. The expert signatures also symbolize a promise to our readers: you are reading a future classic.

THE ADDISON–WESLEY SIGNATURE SERIES
SIGNERS: KENT BECK AND MARTIN FOWLER

Kent Beck has pioneered people-oriented technologies like JUnit, Extreme Programming, and patterns for software development. Kent is interested in helping teams do well by doing good — finding a style of software development that simultaneously satisfies economic, aesthetic, emotional, and practical constraints. His books focus on touching the lives of the creators and users of software.

Martin Fowler has been a pioneer of object technology in enterprise applications. His central concern is how to design software well. He focuses on getting to the heart of how to build enterprise software that will last well into the future. He is interested in looking behind the specifics of technologies to the patterns, practices, and principles that last for many years; these books should be usable a decade from now. Martin's criterion is that these are books he wished he could write.

TITLES IN THE SERIES

Test-Driven Development: By Example
Kent Beck, ISBN: 0321146530

User Stories Applied: For Agile Software Development
Mike Cohn, ISBN: 0321205685

Patterns of Enterprise Application Architecture
Martin Fowler, ISBN: 0321127420

Beyond Software Architecture: Creating and Sustaining Winning Solutions
Luke Hohmann, ISBN: 0201775948

Enterprise Integration Patterns: Designing, Building, and Deploying Messaging Solutions
Gregor Hohpe and Bobby Woolf, ISBN: 0321200683

Refactoring to Patterns

Joshua Kerievsky

✦ Addison-Wesley

Boston • San Francisco • New York • Toronto • Montreal
London • Munich • Paris • Madrid
Capetown • Sydney • Tokyo • Singapore • Mexico City

Figures on pages 26 and 28 (top figure) of this book were previously published on pages 108 and 164 of *Design Patterns: Elements of Reusable Object-Oriented Software* by Erich Gamma, Richard Helm, Ralph Johnson, and John M. Vlissides. Copyright 1995 by Pearson Education, Inc. Republished by permission of Pearson Education, Inc., Publishing as Pearson Addison-Wesley.

Excerpted text on pages 3 and 4 was previously published in *Pattern Languages of Program Design 3* by Robert Martin, Dirk Riehle, and Frank Buschmann (Addison-Wesley, 1998). Republished by permission. All rights reserved.

The publisher offers discounts on this book when ordered in quantity for bulk purchases and special sales. For more information, please contact:

U.S. Corporate and Government Sales
(800) 382-3419
corpsales@pearsontechgroup.com

For sales outside of the U.S., please contact:

International Sales
(317) 581-3793
international@pearsontechgroup.com

Visit Addison-Wesley on the Web: www.awprofessional.com

Library of Congress Cataloging-in-Publication Data

Kerievsky, Joshua.
    Refactoring to patterns / Joshua Kerievsky.
        p.   cm. — (Addison-Wesley signature series)
    ISBN 0-321-21335-1
    1. Software refactoring. 2. Software patterns. I. Title. II. Series.

    QA76.76.R42K47 2004
    005.1'6—dc22   2004012166

ISBN: 0-321-21335-1
Text printed in the United States on recycled paper at Courier in Westford, Massachusetts.
4 5 6 7 8 9 10 11—CRW—09080706
Fourth printing, July 2006

For Tracy, Sasha, and Sophia

Contents

Foreword

Design Patterns described several ways to use patterns. Some people plan for patterns long before they write any code, while other people add a pattern after a lot of code has been written. The second way of using patterns is refactoring, because you are changing the design of the system without adding features or changing the external behavior. Some people put a pattern into a program because they think the pattern will make the program easier to change, but other people do it as a way to simplify the current design. If code has been written, then both of these are refactorings, because the first is refactoring to make a change easier, while the second is refactoring to clean up after a change.

Although a pattern is something you can see in a program, a pattern is also a program transformation. Each pattern can be explained by showing a program before the pattern was used and then afterwards. This is another way that patterns can be thought of as refactorings.

Unfortunately, many readers missed the connection between design patterns and refactoring. They thought of patterns as entirely related to design, not to code. I suppose that the name might have misled them, but the fact that the book was mostly C++ code should have indicated that patterns are about code as well as design, and adding a pattern usually requires changing code.

Joshua Kerievsky got the connection right away. I met him soon after he started the Design Patterns Study Group of New York City. He introduced the idea of a "before and after" study of a pattern, an example that shows the effect of a pattern on a system. Before he left town, his infectious enthusiasm had led to a group of over sixty people meeting several times a month. He started teaching patterns courses to companies and has taught them on-site, at his own location, and on the Internet. He has even taught other people how to teach them.

Joshua has gone on to become an XP practitioner and teacher as well. So, it is perfectly fitting that he has written a book that shows the connection between design patterns and refactoring, one of the core XP practices. Refactoring is not orthogonal to patterns—it is intimately related. Not all of the patterns that he talks about are from *Design Patterns*, but they all are in the style of *Design Patterns*. Joshua's book shows how patterns can help you design without causing you to create an up-front design.

If you practice what this book teaches, you will improve both your ability to create good designs and your ability to think about them.

—Ralph Johnson

Foreword

For several years now, I've been involved with advocating agile methods in general and extreme programming in particular. When I do, people often question how this fits in with my long-running interest in design patterns. Indeed, I've heard people claim that by encouraging refactoring and evolutionary design, I'm recanting what I've previously written about analysis and design patterns.

Yet all it takes is a quick look at people to realize that this view is flawed. Look at the leading members of the patterns community and at the leading members of the agile and XP communities, and you see a huge intersection. The truth is that patterns and evolutionary design have had a close relationship since their very beginnings.

Josh Kerievsky has been at the heart of this overlap. I first met him when he organized the successful patterns study groups in New York City. These groups did a collaborative study of the growing literature on design patterns. I quickly learned that Josh's understanding of design patterns was second to none, and I gained a lot of insight into those patterns by listening to him. Josh adopted refactoring early and was an extremely helpful reviewer on my book. As such it was no surprise to me that he also was a pioneer of extreme programming. His paper on patterns and extreme programming at the first XP conference is one of my favorites.

So if anyone is perfectly suited to write about the interplay of patterns and refactoring, Josh is. It's territory I explored a little bit in *Refactoring*, but I didn't take it too far because I wanted to concentrate on the basic refactorings. This book greatly expands that area, discussing in good detail how to evolve most of the popular patterns used in *Design Patterns* [DP], showing that they need not be designed into a system up front but can be evolved to as a system grows.

As well as the specific knowledge about these refactorings that you can gain from studying them, this book also tells you more about patterns and refactoring in general. Many people have said they find a refactoring approach to be a

better way of learning about patterns because they see in gradual stages the interplay of problem and solution. These refactorings also reinforce the critical fact that refactoring is all about making large changes in tiny steps.

So I'm pleased to be able to present this book to you. I've spent a long time cajoling Josh to write a book and then working with him on this one. I'm delighted with the result, and I think you will be too.

—Martin Fowler

Preface

What Is This Book About?

This book is about the marriage of refactoring—the process of improving the design of existing code—with patterns, the classic solutions to recurring design problems. *Refactoring to Patterns* suggests that using patterns to improve an existing design is better than using patterns early in a new design. This is true whether code is years old or minutes old. We improve designs with patterns by applying sequences of low-level design transformations, known as refactorings.

What Are the Goals of This Book?

This book was written to help you:

- Understand how to combine refactoring and patterns
- Improve the design of existing code with pattern-directed refactorings
- Identify areas of code in need of pattern-directed refactorings
- Learn why using patterns to improve existing code is better than using patterns early in a new design

To achieve these goals, this book includes the following features:

- A catalog of 27 refactorings
- Examples based on real-world code, not the toy stuff
- Pattern descriptions, including real-world pattern examples

- A collection of smells (i.e., problems) that indicate the need for pattern-directed refactorings

- Examples of different ways to implement the same pattern

- Advice for when to refactor to, towards, or away from patterns

To help individuals or groups learn the 27 refactorings in the book, you'll find a suggested study sequence on the inside back cover of the book. For the latest information about this book, please go to its home on the Web at http://industriallogic.com/xp/refactoring/.

Who Should Read This Book?

This book is for object-oriented programmers engaged in or interested in improving the design of existing code. Many of these programmers use patterns and/or practice refactoring but have never implemented patterns by refactoring; others know little about refactoring and patterns and would like to learn more.

This book is useful for both greenfield development, in which you are writing a new system or feature from scratch, and legacy development, in which you are mostly maintaining a legacy system.

What Background Do You Need?

This book assumes you are familiar with design concepts like tight coupling and loose coupling as well as object-oriented concepts like inheritance, polymorphism, encapsulation, composition, interfaces, abstract and concrete classes, abstract and static methods, and so forth.

I use Java examples in this book. I find that Java tends to be easy for most object-oriented programmers to read. I've gone out of my way to not use fancy Java features, so whether you code in C++, C#, Visual Basic .NET, Python, Ruby, Smalltalk, or some other object-oriented language, you ought to be able to understand the Java code in this book.

This book is closely tied to Martin Fowler's classic book *Refactoring* [F]. It contains references to low-level refactorings, such as:

- *Extract Method*

- *Extract Interface*

- *Extract Superclass*

- *Extract Subclass*

- *Pull Up Method*
- *Move Method*
- *Rename Method*

Refactoring also contains references to more sophisticated refactorings, such as:

- *Replace Inheritance with Delegation*
- *Replace Conditional with Polymorphism*
- *Replace Type Code with Subclasses*

To understand the pattern-directed refactorings in this book, you don't need to know every refactoring listed above. Instead, you can follow the example code that illustrates how the listed refactorings are implemented. However, if you want to get the most out of this book, I do recommend that you have *Refactoring* close by your side. It's an invaluable refactoring resource, as well as a useful aid for understanding this book.

The patterns I write about come from the classic book *Design Patterns* [DP], as well as from authors such as Kent Beck, Bobby Woolf, and myself. These are patterns that my colleagues and I have refactored to, towards, or away from on real-world projects. By learning the art of pattern-directed refactorings, you'll understand how to refactor to, towards, or away from patterns not mentioned in this book.

You don't need expert knowledge of these patterns to read this book, though some knowledge of patterns is useful. To help you understand the patterns I've written about, this book includes brief pattern summaries, UML sketches of patterns, and many example implementations of patterns. To get a more detailed understanding of the patterns, I recommend that you study this book in conjunction with the patterns literature I reference.

This book uses UML 2.0 diagrams. If you don't know UML very well, you're in good company. I know the basics. While writing this book, I kept the third edition of Fowler's *UML Distilled* [Fowler, UD] close by my side and referred to it often.

How to Use This Book

To get a high-level understanding of the refactorings in this book, you can begin by studying each refactoring's summary (see Format of the Refactorings, 47), as well as its Benefits and Liabilities box, which appears at the end of each refactoring's Motivation section.

To get a deeper understanding of the refactorings, you'll want to study every part of a refactoring, with the exception of the Mechanics section. The Mechanics section is special. It's intended to help you implement a refactoring by suggesting what low-level refactorings to follow. To understand a refactoring in this book, you don't have to read the Mechanics section. You're more likely to use the Mechanics section as a reference when you're actually refactoring.

The coding smells described in this book and in *Refactoring* [F] provide a useful way to identify a design problem and find associated refactorings to help fix the problem. You can also scan the alphabetized listing of refactorings (on the inside covers of this book and *Refactoring*) to find a refactoring that can help improve a design.

This book documents the refactorings that take a design either to, towards, or away from a pattern. To help you figure out what direction to go in, you'll find a section on this subject (called Refactoring to, towards, and away from Patterns, 29) as well as a table (listed on the inside front cover) that shows each pattern name and the refactorings you can apply to take a design to, towards, or away from the pattern.

The History of This Book

I began writing this book sometime in 1999. At the time, there were several forces driving me to write about patterns, refactoring, and extreme programming (XP) [Beck, XP]. First, I was surprised that patterns had not been mentioned in the XP literature. This led me to write a paper called "Patterns & XP" [Kerievsky, PXP] in which I publicly discussed the subject and offered some suggestions on how to integrate these two great contributions to our field.

Second, I knew that Martin Fowler had included only a few refactorings to patterns in *Refactoring* [F], and he clearly stated that he hoped someone would write more. That seemed like a worthwhile goal.

Finally, I noticed that people in The Design Patterns Workshop, a class that my colleagues and I teach, needed more help in figuring out when to actually apply a pattern to a design. It's one thing to learn what a pattern is and an altogether different thing to really understand when and how to apply the pattern. I thought that these students needed to study real-world examples of cases where applying a pattern to a design makes sense, and thus I began compiling a catalog of such examples.

As soon as I began writing this book, I followed Bruce Eckel's lead and placed my rather rough contents on the Web to obtain feedback. The Web is indeed a beautiful thing. Many folks responded with suggestions, encouragement, and appreciation.

As my writings and ideas matured, I began presenting the subject of *Refactoring to Patterns* in conference tutorials and during Industrial Logic's intensive patterns and refactoring workshops. This led to more suggestions for improvement and many ideas on what programmers needed to understand this subject.

Gradually I came to see that patterns are best viewed in the light of refactoring and that they are destinations best reached by applying sequences of low-level refactorings.

When my writings began to resemble a book, rather than a long paper, I was fortunate enough to have many experienced practitioners review my work and offer suggestions for improvement. You can read more about these folks in the Acknowledgments section.

Standing on the Shoulders of Giants

In the summer of 1995, I walked into a bookstore, encountered the book *Design Patterns* [DP] for the first time, and fell in love with patterns. I wish to thank the authors, Erich Gamma, Richard Helm (whom I still haven't met), Ralph Johnson, and John Vlissides for writing such an excellent piece of literature. The wisdom you shared in your book has helped me become a much better software designer.

Somewhere around 1996, before he became famous, I met Martin Fowler at a patterns conference. It was to be the beginning of a long friendship. I doubt whether I would have written this book if Martin (and his colleagues, Kent Beck, William Opdyke, John Brant, and Don Roberts) had not written the classic book *Refactoring* [F]. Like *Design Patterns*, *Refactoring* utterly changed the way I approach software design.

My writings in this book could only have happened because of the hard work of the authors of *Design Patterns* and *Refactoring*. I can't thank you all enough for your great books.

Acknowledgments

I am most fortunate to have a wife who has lovingly supported me during the writing of this book. Tracy, you are the greatest. I'm looking forward to spending many more decades together.

Our two daughters, Sasha and Sophia, were born during the time I wrote this book. I thank both of them for their patience while their dad wrote and wrote and wrote.

In the 1970s, Bruce Kerievsky, my father, brought my brother and me to work so we could draw pictures of the enormous computers in the refrigerated rooms. He also brought us huge green and white computer listings with our names printed in giant letters. His work inspired me to get into this great field— thank you.

Now that I'm past the gushy thanks to my family, I can focus on the technical acknowledgments. And there are many.

John Brant made the largest contribution to this book. He and his colleague Don Roberts are two of the world's most knowledgeable refactoring people. John, who reviewed four versions of the evolving manuscript, contributed many great ideas and encouraged me to remove many not-so-great ideas. His insights pervade the mechanics for nearly every refactoring in the catalog. Don, who was busy on other projects, could not contribute as much, yet he reviewed John's feedback, and I thank him for that. I also thank both of them for writing this book's Afterword.

Martin Fowler helped with numerous reviews and suggestions, including how to simplify sketches and clarify technical discussions. He helped fix some of my broken UML diagrams and update them to reflect UML 2.0. I'm honored that Martin chose this book for his signature series and grateful for the Foreword he wrote for the book.

Sven Gorts downloaded many versions of the evolving manuscript and sent me a flood of thoughtful feedback. He contributed many useful ideas that have improved this book's writings, diagrams, and code.

Somik Raha helped a great deal in improving the content of this book. His open source htmlparser project, which he started before he had thoroughly learned patterns, turned out to be a gold mine of code that needed refactorings to patterns. Somik and I paired on many of these refactorings, and I can't thank him enough for his support, encouragement, and suggestions.

Eric Evans, the author of *Domain-Driven Design*, provided feedback on early versions of this book. While each of us was writing our books, we would meet at coffee shops in and around San Francisco. Then we would write, exchange laptops, and comment on each other's writings. Thanks for the feedback and companionship, Eric.

Chris Lopez, who is a member of the Silicon Valley Patterns Group (SVPG), provided a great deal of highly detailed and useful feedback on my writings, diagrams, and code. While other members of the SVPG also deserve thanks, Chris went above and beyond the call of duty in his reviews of this book.

Russ Rufer, Tracy Bialik, and the rest of the programmers in the SVPG (including Ted Young, Phil Goodwin, Alan Harriman, Charlie Toland, Bob Evans, John Brewer, Jeff Miller, David Vydra, David W. Smith, Patrick Manion, John Wu, Debbie Utley, Carol Thistlethwaite, Ken Scott-Hlebek, Summer Misherghi, and Siqing Zhang) spent numerous sessions reviewing early and more mature versions of this book. They contributed a good deal of wisdom, which helped me realize what needed to be clarified, extended, or removed. Particular thanks goes to Russ for scheduling so many meetings on the book and to Jeff for recording the group's thoughts.

Ralph Johnson and his Patterns Reading Group at the University of Illinois at Urbana-Champaign provided incredibly useful feedback on the early version of the manuscript. This group sent me feedback on MP3 files. I spent lots of time listening to their recordings and acting on their advice. I'm particularly thankful to Ralph, Brian Foote, Joseph Yoder, and Brian Marick for their thoughts and suggestions. I know there are others in the group—yet I don't have your names; I apologize and offer my thanks. Thanks also to Ralph for writing a Foreword to this book.

John Vlissides provided extremely useful feedback on several occasions, including many detailed notes on the first draft of the manuscript. He was enormously encouraging of my work, which helped a great deal.

Erich Gamma made some excellent suggestions for the introductory material in this book, as well as the refactorings.

Kent Beck reviewed several refactorings in this book and contributed a sidebar for *Inline Singleton (114)*. I thank him for pair-programming with me on the *State* pattern refactoring during the XP2002 conference in Alghero, Italy.

Ward Cunningham contributed a sidebar for *Inline Singleton (114)* and provided some helpful, last-minute advice on where to locate a chapter in the introductory material.

Dirk Baumer, the lead programmer for producing automated refactorings in Eclipse, and Dmitry Lomov, the lead programmer for producing automated refactorings in IntelliJ, both contributed valuable insights and suggestions for many of the refactorings in this book.

Kyle Brown reviewed an early first draft of the manuscript and provided some excellent insights.

Ken Shirriff and John Tangney provided extensive, thoughtful feedback on versions of the manuscript.

Ken Thomases pointed out a critical error in an older version of the mechanics for *Replace Type Code with Class (286)*.

Robert Hirshfeld helped clarify mechanics in a very early version of *Move Embellishment to Decorator (144)*.

Ron Jeffries helped me articulate this book's message by engaging in countless arguments on extremeprogramming@yahoogroups.com. He also helped me refactor my language in a tricky section of the introductory material for this book.

Dmitri Kerievsky helped me clarify the language in this Preface.

The following folks also provided useful feedback along the way: Gunjan Doshi, Jeff Grigg, Kaoru Hosokawa, Don Hinton, Andrew Swan, Erik Meade, Craig Demyanovich, Dave Hoover, Rob Mee, Benny Sadeh, and Alex Chaffee.

I'm also grateful to the feedback of folks who discussed refactorings in this book on the refactoring@yahoogroups.com list.

I'd like to thank the students of Industrial Logic's classes, The Design Patterns Workshop and The Testing & Refactoring Workshop, who provided feedback on the refactorings in this book. Many of you helped me learn what needed to be clarified or added to this book.

A special thanks goes to my editor, Paul Petralia, and his team (Lisa Iarkowski, Faye Gemmellaro, John Fuller, Kim Arney Mulcahy, Chrysta Meadowbrooke, Rebecca Rider, and Richard Evans). When other publishers were competing to publish this book, Paul fought hard to make sure Addison-Wesley won the publishing rights. I'm very grateful that happened. I've spent years reading great Addison-Wesley books, and it's now an honor to be part of the family. Paul has become a friend over the course of writing this book. When he wasn't haranguing me to hurry up and finish the book, we talked about our kids, hit tennis balls, had a few laughs and some drinks. Thanks, Paul—I'm fortunate to have you as my editor.

Chapter 1

Why I Wrote This Book

The great thing about software patterns is that they convey many useful design ideas. It follows, therefore, that if you learn a bunch of these patterns, you'll be a pretty good software designer, right? I considered myself just that once I'd learned and used dozens of patterns. They helped me develop flexible frameworks and build robust and extensible software systems. After a couple of years, however, I discovered that my knowledge of patterns and the way I used them frequently led me to over-engineer my work.

Once my design skills had improved, I found myself using patterns in a different way: I began refactoring to, towards, and away from patterns, instead of using them for up-front design or introducing them too early into my code. My new way of working with patterns emerged from my adoption of extreme programming (XP) design practices, which helped me avoid both over- and under-engineering.

Over-Engineering

When you make your code more flexible or sophisticated than it needs to be, you over-engineer it. Some programmers do this because they believe they know their system's future requirements. They reason that it's best to make a design more flexible or sophisticated today, so it can accommodate the needs of tomorrow. That sounds reasonable—if you happen to be psychic.

If your predictions are wrong, you waste precious time and money. It's not uncommon to spend days or weeks fine-tuning an overly flexible or unnecessarily sophisticated software design, leaving you with less time to add new behavior or remove defects.

What typically happens with code you produce in anticipation of needs that never materialize? It *never* gets removed. This happens either because it's inconvenient to remove the code or because you expect that one day the code might

1

be needed. Regardless of the reason, as overly flexible or unnecessarily sophisti-cated code accumulates, you and the rest of the programmers on your team, especially new ones, must operate within a code base that's bigger and more complicated than it needs to be.

To compensate, folks decide to work in discrete areas of a system. This seems to make their jobs easier, yet it has the unpleasant side effect of generating lots of duplicate code because everyone works in his or her own comfortable area of the system, rarely seeking elsewhere for code that already does what he or she needs.

Over-engineered code affects productivity because when programmers inherit an over-engineered design, they must spend time learning the nuances of that design before they can comfortably extend or maintain it.

Over-engineering tends to happen quietly; many architects and programmers aren't even aware they are doing it. And while their organizations may discern a decline in team productivity, few know that over-engineering plays a role in the problem.

Perhaps the main reason programmers over-engineer is that they don't want to get stuck with a bad design. A bad design can weave its way so deeply into code that improving it becomes an enormous challenge. I've been there, and that's why up-front design with patterns appealed to me so much.

The Patterns Panacea

When I first began learning patterns, they represented a flexible, sophisticated, even elegant way to do object-oriented design that I very much wanted to mas-ter. After thoroughly studying numerous patterns and pattern languages, I used them to improve systems I had already built and to formulate designs for sys-tems I was about to build. Because the results of these efforts were promising, I felt sure I was on the right path.

But over time, the power of patterns led me to lose sight of simpler ways to write code. After learning that there were two or three different ways to do a calculation, I'd immediately race towards implementing the Strategy pattern, when, in fact, a simple conditional expression would have been easier and faster to program—a perfectly sufficient solution.

On one occasion, my preoccupation with patterns became quite apparent. I was pair-programming, and my partner and I had written a class that imple-mented Java's TreeModel interface in order to display a graph of Spec objects in a tree widget. Our code worked, but the tree widget was displaying each Spec object by calling its toString() method, which didn't return the Spec information we wanted. We couldn't change Spec's toString() method because other parts of the system relied on its contents. So we reflected on how to proceed. As was my habit, I considered which patterns could help. The Decorator pattern came to mind, and I suggested that we use it to wrap Spec with an object that could override the toString() method. My partner's response to this suggestion surprised me. "Using a Decorator here would be like applying a sledgehammer to the problem when a few light taps with a small hammer would do." His solution was to create a small class called NodeDisplay, whose constructor took a Spec instance and whose one public method, toString(), obtained the correct display information from the Spec instance. NodeDisplay took no time to program because it was less than 10 simple lines of code. My Decorator solution would have involved creating over 50 lines of code, with many repetitive delegation calls to the Spec instance.

Experiences like this made me aware that I needed to stop thinking so much about patterns and refocus on writing small, simple, understandable code. I was at a crossroads: I'd worked hard to learn patterns to become a better software designer, but now I needed to relax my reliance on them in order to become truly better.

Under-Engineering

Under-engineering is far more common than over-engineering. We under-engineer when we produce poorly designed software. This may occur for several reasons.

- We don't have time, don't make time, or aren't given time to refactor.

- We aren't knowledgeable about good software design.

- We're expected to quickly add new features to existing systems.

- We're made to work on too many projects at once.

Over time, under-engineered software becomes an expensive, difficult-to-maintain or unmaintainable mess. Brian Foote and Joseph Yoder, who authored a pattern language called Big Ball of Mud, describe such software like this:

Data structures may be haphazardly constructed, or even next to non-existent. Everything talks to everything else. Every shred of important state data may be global. Where state information is compartmentalized, it may be passed promiscuously about though Byzantine back channels that circumvent the system's original structure.

Variable and function names might be uninformative, or even misleading. Functions themselves may make extensive use of global variables, as well as long lists of poorly defined parameters. The functions themselves are lengthy and convoluted, and perform several unrelated tasks. Code is duplicated. The flow of control is hard to understand, and difficult to follow. The programmer's intent is next to impossible to discern. The code is simply unreadable, and borders on indecipherable. The code exhibits the unmistakable signs of patch after patch at the hands of multiple maintainers, each of whom barely understood the consequences of what he or she was doing. [Foote and Yoder, 661]

While systems you've worked on may not be so gruesome, it's likely you've done some under-engineering. I know I have. There's simply an overwhelming urge to get code working quickly, and it's often coupled with powerful forces that impede our ability to improve the design of our existing code. In some cases, we consciously don't improve our code because we know (or think we know) it won't have a long shelf life. Other times, we're compelled to not improve our code because well-meaning managers explain that our organization will be more competitive and successful if we "don't fix what ain't broke."

Continuous under-engineering leads to the "fast, slow, slower" rhythm of software development, which goes something like this.

1. You quickly deliver release 1.0 of a system with junky code.

2. You deliver release 2.0 of the system, and the junky code slows you down.

3. As you attempt to deliver future releases, you go slower and slower as the junky code multiplies, until people lose faith in the system, the programmers, and even the process that got everyone into this position.

4. Somewhere during or after release 4.0, you realize you can't win. You begin exploring the option of a total rewrite.

This kind of experience is far too common in our industry. It's costly and it makes organizations far less competitive than they could be. Fortunately, there is a better way.

Test-Driven Development and Continuous Refactoring

Test-driven development [Beck, TDD] and continuous refactoring, two of the many excellent XP practices, have dramatically improved the way I build software. I've found that these two practices have helped me and the organizations

I've worked for spend less time over-engineering and under-engineering and more time creating high-quality, function-rich code, produced on time.

Test-driven development (TDD) and continuous refactoring enable the efficient evolution of working code by turning programming into a dialogue.

- *Ask:* You ask a question of a system by writing a test.

- *Respond:* You respond to the question by writing code to pass the test.

- *Refine:* You refine your response by consolidating ideas, weeding out inessentials, and clarifying ambiguities.

- *Repeat:* You keep the dialogue going by asking the next question.

This rhythm of programming put my head into a totally new place. By using TDD, instead of spending lots of time thinking about a design that would work for every nuance of a system, I now spend seconds or minutes making a primitive piece of behavior work correctly before refactoring and evolving it to the next necessary level of sophistication.

Kent Beck's mantra of TDD and continuous refactoring is "red, green, refactor." The colors refer to what you see when you write and run a test in a unit-testing tool (like JUnit). The process goes like this.

1. *Red:* You create a test that expresses what you expect your code to do. The test fails (turns red) because you haven't created code to make the test pass.

2. *Green:* You program whatever is expedient to make the test pass (turn green). You don't pain yourself to come up with a duplication-free, simple, clear design at this point. You'll drive towards such a design later, when your test is passing and you can comfortably experiment with better designs.

3. *Refactor:* You improve the design of the code that passed the test.

Simple as this sounds, TDD and continuous refactoring turn the world of programming upside down. The inexperienced programmer may think, "Write a test for code that doesn't exist? Write code that passes a test yet needs immediate refactoring? Is this a wasteful, haphazard approach to software development or what?"

Actually, it's just the opposite. TDD and continuous refactoring provide a lean, iterative, and disciplined style of programming that maximizes focus, relaxation, and productivity. "Rapid unhurriedness" is how Martin Fowler describes it [as quoted in Beck, TDD], while Ward Cunningham explains that it's more about continuous analysis and design than it is about testing.

Learning the right rhythm of TDD and continuous refactoring requires practice. Tony Mobley, a programmer I know, described this style of development as a paradigm shift as great, if not greater, than moving from structured programming to object-oriented programming. However long it takes you to get used to this style of development, once you do, you'll find that producing production code any other way feels odd, uncomfortable, even unprofessional. Many of us who program using TDD and continuous refactoring find that it helps us:

- Keep defect counts low

- Refactor without fear

- Produce simpler, better code

- Program without stress

To learn the ins and outs of TDD, study *Test-Driven Development* [Beck, TDD] or *Test-Driven Development: A Practical Guide* [Astels]. For a taste of what it's like to do TDD, see the example sections from *Replace Implicit Tree with Composite (178)* and *Encapsulate Composite with Builder (96)*. To learn how to continuously refactor, you'll want to study *Refactoring* [F] (particularly the first chapter) as well as the refactorings in this book.

Refactoring and Patterns

On various projects, I've observed what and how my colleagues and I refactor. While we use many of the refactorings described in *Refactoring* [F], we also find places where patterns help us improve our designs. At such times, we refactor to or towards patterns, being careful not to produce overly flexible or unnecessarily sophisticated solutions.

When I explored the motivations for applying pattern-directed refactorings, I found they are identical to the general motivations for implementing low-level refactorings: to reduce or remove duplication, to simplify what is complicated, and to make code better at communicating its intention.

This motivation can easily be missed if you study only a portion of a design pattern. For example, every pattern in *Design Patterns* [DP] includes a section known as the Intent. The authors of *Design Patterns* describe the Intent as follows: "A short statement that answers the following questions: What does the design pattern do? What is its rationale and intent? What particular design issues or problem does it address?" [DP, 6]. Despite this description, the Intent sections for many design patterns only hint at the main problem the pattern solves. Instead, more of the focus is put on what the pattern does. Here are two examples.

Intent of Template Method
Define the skeleton of an algorithm in an operation, deferring some steps to subclasses. Template Method lets subclasses redefine certain steps of an algorithm without changing the algorithm's structure. [DP, 325]

Intent of State
Allow an object to alter its behavior when its internal state changes. The object will appear to change its class. [DP, 315]

These Intent descriptions don't say that a *Template Method* helps reduce or remove duplicated code in similar methods of subclasses in a hierarchy or that the *State* pattern helps simplify complex conditional state-changing logic. If programmers study all of the sections of a design pattern, particularly the Applicability section, they'll learn about the problems the pattern addresses.

However, when using the *Design Patterns* book during design, many programmers, myself included, have read the Intent section of a pattern to see whether the pattern could provide a good fit for a given situation. This method of choosing a pattern doesn't work as well as a method that helps you match a design problem to the problems addressed by a pattern. Why? Because patterns exist to solve problems, and learning whether they really can help in a given situation involves understanding what problems they help solve.

The refactoring literature tends to focus more on specific design problems than the patterns literature does. If you study the first page of a refactoring, you'll see the kind of problem the refactoring helps solve. The catalog of pattern-directed refactorings presented in this book, which is a direct continuation of work started in *Refactoring*, is intended to help you see what kinds of specific problems the patterns help solve.

While this book bridges the gap between patterns and refactoring, the connection between the two was noted by the authors of *Design Patterns* in the conclusion to their great book:

> Our design patterns capture many of the structures that result from refactoring. . . . Design patterns thus provide targets for your refactorings. [DP, 354]

Martin Fowler makes a similar observation near the beginning of *Refactoring*:

> There is a natural relation between patterns and refactorings. Patterns are where you want to be; refactorings are ways to get there from somewhere else. [F, 107]

Evolutionary Design

Today, after having become quite familiar with patterns, the "structures that result from refactoring," I know that understanding good reasons to refactor to or towards a pattern are more valuable than understanding the end result of a pattern or the nuances of implementing that end result.

If you'd like to become a better software designer, studying the evolution of great software designs will be more valuable than studying the great designs themselves. For it is in the evolution that the real wisdom lies. The structures that result from the evolution can help you, but without knowing why they were evolved into a design, you're more likely to misapply them or over-engineer with them on your next project.

To date, our software design literature has focused more on teaching great solutions than on teaching evolutions to great solutions. We need to change that. As the great poet Goethe said, "That which thy fathers have bequeathed to thee, earn it anew if thou wouldst possess it." The refactoring literature is helping us reacquire a better understanding of good design solutions by revealing sensible evolutions to those solutions.

If you want to get the most out of patterns, you must do the same thing: See patterns in the context of refactoring, not just as reusable elements that exist apart from refactoring. This is my primary reason for producing a catalog of pattern-directed refactorings.

By learning to evolve your designs, you can become a better software designer and reduce the amount of work you over- or under-engineer. TDD and continuous refactoring are the key practices of evolutionary design. Instill pattern-directed refactorings into your knowledge of how to refactor and you'll find yourself even better equipped to evolve great designs.

Chapter 2

Refactoring

In this chapter I offer a few thoughts on what refactoring is and what you need to do to be good at it. This chapter is best read in accompaniment with the chapter "Principles in Refactoring" [F].

What Is Refactoring?

A **refactoring** is a "behavior-preserving transformation" or, as Martin Fowler defines it, "a change made to the internal structure of software to make it easier to understand and cheaper to modify without changing its observable behavior" [F, 53].

The **process of refactoring** involves the removal of duplication, the simplification of complex logic, and the clarification of unclear code. When you refactor, you relentlessly poke and prod your code to improve its design. Such improvements may involve something as small as changing a variable name or as large as unifying two hierarchies.

To refactor safely, you must either manually test that your changes didn't break anything or run automated tests. You will have more courage to refactor and be more willing to try experimental designs if you can quickly run automated tests to confirm that your code still works.

Refactoring in small steps helps prevent the introduction of defects. Most refactorings take seconds or minutes to perform. Some large refactorings can require a sustained effort for days, weeks, or months until a transformation has been completed. Even such large refactorings are implemented in small steps.

It's best to refactor continuously, rather than in phases. When you see code that needs improvement, improve it. On the other hand, if your manager needs you to finish a feature before a demo that just got scheduled for tomorrow, finish the feature and refactor later. Business is well served by continuous refactoring, yet the practice of refactoring must coexist harmoniously with business priorities.

What Motivates Us to Refactor?

While we refactor code for many reasons, the following motivations are among the most common.

- *Make it easier to add new code.*
  When we add a new feature to a system, we have a choice: we can quickly program the feature without regard to how well it fits with an existing design, or we can modify the existing design so it can easily and gracefully accommodate the new feature. If we go with the former approach, we incur design debt (see *Design Debt*, 15), which can be paid down later by refactoring. If we go with the latter approach, we analyze what will need to change to best accommodate the new feature and then make whatever changes are necessary. Neither approach is better than the other. If you have little time, it may make more sense to quickly add the feature and refactor later. If you have more time or you perceive that you'll go faster by paving the way for the feature prior to programming it, by all means refactor before adding the feature.

- *Improve the design of existing code.*
  By continuously improving the design of code, we make it easier and easier to work with. This is in sharp contrast to what typically happens: little refactoring and a great deal of attention paid to expediently adding new features. Continuous refactoring involves constantly sniffing for coding smells (see Chapter 4, 37) and removing smells immediately after (or soon after) finding them. If you get into the hygienic habit of refactoring continuously, you'll find that it is easier to extend and maintain code. You may even enjoy your job more.

- *Gain a better understanding of code.*
  Sometimes we look at code and have no idea what it does or how it works. Even if someone could stand next to us and explain the code, the next person to look at it could also be totally confused. Is it best to write a comment for such code? No. If the code isn't clear, it's an odor that needs to be removed by refactoring, not by deodorizing the code with a comment.

  When we refactor such code, it is usually best to do so in the presence of someone who fully understands the code. If that person isn't available, see if he or she can help explain the code by e-mail, chat, or phone. Failing that, refactor only what you truly understand. In the end, your efforts will make it easier for everyone to understand the code.

- *Make coding less annoying.*
  I've often wondered what propels me to refactor code. Sure, I can say that I refactor to remove duplication, to simplify or clarify the code. But what actually propels me to refactor? Emotions. I often refactor simply to make code less annoying to work with.

  For example, I once joined a project that had some significant design debt. In particular, there was one enormous class with way too many responsibilities. Because much of what we did involved changing this enormous class, every time we checked in code (which was often, since we practiced continuous integration), we would have to deal with a complex merge involving the enormous class. As a result, everyone took longer than necessary to integrate code. This was very annoying. So another programmer and I set off on a three-week odyssey to break apart the enormous class into smaller classes. It was hard work that just had to be done. When we finished this work, integrating code took far less time and the overall programming experience was much more pleasant.

Many Eyes

When the Declaration of Independence was still a draft, Benjamin Franklin, sitting beside Thomas Jefferson, revised Jefferson's wording of "We hold these truths to be sacred and undeniable" to the now-famous phrase, "We hold these truths to be self-evident." According to biographer Walter Isaacson, Jefferson was distraught by Franklin's edits. So Franklin, aware of his friend's state, sought to console Jefferson by telling him the tale of his friend John Thompson.

John had just started out in the hat-making business and wanted a sign for his shop. He composed his sign like so:

John Thompson, hatter, makes
and sells hats for ready money.

Before using the new sign, John decided to show it to some friends to seek their feedback. The first friend thought that the word "hatter" was repetitive and unnecessary because it was followed by the words "makes . . . hats," which showed that John was a hatter. The word "hatter" was struck out. The next friend observed that the word "makes" could be removed because his customers would not care who made the hats. So "makes" was struck out. A third friend said he thought the words "for ready money" were useless, as it was not the custom to sell hats on credit. People were expected to purchase hats with money. So those words were omitted.

The sign now read, "John Thompson sells hats."

"Sells hats!" said his next friend. "Why, nobody will expect you to give them away. What then is the use of that word?" "Sells" was stricken. At this point there was no use for the word "hats" since a picture of one was painted on the sign. So the sign was ultimately reduced to:

John Thompson

In his book *Simple and Direct*, Jacques Barzun explains that all good writing is based upon revision [Barzun, 227]. Revision, he points out, means to re-see. John Thompson's sign was gradually revised by his friends, who helped him remove duplicate words, simplify his language, and clarify his intent. Jefferson's words were revised by Franklin, who saw a simpler, better way to express Jefferson's intent. In both cases, having many eyes revise one individual's work helped produce dramatic improvements.

The same is true of code. To get the best refactoring results, you'll want the help of many eyes. This is one reason why extreme programming suggests the practices of pair-programming and collective code ownership [Beck, XP].

Human-Readable Code

Every now and then I run across a piece of code that so impresses me, I spend the next several months and years telling people about it. Such was the case when I studied a piece of code written by Ward Cunningham. If you don't know Ward, you may know one of his many excellent innovations. Ward pioneered Class-Responsibility-Collaboration (CRC) cards, the Wiki Web (a simple, fast, read/write Web site), extreme programming (XP), and the FIT testing framework (*http://fit.c2.com*).

The code I was studying came from a fictional payroll system that was meant for use in a refactoring workshop. As one of the workshop instructors, I needed to study this code prior to teaching. I began by looking over the test code. The first test method I studied checked a payroll amount based on a date. What immediately struck my eye was the date. The code said:

```
november(20, 2005)
```

This code called the following method:

```
public Date november(int day, int year)
```

I was surprised and delighted. Even in a piece of test code, Ward had taken the trouble to produce a thoroughly human-readable method. If he had not cared to produce code that was simple and easy to understand, he could have written this:

```
java.util.Calendar c = java.util.Calendar.getInstance();
c.set(2005, java.util.Calendar.NOVEMBER, 20);
c.getTime();
```

While the above code produces the same date, it doesn't do what Ward's november() method does, which:

- Reads like spoken language

- Separates important code from distracting code

Now here's a very different story. It involves a method called w44(). I discovered the w44() function in a heap of Turbo Pascal spaghetti code that passed for a loan risk calculator for a large Wall Street bank. I spent the first three weeks of my professional programming career exploring this morass of code. I eventually figured out that 44 is the ASCII symbol for a comma, and "w" stands for "with." So w44() was the programmer's way of communicating that his routine returned a number, formatted as a string with commas. How intuitive! Either the programmer was shooting for big-time job security or he just didn't have a way with names.

Martin Fowler said it best:

> Any fool can write code that a computer can understand. Good programmers write code that humans can understand. [F, 15]

Keeping It Clean

Keeping code clean is a lot like keeping a room clean. Once your room becomes a mess, it becomes harder to clean. The worse the mess becomes, the less you want to clean it.

Suppose you do one giant cleanup of your room. Now what? If you want your room to remain clean, you can't leave things on the floor (like those socks) or allow books, magazines, glasses, or toys to pile up on tables. You must practice continuous hygiene.

Have you ever been in this situation? I have. If I can keep my room clean for several weeks, continuous hygiene starts to become a habit. Then I don't have to think so hard about whether I should throw my socks on the floor or deposit them in the laundry hamper. My habit propels me to put the socks in the hamper.

Unfortunately, new habits often run the risk of being compromised by old habits. One day you're too tired to pick your clothes up off the floor. Then several books get knocked off a shelf by a certain toddler. Before you know it, your room is a mess again.

To keep code clean, we must continuously remove duplication and simplify and clarify code. We must not tolerate messes in code, and we must not backslide into bad habits. Clean code leads to better design, which leads to faster development, which leads to happy customers and programmers. Keep your code clean.

Small Steps

Once upon a time a young, bright programmer was attending an intensive testing and refactoring workshop I was teaching. Everyone in this class was participating in a coding challenge that involved refactoring code with nearly all of the coding smells (see Chapter 4, 37) described in this book and in *Refactoring* [F]. During this challenge, pairs of programmers must discover a smell, find a refactoring for the smell, and demonstrate the refactoring by programming it on a projector while the rest of the class watches.

At about five minutes before noon, the class had been refactoring for nearly an hour. Since lunch had already been brought into the room, I asked if anyone had a small refactoring they'd like to complete before we broke for lunch. The young programmer raised his hand and said he had a small refactoring in mind. Without mentioning a specific smell or associated refactoring, this fellow described a rather large problem in the code and explained what he intended to do to fix it. A few students expressed their doubt that such a problem could be fixed in only five minutes, but the programmer insisted that he could complete the work, so we all agreed to let him and his pair partner try it.

Five minutes pass very quickly when you're refactoring something that is complicated.

The programmer and his partner found that after moving and altering some code, many of the unit tests were now failing. Failing unit tests show up as a big red bar in the unit-testing tool, which looks awfully big and red when it is being projected onto a large screen. As the programmers attempted to fix the broken unit tests, one by one people began to leave so they could eat lunch at a nearby table. Fifteen minutes later I took a break too. As I stood in the lunch line, I watched the programming action on the projector.

Twenty minutes into their work, the big red bar still hadn't turned green (which signals that all tests are passing). At that point the young programmer and his partner got up to get some food. Then they quickly returned to the computer. Many of us watched as one programmer attempted to eat his lunch with one hand while continuing to refactor with the other. Meanwhile, the minutes were ticking by.

At ten minutes to one (nearly fifty-five minutes after beginning their refactoring), the big red bar turned green. The refactoring was complete. As the class reassembled, I asked everyone what had gone wrong. The young programmer provided the answer: he had not taken small steps. By combining several refactorings into a single, large step, he thought he would go faster; but just the opposite was true. Each big step generated failures in the unit tests, which took a good deal of time to fix, not to mention that some of the fixes needed to be undone during later steps.

Many of us have had similar experiences—we take steps that are too large and then struggle for minutes, hours, or even days to get back to a green bar. The better I get at refactoring, the more I proceed by taking very small, safe steps. In fact, the green bar has become a gyroscope, a device that helps me stay on course. If the bar stays red for too long—more than a few minutes—I know that I'm not taking small enough steps. Then I backtrack and begin again. I nearly always find smaller, simpler steps I can take that will get me to my goal faster than if I'd taken bigger steps.

Design Debt

If you ask your manager to let you spend time continuously refactoring your code to "improve its design," what do you think the response will be? Probably "No" or an extended outburst of laughter or a harsh look. Keeping up with an endless stream of feature requests and defect reports is hard enough! Who has time for design improvements? What planet are you living on?

The technical language of refactoring doesn't communicate effectively with the vast majority of management. Instead, Ward Cunningham's financial metaphor of design debt [F, 66] works infinitely better. Design debt occurs when you don't consistently do three things.

1. Remove duplication.

2. Simplify your code.

3. Clarify you code's intent.

Few systems remain completely free of design debt. Wired as we are, humans just don't write perfect code the first time around. We naturally accumulate design debt. So the question becomes, "When do you pay it down?"

Due to ignorance or a commitment to "not fix what ain't broken," many programmers and teams spend little time paying down design debt. As a result, they create a Big Ball of Mud [Foote and Yoder]. In financial terms, if you don't pay off a debt, you incur late fees. If you don't pay your late fees, you incur higher late fees. The more you don't pay, the worse your fees and payments become. Compound interest kicks in, and as time goes on, getting out of debt becomes an impossible dream. So it is with design debt.

Discussing technical problems using the financial metaphor of design debt is a proven way to get through to management. I routinely take out a credit card and show it to managers when I'm speaking about design debt. I ask them, "How many months in a row do you not pay down your debt?" While some don't always pay off their debt in full each month, nearly all don't let debt accumulate for long. Discussions like this help managers acknowledge the wisdom of continuously paying down design debt.

Once management accepts the importance of continuous refactoring, the organization's entire way of building software can change. Suddenly, everyone from executives to managers to programmers agrees that going too fast hurts everyone. Programmers now have management's blessing to refactor. Over time, the small, hygienic acts of refactoring accumulate to make systems easier and easier to extend and maintain. When that happens, everyone benefits, including the makers, managers, and users of the software.

Evolving a New Architecture

There was once a company that had an older system, with the all-too-common problems of poor design, instability, and difficult maintenance. The company decided to refactor the system's architecture rather than rewrite everything from scratch.

Common code would be accessible from a new framework layer. Applications would use the framework layer for common services. This separation would allow framework programmers to gradually improve underlying framework code, with minimal impact on applications.

The company decided to form a framework team. Application teams would rely on the framework team for common services.

While this plan sounds reasonable, it's actually quite risky. If the framework team members lose touch with application needs, they can easily build the wrong code. If the application team members don't get what they need, they may bypass the framework to meet deadlines or slow down just to wait for what they need. Bypassing the framework is a return to the legacy architecture, while waiting for code is also a poor option.

Evolutionary design provides a better way. It suggests that you:

- Form one team

- Drive the framework from application needs

- Continuously improve applications and the framework by refactoring

With one team, the framework and the applications can't fall out of alignment. With the framework driven by real application needs, only valuable framework code gets produced. Continuous refactoring is essential to this process, for it's what keeps framework and application parts separate.

The company in this story decided to follow this evolutionary path, hiring coaches to train and guide them. Despite initial concerns about not having one team focus exclusively on framework development, the process resulted in continuous improvement in architecture, continuous delivery of high-quality applications, and evolution of a lean, general-purpose framework.

Refactoring is the essential ingredient here. It's what allows the team to effectively and efficiently evolve a new architecture.

Composite and Test-Driven Refactorings

Composite refactorings are high-level refactorings composed of low-level refactorings. Much of the work performed by low-level refactorings involves moving code around. For example, *Extract Method* [F] moves code to a new method, *Pull Up Method* [F] moves a method from a subclass to a superclass, *Extract*

Class [F] moves code to a new class, and *Move Method* [F] moves a method from one class to another.

Nearly all of the refactorings in this book are composite refactorings. You begin with a piece of code you want to change and then incrementally apply various low-level refactorings until a desired change has occurred. Between applying low-level refactorings, you run tests to confirm that modified code continues to behave as expected. Testing is thus an integral part of composite refactoring; if you don't run tests, you'll have a hard time applying low-level refactorings with confidence.

Testing also plays an altogether different role in refactoring; it can be used to rewrite and replace old code. A **test-driven refactoring** involves applying test-driven development to produce replacement code and then swap out old code for new code (while retaining and rerunning the old code's tests).

Composite refactorings are used far more frequently than test-driven refactorings because a good deal of refactoring work simply involves relocating existing code. When it isn't possible to improve a design this way, test-driven refactorings can help you produce a better design safely and effectively.

Substitute Algorithm [F] is a good example of a refactoring that is best implemented using test-driven refactorings. It essentially involves completely changing an existing algorithm for one that is simpler and clearer. How do you produce the new algorithm? You can't produce it by transforming the old algorithm into the new one because your logic for the new algorithm is different. You can program the new algorithm, substitute it for the old algorithm, and then see if the tests pass. But if the tests don't pass, you're likely to find yourself on a long date with a debugger. A better way to program the algorithm is to use test-driven development. This tends to produce simple code, and it also produces tests that later allow you or others to confidently apply low-level or composite refactorings.

Encapsulate Composite with Builder (96) is another example of a test-driven refactoring. In this case, you want to make it easier for clients to build a Composite by simplifying the build process. A Builder, which provides a simpler way of building a Composite, is where you'd like to take the design. Yet if that design is far different from the existing design, you will likely be unable to use low-level or composite refactorings to produce the new design. Once again, test-driven development provides an effective way to reimplement and replace old code.

The refactoring *Replace Implicit Tree with Composite (178)* is both a composite refactoring and a test-driven refactoring. Choosing how to implement this refactoring depends on the nature of the code you encounter. In general, if it's difficult to implement the *Extract Class* [F] refactoring on the code, the test-driven approach may be easier. *Replace Implicit Tree with Composite (178)* includes an example that uses test-driven refactoring.

Move Embellishment to Decorator (144) is not a test-driven refactoring; however, the example for this refactoring shows how test-driven refactoring is used to move behavior from outside a framework to inside the framework. This example involves moving code around, so you might think it would be more convenient to use composite refactorings to implement it. In fact, because the changes involve updating numerous classes, it turns out to be easier to use test-driven development to make the design transformation.

In your practice of refactoring, you're likely to use low-level and composite refactorings most of the time. Just remember that the "reimplement and replace" technique, as performed by using test-driven refactoring, is another useful way to refactor. While it tends to be most helpful when you're designing a new algorithm or mechanism, it may also provide an easier path than applying low-level or composite refactorings.

The Benefits of Composite Refactorings

The composite refactorings in this book, each of which targets a particular pattern, have some of the following benefits.

- *They describe an overall plan for a refactoring sequence.*
  The mechanics of a composite refactoring describe the sequence of low-level refactorings you can apply to improve a design in a particular way. Do you need such a sequence? If you already know the low-level refactorings, you can certainly apply them in whatever order you see fit.

  However, the refactoring sequences in this catalog may prove to be more safe, effective, or efficient in improving your design than your own refactoring sequences are. I once followed certain low-level refactorings to refactor to the State [DP] pattern. Then I learned a better, safer sequence. Then someone suggested improvements to that sequence. By the time I got to the fifth version of the sequence, I knew I had a much better way of refactoring to the State pattern, and it was far different from my initial approach.

- *They suggest nonobvious design directions.*
  Composite refactorings begin at a source and take you to a destination. The destination may or may not be obvious, given your source. Much depends on your familiarity with patterns, each of which defines a destination as well as the forces that suggest the need to go towards or to that

destination. The composite refactorings in this book make these nonobvious design directions clearer by describing real-world cases in which it made sense to move in the direction of a pattern.

- *They provide insights into implementing patterns.*
  Because there is no right way to implement a pattern (see *There Are Many Ways to Implement a Pattern*, 26), it's useful to consider alternative pattern implementations. This is particularly true of patterns that solve different kinds of design problems. For example, this book contains three different refactorings to Composite [DP] and three different ways to refactor to Visitor [DP]. How you refactor to these patterns and others will vary depending on the initial problem you face. In recognition of that, the refactoring sequences in this book vary in how they ultimately implement a pattern.

Refactoring Tools

The early pioneers of refactoring tools—people like William Opdyke, Ralph Johnson, John Brant, and Don Roberts—envisioned a world in which we could look at code that needed a refactoring and simply ask a tool to perform the refactoring for us. In the mid-1990s, John and Don built such a tool for Smalltalk. Software development hasn't been the same since.

After the 1999 publication of *Refactoring* [F], Martin Fowler challenged tool vendors to produce automated refactoring tools for mainstream languages such as Java. These tool vendors responded, and before long, many programmers throughout the world could execute automated refactorings from their integrated development environments (IDEs). Over time, even die-hard users of programming editors began transitioning to IDEs, largely due to automated refactoring support.

As refactoring tools continue to implement low-level refactorings, like *Extract Method* [F], *Extract Class* [F], and *Pull Up Method* [F], it becomes easier to transform designs by executing sequences of automated refactorings. This has important implications for pattern-directed refactorings because the mechanics for these refactorings are composed of low-level refactorings. When tool vendors automate the majority of low-level refactorings, they will automatically create support for the refactorings in this book.

Using automated refactorings to move towards, to, or away from a pattern is completely different from using a tool to generate pattern code. In general, I've found that pattern code generators provide an excellent way to over-engineer your code. In addition, they generate code that doesn't contain tests, which further limits your ability to refactor as and when needed. By contrast, refactoring lets you discover small design improvements you can safely make to go towards, to, or away from a pattern implementation.

Because refactoring is the act of performing behavior-preserving transformations, you might think that you would not need to run test code after you perform an automated refactoring. Well, you do, much of the time. You may have complete confidence in your automated refactoring tool for some refactorings, while you may not completely trust it for other refactorings. Many automated refactorings prompt you to make choices; if you make the wrong choices, you can easily cause your test code to stop running correctly (which is another way to say that the automated refactoring you performed did add or remove some behavior). In general, it's useful to run all of your tests after refactoring to confirm that the code is behaving as you expect.

If you lack tests, can you trust automated refactoring tools to preserve behavior in your code and not introduce unwanted behavior? You may be able to trust many of the refactorings, while others, which may be just out of production, are less stable or trustworthy. In general, if you lack test coverage for your code, you really won't have much success with refactoring, unless the tools become substantially more intelligent.

Advances in automated refactorings can impact what steps you follow in the mechanics of a refactoring. For example, a recent automation of *Extract Method* [F] is so smart that if you extract a chunk of code from one method and that same chunk of code exists in another method, both chunks of code will be replaced by a call to the newly extracted method. That capability may change how you approach the mechanics from a refactoring, given that some of the work from multiple steps may be automated for you.

What is the future of refactoring tools? I hope that we see more automated support for low-level refactorings, tools that suggest which refactorings could help improve certain pieces of code, and tools that allow you to explore how your design would look if several refactorings were applied together.

Chapter 3

Patterns

This chapter looks at what a pattern is; what it means to be patterns happy; the importance of understanding that patterns can be implemented in many ways; considerations for refactoring to, towards, or away from patterns; whether or not patterns make code more complex; what it means to have "pattern knowledge"; and when it may make sense to do up-front design with patterns.

What Is a Pattern?

Christopher Alexander, an architect, professor, and social commentator, inspired the software patterns movement with two literary masterpieces, *A Timeless Way of Building* [Alexander, TWB] and *A Pattern Language* [Alexander, PL]. Beginning in the late 1980s, software practitioners with years of experience began studying Alexander's works and sharing their knowledge in the form of patterns and intricate networks of patterns, known as **pattern languages**. This led to the publication of valuable papers and books about patterns and pattern languages in such areas as object-oriented design, analysis and domain design, process and organizational design, and user interface design.

Pattern authors have often debated how to define a pattern, and many of the disagreements stem from how close to or far from Alexander's view the debaters are. As I'm partial to Alexander's view, I'll quote him directly:

Each pattern is a three-part rule, which expresses a relation between a certain context, a problem, and a solution.

As an element in the world, each pattern is a relationship between a certain context, a certain system of forces which occurs repeatedly in that context, and a certain spatial configuration which allows these forces to resolve themselves.

As an element of language, a pattern is an instruction, which shows how this spatial configuration can be used, over and over again, to resolve the given system of forces, wherever the context makes it relevant.

The pattern is, in short, at the same time a thing, which happens in the world, and the rule which tells us how to create that thing, and when we must create it. It is both a process and a thing; both a description of a thing which is alive, and a description of the process which will generate that thing. [Alexander, TWB, 247]

Our industry's view of patterns has mostly been influenced by catalogs of individual patterns, such as those found in *Design Patterns* [DP] and Martin Fowler's *Patterns of Enterprise Application Architectures* [Fowler, PEAA]. Such catalogs don't actually contain stand-alone patterns because authors typically discuss which alternative patterns to consider if a pattern doesn't provide a good fit. In recent years, we've also seen the emergence of literature that resembles Alexander's pattern languages. Such works include *Extreme Programming Explained* [Beck, XP], *Domain-Driven Design* [Evans], and *Checks: A Pattern Language of Information Integrity* [Cunningham].

Patterns Happy

On the back cover of *Contributing to Eclipse* [Gamma and Beck], a brief biography of Erich Gamma says, "Erich Gamma shared his joy in the order and beauty of software design as coauthor of the classic *Design Patterns*." If you've ever produced or encountered an excellent design using patterns, you know this joy.

On the other hand, if you've ever produced or encountered patterns-dense code that is poorly designed because it doesn't require the flexibility or sophistication of patterns, you know the dread of patterns.

The overuse of patterns tends to result from being patterns happy. We are **patterns happy** when we become so enamored of patterns that we simply must use them in our code. A patterns-happy programmer may work hard to use patterns on a system just to get the experience of implementing them or maybe to gain a reputation for writing really good, complex code.

A programmer named Jason Tiscione, writing on SlashDot (see *http://developers.slashdot.org/comments.pl?sid=33602&cid=3636102*), perfectly caricatured patterns-happy code with the following version of Hello World.

```
interface MessageStrategy {
    public void sendMessage();
}

abstract class AbstractStrategyFactory {
    public abstract MessageStrategy createStrategy(MessageBody mb);
}
```

```
class MessageBody {
   Object payload;
   public Object getPayload() {
      return payload;
   }
   public void configure(Object obj) {
      payload = obj;
   }
   public void send(MessageStrategy ms) {
      ms.sendMessage();
   }
}

class DefaultFactory extends AbstractStrategyFactory {
   private DefaultFactory() {
   }
   static DefaultFactory instance;
   public static AbstractStrategyFactory getInstance() {
      if (instance == null)
         instance = new DefaultFactory();
      return instance;
   }

   public MessageStrategy createStrategy(final MessageBody mb) {
      return new MessageStrategy() {
         MessageBody body = mb;
         public void sendMessage() {
            Object obj = body.getPayload();
            System.out.println(obj);
         }
      };
   }
}

public class HelloWorld {
   public static void main(String[] args) {
      MessageBody mb = new MessageBody();
      mb.configure("Hello World!");
      AbstractStrategyFactory asf = DefaultFactory.getInstance();
      MessageStrategy strategy = asf.createStrategy(mb);
      mb.send(strategy);
   }
}
```

Have you ever seen code that resembles Jason's Hello World program? I certainly have, on too many occasions.

The patterns-happy malady isn't limited to beginner programmers. Intermediate and advanced programmers fall prey to it too, particularly after they read sophisticated patterns books or articles. For example, I discovered an implementation of the Closure pattern on a system I was helping to develop. It turned out that a programmer on the project had just learned the Closure pattern by studying it on the Wiki Web (*http://c2.com/cgi/wiki?UseClosuresNot-Enumerations*).

As I studied this Closure implementation, I could not find a good justification for using it. The Closure pattern just wasn't necessary. So I refactored the Closure pattern out of the code and replaced it with simpler code. When I finished, I asked the programmers on the team if they thought the newer code was simpler than the Closure code. They said yes. Eventually the author of the code also acknowledged that the refactored code was simpler.

It is perhaps impossible to avoid being patterns happy on the road to learning patterns. In fact, most of us learn by making mistakes. I've been patterns happy on more than one occasion.

The true joy of patterns comes from using them wisely. Refactoring helps us do that by focusing our attention on removing duplication, simplifying code, and making code communicate its intention. When patterns evolve into a system by means of refactoring, there is less chance of over-engineering with patterns. The better you get at refactoring, the more chance you'll have to find the joy of patterns.

There Are Many Ways to Implement a Pattern

Every pattern describes a problem which occurs over and over again in our environment, and then describes the core of the solution to that problem, in such a way that you can use this solution a million times over, without ever doing it the same way twice. [Alexander, PL, x]

Every pattern in the classic book *Design Patterns* [DP] contains a Structure diagram. For example, the Structure diagram for the Factory Method pattern looks like this:

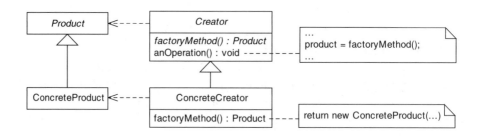

This diagram indicates that the Creator and Product classes are abstract, while the ConcreteCreator and ConcreteProduct classes are concrete. Is this the only way to implement the Factory Method pattern? By no means!

In fact, the authors of *Design Patterns* go to great pains to explain different ways to implement each pattern in a section called Implementation Notes. If you read the implementation notes for the Factory Method pattern, you'll find that there are plenty of ways to implement a Factory Method. For example, the following diagram shows another way:

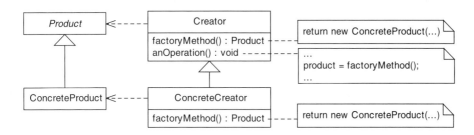

In this case, the Product class is abstract, while every other class is concrete. In addition, the Creator class implements its own factoryMethod(), which the Concrete-Creator overrides.

There are even more ways to implement the Factory Method pattern. Here's another one:

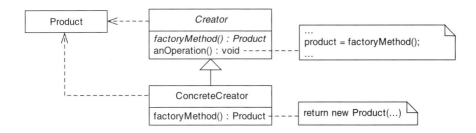

In this case, the Product class is concrete and has no subclass. The Creator, which is abstract, defines an abstract version of the Factory Method, which the ConcreteCreator implements to return an instance of Product.

The main point? There are many ways to implement a pattern.

Unfortunately, when programmers look at the solitary Structure diagram accompanying each pattern in the *Design Patterns* book, they often jump to the conclusion that the Structure diagram is *the* way to implement the pattern. If they'd only read the crucial implementation notes, they'd know better. Yet many a programmer picks up *Design Patterns*, gazes at a Structure diagram, and then begins coding. The result is code that exactly mirrors the Structure diagram, instead of a pattern implementation that best matches the need at hand.

A few years after the publication of *Design Patterns*, John Vlissides, one of the book's coauthors, wrote:

> It seems you can't overemphasize that a pattern's Structure diagram is just an example, not a specification. It portrays the implementation we see most often. As such the Structure diagram will probably have a lot in common with your own implementation, but differences are inevitable and actually desirable. At the very least you will rename the participants as appropriate for your domain. Vary the implementation trade-offs, and your implementation might start looking a lot different from the Structure diagram. [Vlissides]

In this book, you'll find pattern implementations that look quite different from their Structure diagrams in *Design Patterns*. For example, here's the Structure diagram for the Composite pattern:

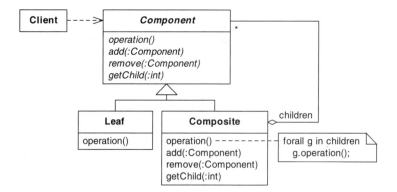

And here is a particular implementation of the Composite pattern:

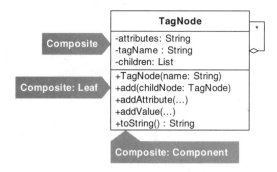

As you can see, this implementation of Composite bears little resemblance to the Structure diagram for Composite. It is a minimalistic Composite implementation that resulted from coding only what was necessary.

Being minimalistic in your pattern implementations is part of the practice of evolutionary design. In many cases, a non-patterns-based implementation may need to evolve to include a pattern. In that case, you can refactor the design to a simple pattern implementation. I use this approach throughout this book.

Refactoring to, towards, and away from Patterns

Good designers refactor in many directions, always with the goal of reaching a better design. While many of the refactorings I apply don't involve patterns (i.e., they're small, simple transformations, like *Extract Method* [F], *Rename Method* [F], *Move Method* [F], *Pull Up Method* [F], and so forth), when my refactorings do involve patterns, I refactor to, towards, and even away from patterns.

The direction a pattern-directed refactoring takes is often influenced by the nature of a pattern. For example, *Compose Method (123)* is a refactoring based on Kent Beck's Composed Method [Beck, SBPP] pattern. When I apply *Compose Method (123)*, which I do often, I refactor *to* a Composed Method, not *towards* one. Refactoring towards a Composed Method doesn't sufficiently improve a method. You must refactor all the way to this pattern to achieve a genuine improvement.

The same is true of the Template Method pattern [DP]. People generally apply the refactoring *Form Template Method (205)* to remove duplicate code in subclasses. You can't refactor towards a Template Method and expect to remove duplication. Either you implement a Template Method or you don't, and if you don't, you won't be removing duplicate code in your subclasses.

On the other hand, this book contains numerous refactorings that provide acceptable design improvements whether you go towards or all the way to a pattern implementation. *Move Embellishment to Decorator (144)* provides a good example. An early step in the mechanics for this refactoring suggests that you use the *Replace Conditional with Polymorphism* [F] refactoring. Once you've done that, you can decide whether you've made a good enough design improvement to stop. If you happen to see a benefit from taking the next step, the mechanics suggest that you use the *Replace Inheritance with Delegation* [F] refactoring. If doing so provides a sufficient design improvement, you can stop. Or, if you see a benefit in applying all of the mechanics, you will refactor all the way to a Decorator.

Similarly, if you suspect that you need to use *Replace Conditional Dispatcher with Command (191)*, the steps you take towards a Command [DP] implementation can improve your design, regardless of whether you refactor all the way to the Command pattern.

Once you've refactored to or towards a pattern, you must evaluate whether your design has indeed improved. If it hasn't, you'd better backtrack or refactor in another direction, such as away from a pattern or to another pattern. *Inline Singleton (114)* removes the Singleton [DP] pattern from a design. *Encapsulate Composite with Builder (96)* changes client code to interact with a Builder [DP] rather than a Composite. *Move Accumulation to Visitor (320)* replaces awkward and/or duplication-ridden Iterator [DP] code with a Visitor [DP] solution.

By applying the refactorings in this book, you may refactor to, towards, or away from patterns. Just remember that the goal is always to obtain a better design, not to implement patterns. Table 3.1 lists the directions I often take when applying the patterns-based refactorings in this book.

Table 3.1

Pattern	To	Towards	Away
Adapter	*Extract Adapter (258), Unify Interfaces with Adapter (247)*	*Unify Interfaces with Adapter (247)*	
Builder	*Encapsulate Composite with Builder (96)*		
Collecting Parameter	*Move Accumulation to Collecting Parameter (313)*		
Command	*Replace Conditional Dispatcher with Command (191)*	*Replace Conditional Dispatcher with Command (191)*	
Composed Method	*Compose Method (123)*		
Composite	*Replace One/Many Distinctions with Composite (224), Extract Composite (214), Replace Implicit Tree with Composite (178)*		*Encapsulate Composite with Builder (96)*
Creation Method	*Replace Constructors with Creation Methods (57)*		
Decorator	*Move Embellishment to Decorator (144)*	*Move Embellishment to Decorator (144)*	

Table 3.1 *(continued)*

Pattern	To	Towards	Away
Factory	*Move Creation Knowledge to Factory (68), Encapsulate Classes with Factory (80)*		
Factory Method	*Introduce Polymorphic Creation with Factory Method (88)*		
Interpreter	*Replace Implicit Language with Interpreter (269)*		
Iterator			*Move Accumulation to Visitor (320)*
Null Object	*Introduce Null Object (301)*		
Observer	*Replace Hard-Coded Notifications with Observer (236)*	*Replace Hard-Coded Notifications with Observer (236)*	
Singleton	*Limit Instantiation with Singleton (296)*		*Inline Singleton (114)*
State	*Replace State-Altering Conditionals with State (166)*	*Replace State-Altering Conditionals with State (166)*	
Strategy	*Replace Conditional Logic with Strategy (129)*	*Replace Conditional Logic with Strategy (129)*	
Template Method	*Form Template Method (205)*		
Visitor	*Move Accumulation to Visitor (320)*	*Move Accumulation to Visitor (320)*	

Do Patterns Make Code More Complex?

One team I worked with included programmers who knew patterns and programmers who didn't know patterns. Bobby knew patterns well and had ten years of programming experience. John had little exposure to patterns and had four years of programming experience.

One day John looked over a significant refactoring Bobby had completed and exclaimed, "I liked the code better before! Now the code is way more complex!"

Bobby had refactored a large amount of conditional logic associated with validating data entry screens. His refactoring led him to the Composite pattern. Bobby had converted many pieces of validation logic into separate validation objects, all of which shared the same interface. For a given data entry screen, the appropriate validation objects were now assembled into a single Composite validation object. At runtime, a data entry screen's Composite validation object would be queried to discover which validation rules passed or failed.

I happened to be pair-programming with John when he expressed his discontent with Bobby's refactoring. I wanted to understand the root of John's discontent, so I asked John some questions. I quickly learned that John was not familiar with the Composite pattern. That explained a lot.

John was open to learning the Composite pattern when I offered to teach it to him. After I felt that he had grasped the pattern, we went back to looking over Bobby's refactored code. I then asked John whether he felt differently about the refactoring. Reluctantly, he agreed that the code wasn't as complex as he had thought, yet he didn't go so far as to say it was better than the previous code.

From my perspective, Bobby's refactoring represented a vast improvement over the previous code. Bobby had removed large chunks of conditional logic and duplicate code in classes associated with data entry screens. He had also dramatically simplified the way to discover passing and failing validation rules.

My own comfort and familiarity with the Composite pattern influenced my perspective on Bobby's refactoring. Unlike John, I found the refactored code to be simpler and cleaner than the previous code.

In general, pattern implementations ought to help remove duplicate code, simplify logic, communicate intention, and increase flexibility. However, as this story reveals, people's familiarity with patterns plays a major role in how they perceive patterns-based refactorings. I prefer that teams learn patterns rather than avoid using them because the teams view patterns as being too complex. On the other hand, some pattern implementations can make code more complex than it needs to be; when that happens, backtracking or more refactoring is necessary.

Pattern Knowledge

If you don't know patterns, you're less likely to evolve great designs. Patterns capture wisdom. Reusing that wisdom is extremely useful.

Maynard Solomon, a biographer of Mozart, observed that Mozart didn't invent new forms of music—he simply combined existing forms to produce stunningly good results [Solomon]. Patterns are like new forms of music you can use and combine to produce excellent software designs.

Knowledge of the Builder pattern once played a crucial role in the evolution of a system I helped develop. The system needed to run in two completely different environments. Had we not evolved the system to use the Builder pattern relatively early in our design, I shudder to think of how our design would have turned out.

JUnit, an excellent testing framework that enables test-driven development and unit testing, is dense with patterns. Its authors, Kent Beck and Erich Gamma, didn't try to put as many patterns into JUnit as they could. They simply evolved the framework and reused the wisdom of patterns as they designed. Since JUnit is an open source tool, I've been able to follow its evolution from version 1.0 to the latest version. By studying each version and by talking to Kent and Erich about their work, I can tell you that they definitely refactored to and towards patterns. Their knowledge of patterns most certainly aided them in their refactoring work.

Yet as I mentioned at the start of this book, having knowledge of patterns isn't enough to evolve great software. You must also know how to intelligently use patterns, which is the subject of this book. Nevertheless, if you don't study patterns, you'll lack access to important, even beautiful, design ideas.

My preferred way to gain knowledge of patterns is to choose great pattern books to study and then study one pattern a week in a study group. "Pools of Insight" [Kerievsky, PI], a pattern language I once wrote, describes how to set up a long-lasting patterns study group.

A study group I founded in 1995, called the Design Patterns Study Group of New York City, is still going strong today. The Silicon Valley Patterns Group is another long-running patterns study group. Some of its members enjoy it so much that they've actually moved closer to where the group meets, to make it easier to attend meetings.

Folks in these study groups love to become better software designers. Meeting and discussing important design ideas each week is a great way to do that.

If you think there are already too many patterns books to study, don't worry. Follow the advice of Jerry Weinberg. I once asked him how he keeps up with all the books that come out. He said, "Easy—I only read the great ones."

Up-Front Design with Patterns

In spring 1996, a well-known music and television company sought to create a Java version of its Web site. The company's managers knew how they wanted the site to look and behave but lacked the Java expertise to build the site. So they began looking for a development partner.

Industrial Logic, my company, was contacted by this organization. At our first meeting, I was led through the user interface design. I also learned that the company would want to modify the behavior of the future site without having to call programmers to make every little change. The managers had one question for me: How would I program the site to meet their needs?

Over the next few weeks, I worked with my colleagues to consider designs for the site. All of us were members of the Design Patterns Study Group I had started six months earlier. Our newfound knowledge of patterns was most helpful in our design work. For each of the requirements of the site, we considered what patterns could help us.

It soon became apparent that the Command [DP] pattern would play an essential role in our design. We would program the site in such a way that Command objects would control all behavior. If you clicked somewhere on the screen, a Command object (or many Command objects) would execute. We'd also invent a simple Interpreter [DP] to allow our clients to configure their site to run whatever Command objects they wanted, thereby allowing them to modify their site's behavior without having to call us.

We spent several days documenting our design. Then we had a second big meeting with the music and television folks. The meeting went well and we were asked to return for a third meeting to get into more technical details about our design.

As the weeks ticked by, we had our next meeting and then our next one. By mid-summer, we had not programmed any code for the site; we simply had a growing body of design documents. Finally, sometime in mid-August, we learned that we had won the bid to develop the site.

Over the coming months, we programmed the site, following our design very closely. As we programmed, we found places where we could improve the design by refactoring to the Composite [DP], Iterator [DP], and Null Object [Woolf] patterns. For an example of how and why we refactored to Null Object, see the discussion in *Introduce Null Object (301)*.

By mid-December, about one month beyond the scheduled delivery date, we were done. The site went live. We all celebrated.

I often think of this experience when I consider refactoring and the role of patterns. If we had to do it all over again, would it have been better to evolve our design, instead of doing big design up-front (BDUF)? Would we have been more successful had we exclusively refactored to or towards patterns rather than using a few patterns early in our design?

No. We would not have won the bid for this project had we not thought of a design and presented it, in detail, to the client. BDUF was essential in this context, and our up-front design with the Command and Interpreter patterns was a critical part of our success.

The typical problem with BDUF is that it often wastes time. You come up with a design for requirements and then those requirements change, get dropped, or are deferred to some later date. Or your requirements don't change, but you spend lots of time coming up with a design that's more elegant or sophisticated than it needs to be.

In this case, we didn't encounter such BDUF problems. Our project was small with very fixed requirements. We used every aspect of our up-front design in our programming work. Our code did just what our clients needed and wasn't overly complicated or sophisticated.

However, we were late to deliver the site by one month because of numerous defects we encountered in the Internet browsers. We began testing the Mac version of the site midway through the project and soon found that Netscape on the Mac had serious defects that we needed to program around. In addition, we encountered numerous differences between Internet Explorer and Netscape, which caused us to make many time-consuming modifications to our code.

Being one month late to deliver wasn't a serious problem, though it did cause us some stress. If we had begun programming sooner, before we won the bid, we may have encountered the browser defects earlier. Yet at the time we were reluctant to code anything until we had a client who would pay us for our work.

Since 1996, I've done very little up-front design with patterns. The approach I've taken on project after project has been to evolve a system, refactoring to, towards, or away from patterns as necessary. The Command pattern remains the major exception. Since 1996, I've used it on two or three systems very early in a design because it was easy to implement and the systems clearly required the behavior supplied by the Command pattern.

I included this story in this chapter because I believe it helps illustrate when it makes sense to ignore the ideas in this book. While I don't generally favor up-front design with patterns, I know that it has some place in a designer's toolkit. I use up-front design with patterns rarely and most judiciously, and I recommend you do so as well.

Chapter 4

Code Smells

> When you have learned to look at your words with critical detachment, you will find that rereading a piece five or six times in a row will each time bring to light fresh spots of trouble. [Barzun, 229]

Refactoring, or improving the design of existing code, requires that you know what code needs improvement. Catalogs of refactorings help you gain this knowledge, yet your situation may be different from what you see in a catalog. It's therefore necessary to learn common design problems so you can recognize them in your own code.

The most common design problems result from code that

- Is duplicated

- Is unclear

- Is complicated

These criteria can certainly help you discover places in code that need improvement. On the other hand, many programmers find this list to be too vague; they don't know how to spot duplication in code that isn't outwardly the same, they aren't sure how to tell when code is clearly communicating its intent, and they don't know how to distinguish simple code from complicated code.

In their chapter "Bad Smells in Code" in *Refactoring* [F], Martin Fowler and Kent Beck provide additional guidance for identifying design problems. They liken design problems to smells and explain which refactorings, or combinations of refactorings, work best to eliminate odors.

Fowler and Beck's code smells target problems that occur everywhere: in methods, classes, hierarchies, packages (namespaces, modules), and entire systems. The names of their smells, such as Feature Envy, Primitive Obsession, and Speculative Generality, provide a rich and colorful vocabulary with which programmers may rapidly communicate about design problems.

37

I decided it would be useful to discover which of Fowler and Beck's 22 code smells are addressed by the refactorings I present in this book. While completing this task, I discovered 5 new code smells that suggest the need for pattern-directed refactorings. In all, the refactorings in this book address 12 code smells.

Table 4.1 lists the 12 smells and some refactorings to consider when you want to remove the smells. Deodorizing such smells is best done by considering the associated refactorings. The sections in this chapter discuss each of the 12 smells in turn and provide guidance for when to use the different refactorings.

Table 4.1

Smell[a]	Refactoring
Duplicated Code (39) [F]	*Form Template Method (205)* *Introduce Polymorphic Creation with Factory Method (88)* *Chain Constructors (340)* *Replace One/Many Distinctions with Composite (224)* *Extract Composite (214)* *Unify Interfaces with Adapter (247)* *Introduce Null Object (301)*
Long Method (40) [F]	*Compose Method (123)* *Move Accumulation to Collecting Parameter (313)* *Replace Conditional Dispatcher with Command (191)* *Move Accumulation to Visitor (320)* *Replace Conditional Logic with Strategy (129)*
Conditional Complexity (41)	*Replace Conditional Logic with Strategy (129)* *Move Embellishment to Decorator (144)* *Replace State-Altering Conditionals with State (166)* *Introduce Null Object (301)*
Primitive Obsession (41) [F]	*Replace Type Code with Class (286)* *Replace State-Altering Conditionals with State (166)* *Replace Conditional Logic with Strategy (129)* *Replace Implicit Tree with Composite (178)* *Replace Implicit Language with Interpreter (269)* *Move Embellishment to Decorator (144)* *Encapsulate Composite with Builder (96)*
Indecent Exposure (42)	*Encapsulate Classes with Factory (80)*
Solution Sprawl (43)	*Move Creation Knowledge to Factory (68)*
Alternative Classes with Different Interfaces (43) [F]	*Unify Interfaces with Adapter (247)*

Table 4.1 *(continued)*

Smell[a]	Refactoring
Lazy Class (43) [F]	*Inline Singleton (114)*
Large Class (44) [F]	*Replace Conditional Dispatcher with Command (191)* *Replace State-Altering Conditionals with State (166)* *Replace Implicit Language with Interpreter (269)*
Switch Statements (44) [F]	*Replace Conditional Dispatcher with Command (191)* *Move Accumulation to Visitor (320)*
Combinatorial Explosion (45)	*Replace Implicit Language with Interpreter (269)*
Oddball Solution (45)	*Unify Interfaces with Adapter (247)*

a. Page numbers refer to the page of the current book where the smell is discussed further. [F] indicates that the smell is discussed in Fowler and Beck's chapter "Bad Smells in Code" in *Refactoring* [F].

Duplicated Code

Duplicated code is the most pervasive and pungent smell in software. It tends to be either explicit or subtle. Explicit duplication exists in identical code, while subtle duplication exists in structures or processing steps that are outwardly different yet essentially the same.

You can often remove explicit and/or subtle duplication in subclasses of a hierarchy by applying *Form Template Method (205)*. If a method in the subclasses is implemented similarly, except for an object creation step, applying *Introduce Polymorphic Creation with Factory Method (88)* will pave the way for removing more duplication by means of a Template Method.

If the constructors of a class contain duplicated code, you can often eliminate the duplication by applying *Chain Constructors (340)*.

If you have separate code for processing a single object or a collection of objects, you may be able to remove duplication by applying *Replace One/Many Distinctions with Composite (224)*.

If subclasses of a hierarchy each implement their own Composite, the implementations may be identical, in which case you can use *Extract Composite (214)*.

If you process objects differently merely because they have different interfaces, applying *Unify Interfaces with Adapter (247)* will pave the way for removing duplicated processing logic.

If you have conditional logic to deal with an object when it is null and the same null logic is duplicated throughout your system, applying *Introduce Null Object (301)* will eliminate the duplication and simplify the system.

Long Method

In their description of this smell, Fowler and Beck [F] explain several good reasons why short methods are superior to long methods. A principal reason involves the sharing of logic. Two long methods may very well contain duplicated code. Yet if you break those methods into smaller ones, you can often find ways for them to share logic.

Fowler and Beck also describe how small methods help explain code. If you don't understand what a chunk of code does and you extract that code to a small, well-named method, it will be easier to understand the original code. Systems that have a majority of small methods tend to be easier to extend and maintain because they're easier to understand and contain less duplication.

What is the preferred size of small methods? I would say ten lines of code or fewer, with the majority of your methods using one to five lines of code. If you make the vast majority of a system's methods small, you can have a few methods that are larger, as long as they are simple to understand and don't contain duplication.

Some programmers choose not to write small methods because they fear the performance costs associated with chaining calls to many small methods. This is an unfortunate choice for several reasons. First, good designers don't prematurely optimize code. Second, chaining together small method calls often costs very little in performance—a fact you can confirm by using a profiler. Third, if you do happen to experience performance problems, you can often refactor to improve performance without having to give up your small methods.

When I'm faced with a long method, one of my first impulses is to break it down into a Composed Method [Beck, SBPP] by applying the refactoring *Compose Method (123)*. This work usually involves applying *Extract Method* [F]. If the code you're transforming into a Composed Method accumulates information to a common variable, consider applying *Move Accumulation to Collecting Parameter (313)*.

If your method is long because it contains a large switch statement for dispatching and handling requests, you can shrink the method by using *Replace Conditional Dispatcher with Command (191)*.

If you use a switch statement to gather data from numerous classes with different interfaces, you can shrink the size of the method by applying *Move Accumulation to Visitor (320)*.

If a method is long because it contains numerous versions of an algorithm and conditional logic to choose which version to use at runtime, you can shrink the size of the method by applying *Replace Conditional Logic with Strategy (129)*.

Conditional Complexity

Conditional logic is innocent in its infancy, when it is simple to understand and contained within a few lines of code. Unfortunately, it rarely ages well. For example, you implement several new features and suddenly your conditional logic becomes complicated and expansive. Several refactorings in *Refactoring* [F] and this catalog address such problems.

If conditional logic controls which of several variants of a calculation to execute, consider applying *Replace Conditional Logic with Strategy (129)*.

If conditional logic controls which of several pieces of special-case behavior must be executed in addition to the class's core behavior, you may want to use *Move Embellishment to Decorator (144)*.

If the conditional expressions that control an object's state transitions are complex, consider simplifying the logic by applying *Replace State-Altering Conditionals with State (166)*.

Dealing with null cases often leads to the creation of conditional logic. If the same null conditional logic is duplicated throughout your system, you can clean it up by using *Introduce Null Object (301)*.

Primitive Obsession

Primitives, which include integers, strings, doubles, arrays, and other low-level language elements, are generic because many people use them. Classes, on the other hand, may be as specific as you need them to be because you create them for specific purposes. In many cases, classes provide a simpler and more natural way to model things than primitives. In addition, once you create a class, you'll often discover that other code in a system belongs in that class.

Fowler and Beck [F] explain how Primitive Obsession manifests itself when code relies too much on primitives. This typically occurs when you haven't yet seen how a higher-level abstraction can clarify or simplify your code. Fowler's refactorings include many of the most common solutions for addressing this problem. This book builds on those solutions and offers more.

If a primitive value controls logic in a class and the primitive value isn't type-safe (i.e., clients can assign it to an unsafe or incorrect value), consider applying *Replace Type Code with Class (286)*. The result will be code that is type-safe and capable of being extended by new behavior (something you can't do with a primitive).

If an object's state transitions are controlled by complex conditional logic that uses primitive values, you can use *Replace State-Altering Conditionals with State (166)*. The result will be numerous classes to represent each state and simplified state transition logic.

If complicated conditional logic controls which algorithm to run and that logic relies on primitive values, consider applying *Replace Conditional Logic with Strategy (129)*.

If you implicitly create a tree structure using a primitive representation, such as a string, your code may be difficult to work with, prone to errors, and/or filled with duplication. Applying *Replace Implicit Tree with Composite (178)* will reduce these problems.

If many methods of a class exist to support numerous combinations of primitive values, you may have an implicit language. If so, consider applying *Replace Implicit Language with Interpreter (269)*.

If primitive values exist in a class only to provide embellishments to the class's core responsibility, you may want to use *Move Embellishment to Decorator (144)*.

Finally, even if you have a class, it may still be too primitive to make life easy for clients. This may be the case if you have a Composite [DP] implementation that is tricky to work with. You can simplify how clients build the Composite by applying *Encapsulate Composite with Builder (96)*.

Indecent Exposure

This smell indicates the lack of what David Parnas so famously termed "information hiding" [Parnas]. The smell occurs when methods or classes that ought not be visible to clients are publicly visible to them. Exposing such code means that clients know about code that is unimportant or only indirectly important. This contributes to the complexity of a design.

The refactoring *Encapsulate Classes with Factory (80)* deodorizes this smell. Not every class that is useful to clients needs to be public (i.e., have a public constructor). Some classes ought to be referenced only via their common interfaces. You can make that happen if you make the class's constructors non-public and use a Factory to produce instances.

Solution Sprawl

When code and/or data used to perform a responsibility becomes sprawled across numerous classes, Solution Sprawl is in the air. This smell often results from quickly adding a feature to a system without spending enough time simplifying and consolidating the design to best accommodate the feature.

Solution Sprawl is the identical twin brother of Shotgun Surgery, a smell described by Fowler and Beck [F]. You become aware of this smell when adding or updating a system feature causes you to make changes to many different pieces of code. Solution Sprawl and Shotgun Surgery address the same problem, yet are sensed differently. We become aware of Solution Sprawl by observing it, while we become aware of Shotgun Surgery by doing it.

Move Creation Knowledge to Factory (68) is a refactoring that solves the problem of a sprawling object creation responsibility.

Alternative Classes with Different Interfaces

This Fowler and Beck [F] coding smell occurs when the interfaces of two classes are different and yet the classes are quite similar. If you can find the similarities between the two classes, you can often refactor the classes to make them share a common interface.

However, sometimes you can't directly change the interface of a class because you don't have control over the code. The typical example is when you're working with a third-party library. In that case, you can apply *Unify Interfaces with Adapter (247)* to produce a common interface for the two classes.

Lazy Class

When describing this smell, Fowler and Beck write, "A class that isn't doing enough to pay for itself should be eliminated" [F, 83]. It's not uncommon to encounter a Singleton [DP] that isn't paying for itself. In fact, the Singleton may be costing you something by making your design too dependent on what amounts to global data. *Inline Singleton (114)* explains a quick, humane procedure for eliminating a Singleton.

Large Class

Fowler and Beck [F] note that the presence of too many instance variables usually indicates that a class is trying to do too much. In general, large classes typically contain too many responsibilities. *Extract Class* [F] and *Extract Subclass* [F], which are some of the main refactorings used to address this smell, help move responsibilities to other classes. The pattern-directed refactorings in this book make use of these refactorings to reduce the size of classes.

Replace Conditional Dispatcher with Command (191) extracts behavior into Command [DP] classes, which can greatly reduce the size of a class that performs a variety of behaviors in response to different requests.

Replace State-Altering Conditionals with State (166) can reduce a large class filled with state transition code into a small class that delegates to a family of State [DP] classes.

Replace Implicit Language with Interpreter (269) can reduce a large class into a small one by transforming copious code for emulating a language into a small Interpreter [DP].

Switch Statements

Switch statements (or their equivalent, if…elseif…elseif… structures) aren't inherently bad. They become bad only when they make your design more complicated or rigid than it needs to be. In that case, it's best to refactor away from switch statements to a more object-based or polymorphic solution.

Replace Conditional Dispatcher with Command (191) describes how to break down a large switch statement into a collection of Command [DP] objects, each of which may be looked up and invoked without relying on conditional logic.

Move Accumulation to Visitor (320) describes an example where switch statements are used to obtain data from instances of classes that have different interfaces. By refactoring the code to use a Visitor [DP], no conditional logic is needed and the design becomes more flexible.

Combinatorial Explosion

This smell is a subtle form of duplication. It exists when you have numerous pieces of code that do the same thing using different kinds or quantities of data or objects.

For example, say you have numerous methods on a class for performing queries. Each of these methods performs a query using specific conditions and data. The more specialized queries you need to support, the more query methods you must create. Pretty soon you have an explosion of methods to handle the many ways of performing queries. You also have an implicit query language. You can remove all of these methods and the combinatorial explosion smell by applying *Replace Implicit Language with Interpreter (269)*.

Oddball Solution

When a problem is solved one way throughout a system and the same problem is solved another way in the same system, one of the solutions is the oddball or inconsistent solution. The presence of this smell usually indicates subtly duplicated code.

To remove this duplication, first determine your preferred solution. In some cases, the solution used least often may be your preferred solution if it is better than the solution used most of the time. After determining your preferred solution, you can often apply *Substitute Algorithm* [F] to produce a consistent solution throughout your system. Given a consistent solution, you may be able to move all instances of the solution to one place, thereby removing duplication.

The Oddball Solution smell is usually present when you have a preferred way to communicate with a set of classes, yet differences in the interfaces of the classes prevent you from communicating with them in a consistent way. In that case, consider applying *Unify Interfaces with Adapter (247)* to produce a common interface by which you may communicate consistently with all of the classes. Once you do that, you can often discover ways to remove duplicated processing logic.

Chapter 5

A Catalog of Refactorings to Patterns

This chapter looks at the format of the refactorings in this book, the projects referenced in the refactorings, the maturity level of the refactorings, as well as a suggested study sequence for the catalog.

Format of the Refactorings

The format of each refactoring in this book mostly follows the format used by Martin Fowler in *Refactoring* [F], with a few of my own embellishments. Each refactoring generally has most, if not all, of the following parts.

- **Name:** The name is important for building up a vocabulary of refactorings. The refactorings in this book refer to numerous refactorings in *Refactoring* as well as refactorings in this book.

- **Summary:** Each refactoring in this book describes a design transformation. I use textual and diagrammatic descriptions to explain each transformation. I call the diagrammatic portion of the summary a **sketch** because it uses UML to show the essence of a design transformation. The sketches use a variety of UML diagrams, including class, object, collaboration, and sequence diagrams. The sketches rarely show every method or field within a class, as that would distract the reader from the essence of the transformation. Most of the sketches also include gray boxes that contain the names of important participants in a refactoring. For example, the diagram on the next page shows the "after" sketch from *Move Embellishment to Decorator (144)*.

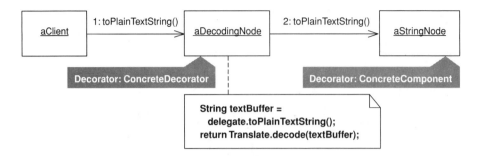

The participants listed in the gray boxes, "Decorator: ConcreteDecorator" and "Decorator: ConcreteComponent," both originate from the Participants section from the *Decorator* pattern in *Design Patterns* [DP]. In some cases, the participants listed in gray boxes originate from the names of classes or methods that I write about in the Mechanics section of a refactoring.

- **Motivation:** This section describes why you'd want to use this refactoring. It also tends to include high-level descriptions that give a good overview of the patterns. If you need further details, it will be best to consult a book that describes the particular pattern in depth.

  At the end of the Motivation section, I include a box that lists the benefits and liabilities associated with the refactoring. A plus sign (+) signifies a benefit, while a minus sign (–) signifies a liability. Here's an example from the refactoring *Replace State-Altering Conditionals with State (166).*

Benefits and Liabilities

+ Reduces or removes state-changing conditional logic.
+ Simplifies complex state-changing logic.
+ Provides a good bird's-eye view of state-changing logic.
– Complicates a design when state transition logic is already easy to follow.

- **Mechanics:** This section lists the step-by-step instructions for implementing the refactoring. Some Mechanics sections include a preamble that describes what ought to be in place before you begin the refactoring. All of the Mechanics sections include numbered steps, so you can easily correlate these steps with the numbered steps in the Example sections.

You'll find that the Mechanics sections reference many of the refactorings in *Refactoring* [F]. To fully understand the Mechanics sections in this book, I suggest that you have *Refactoring* close by your side.

I also advise that you don't treat these sections like gospel. At best, they offer a safe way to get from one design to another. If your situation demands an alternate path, don't hesitate to try it. Also remember that you can often follow the steps in a Mechanics section part way, and if you achieve enough of a design improvement, stop there. Only implement all the steps of a Mechanics section if doing so truly improves your design.

- **Example:** This section is where I go into great depth about how I used the refactoring in question to transform a design. Each step within an Example section is numbered and correlates with the numbered steps in the Mechanics section for that refactoring.

  I follow Martin Fowler's style of using boldface code (`like this`) to highlight changes made to code during the steps of each refactoring. Like Martin, I also use a strikeout font (~~like this~~) to show when I'm deleting code.

- **Variations:** A few refactorings in this book include a section that explains a variation on the refactoring. This section is by no means exhaustive—there are far too many variations on refactorings to describe them all. However, I do document some important ones.

Projects Referenced in This Catalog

The examples in this book either come from real-world projects or are inspired by real-world projects I've worked on. I use real-world code rather than toy code because when we refactor real-world code, our refactoring decisions are constrained by forces present in the code. This doesn't happen as much with toy code. In addition, toy code, which tends to lack these forces or contain only a portion of them, never seems to offer as rich an educational experience as real-world code.

Real-world code can take a little more effort to understand than toy code. I've tried to make it easier to understand the real-world code in this book by removing most of the extraneous details. Yet it's impossible to remove all rough edges in real-world code, and doing so could even diminish what can be learned from real-world refactorings.

The code used in the Example sections comes from diverse projects. Some of these projects are referenced only once, while others are referenced several times in different refactorings. The projects you'll find referenced in multiple refactorings are described briefly in the following subsections.

XML Builders

Many information systems I've worked on have produced XML, and nearly all
of these systems have used the very basics of XML: open and closed tags, with
values and attributes. When you work with the basics of XML, it often makes
little sense to create XML using a sophisticated third-party library, even if it's
free. You can easily write your own code to create XML exactly as you need it.
I've found that my own XML code is simpler than that created by third-party
tools, which must provide complex ways to create or manipulate XML.

Over the years, I've written code to create XML in numerous ways. In this
book, you'll find references to an `XMLBuilder`, a `DOMBuilder`, a `TagBuilder`, and a `Tag-
Node`. The `TagBuilder` is my favorite XML builder; it evolved out of my work on
other XML builders.

The following refactorings contain example code involved in building XML:

- *Replace Implicit Tree with Composite (178)*
- *Introduce Polymorphic Creation with Factory Method (88)*
- *Encapsulate Composite with Builder (96)*
- *Move Accumulation to Collecting Parameter (313)*
- *Unify Interfaces with Adapter (247)*

HTML Parser

The HTML Parser (*http://sourceforge.net/projects/htmlparser*) is an open source
library that allows programs to easily parse HTML. It is the most popular
HTML parser on SourceForge (*http://sourceforge.net*) and is used by many people throughout the world. This project was initiated by Somik Raha. Somik and
others on the project made sure to write many tests as they developed the
parser. When I joined the project, I found areas in the code that required design
improvements. So I began refactoring, often while pair-programming with
Somik. This work yielded many interesting refactorings, including numerous
refactorings to patterns.

The following refactorings contain examples from the parser:

- *Move Embellishment to Decorator (144)*
- *Move Creation Knowledge to Factory (68)*

- *Extract Composite (214)*

- *Move Accumulation to Visitor (320)*

Loan Risk Calculator

I spent the first eight years of my career programming for a bank on Wall Street, creating loan calculators to assess credit, market, and global risk. At the time, I even wore suits! Some of my earliest object-oriented systems were written using Turbo Pascal and C++. While I cannot show code from those systems in this book, I can show code inspired by them. For sensitive calculations, I modified the code to use calculations you might find in any financial textbook.

The following refactorings contain examples related to my work on the loan risk calculator:

- *Chain Constructors (340)*

- *Replace Constructors with Creation Methods (57)*

- *Replace Conditional Logic with Strategy (129)*

A Starting Point

In a section called "How Mature Are These Refactorings?" Martin Fowler writes:

> As you use the refactorings [in this book] bear in mind that they are a starting point. You will doubtless find gaps in them. I'm publishing them now because although they are not perfect, I do believe they are useful. I believe they will give you a starting point that will improve your ability to refactor efficiently. That is what they do for me. [F, 107]

The same can be said of the refactorings in this book. They too are a starting point. With today's evolving tools and variety of object-oriented languages, there are many ways to perform refactorings.

It's best to treat my refactorings as a recipe that you adapt to your environment. This may mean skipping some steps in the mechanics of a refactoring, or it may mean going about the refactoring in a different way. What matters in the end is not the steps you follow but whether or not you improve the design of your code. If this book gives you useful ideas for improving your code, I'll be happy.

This catalog does not describe all of the possible pattern-directed refactorings I could have included. After writing 27 refactorings, it seemed like it was time to ship a book. However, my hope is that other authors will help extend this catalog to document additional pattern-directed refactorings that will be useful to programmers.

A Study Sequence

To thoroughly learn the refactorings in the catalog, you'll want to study every refactoring's example code. Because several refactorings refer to the same project, you'll find it easier to understand the refactorings if you follow them using the study sequence shown in Table 5.1.

Table 5.1

Session	Refactoring(s)
1	*Replace Constructors with Creation Methods (57)* *Chain Constructors (340)*
2	*Encapsulate Classes with Factory (80)*
3	*Introduce Polymorphic Creation with Factory Method (88)*
4	*Replace Conditional Logic with Strategy (129)*
5	*Form Template Method (205)*
6	*Compose Method (123)*
7	*Replace Implicit Tree with Composite (178)*
8	*Encapsulate Composite with Builder (96)*
9	*Move Accumulation to Collecting Parameter (313)*
10	*Extract Composite (214)* *Replace One/Many Distinctions with Composite (224)*
11	*Replace Conditional Dispatcher with Command (191)*
12	*Extract Adapter (258)* *Unify Interfaces with Adapter (247)*
13	*Replace Type Code with Class (286)*
14	*Replace State-Altering Conditionals with State (166)*
15	*Introduce Null Object (301)*
16	*Inline Singleton (114)* *Limit Instantiation with Singleton (296)*

Table 5.1 *(continued)*

Session	Refactoring(s)
17	*Replace Hard-Coded Notifications with Observer (236)*
18	*Move Embellishment to Decorator (144)* *Unify Interfaces (343)* *Extract Parameter (346)*
19	*Move Creation Knowledge to Factory (68)*
20	*Move Accumulation to Visitor (320)*
21	*Replace Implicit Language with Interpreter (269)*

Chapter 6

Creation

While every object-oriented system creates objects or object structures, the creation code is not always free of duplication, simple, intuitive, or as loosely coupled to client code as it could be. The six refactorings in this chapter target design problems in everything from constructors to overly complicated construction logic to unnecessary Singletons [DP]. While these refactorings don't address every creational design problem you'll likely encounter, they do address some of the most common problems.

If there are too many constructors on a class, clients will have a difficult time knowing which constructor to call. One solution is to reduce the number of constructors by applying such refactorings as *Extract Class* [F] or *Extract Subclass* [F]. If that isn't possible or useful, you can clarify the intention of the constructors by applying *Replace Constructors with Creation Methods (57)*.

What is a Creation Method? It is simply a static or nonstatic method that creates and returns an object instance. For this book, I decided to define the Creation Method pattern to help distinguish it from the Factory Method [DP] pattern. A Factory Method is useful for polymorphic creation. Unlike a Creation Method, a Factory Method may not be static and must be implemented by at least two classes, typically a superclass and a subclass. If classes in a hierarchy implement a method similarly, except for an object creation step, you can likely remove duplicate code by first applying *Introduce Polymorphic Creation with Factory Method (88)*.

A class that is a Factory is one that implements one or more Creation Methods. If data and/or code used in object creation become sprawled across numerous classes, you'll likely find yourself frequently updating code in numerous places, a sure sign of the smell *Solution Sprawl (43)*. Applying *Move Creation Knowledge to Factory (68)* will reduce creational sprawl by consolidating creation code and data under a single Factory.

Encapsulate Classes with Factory (80) is another useful refactoring that involves the Factory pattern. The two most common motivations for applying this refactoring are (1) to ensure that clients communicate with instances of classes via a common interface and (2) to reduce client knowledge of classes while making instances of the classes accessible via a Factory.

To simplify the construction of an object structure, there is no better pattern than Builder [DP]. *Encapsulate Composite with Builder (96)* shows how a Builder can provide a simpler, less error-prone way to construct a Composite [DP].

The final refactoring in this section is *Inline Singleton (114)*. It was a joy to write this refactoring, for I often encounter Singletons that do not need to exist. This refactoring, which shows you how to remove a Singleton from your code, features advice about Singletons from Ward Cunningham, Kent Beck, and Martin Fowler.

Replace Constructors with Creation Methods

Constructors on a class make it hard to decide
which constructor to call during development.

Replace the constructors with intention-revealing
Creation Methods that return object instances.

Loan
+Loan(commitment, riskRating, maturity)
+Loan(commitment, riskRating, maturity, expiry)
+Loan(commitment, outstanding, riskRating, maturity, expiry)
+Loan(capitalStrategy, commitment, riskRating, maturity, expiry)
+Loan(capitalStrategy, commitment, outstanding, riskRating, maturity, expiry)

Loan
-Loan(capitalStrategy, commitment, outstanding, riskRating, maturity, expiry)
+createTermLoan(commitment, riskRating, maturity) : Loan
+createTermLoan(capitalStrategy, commitment, outstanding, riskRating, maturity) : Loan
+createRevolver(commitment, outstanding, riskRating, expiry) : Loan
+createRevolver(capitalStrategy, commitment, outstanding, riskRating, expiry) : Loan
+createRCTL(commitment, outstanding, riskRating, maturity, expiry) : Loan
+createRCTL(capitalStrategy, commitment, outstanding, riskRating, maturity, expiry) : Loan

Motivation

Some languages allow you to name constructors any way you like, regardless of
the name of the class. Other languages, such as Java and C++, don't allow this;
each constructor must be named after its class. If you have one simple constructor, this may not be a problem. On the other hand, if you have multiple constructors, programmers will have to choose which constructor to call by studying the
expected parameters and/or poking around at the constructor code. What's
wrong with that? A lot.

Constructors simply don't communicate intention efficiently or effectively. The more constructors you have, the easier it is for programmers to choose the wrong one. Having to choose which constructor to call slows down development, and the code that does call one of the many constructors often fails to sufficiently communicate the nature of the object being constructed.

If you need to add a new constructor to a class with the same signature as an existing constructor, you're out of luck. Because they have to share the same name, you can't add the new constructor—since it isn't possible to have two constructors with the same signature in the same class, despite the fact that they would create different kinds of objects.

It's common, particularly on mature systems, to find numerous constructors that are no longer being used yet continue to live on in the code. Why are these dead constructors still present? Most of the time it's because programmers don't know that the constructors have no caller. Either they haven't checked for callers (perhaps because the search expression they'd need to formulate is too complicated) or they aren't using a development environment that automatically highlights uncalled code. Whatever the reason, dead constructors only bloat a class and make it more complicated than it needs to be.

A Creation Method can help make these problems go away. A Creation Method is simply a static or nonstatic method on a class that instantiates new instances of the class. There are no name constraints on Creation Methods, so you can name them to clearly express what you are creating (e.g., createTermLoan() or createRevolver()). This naming flexibility means that two differently named Creation Methods can accept the same number and type of arguments. And for programmers who lack modern development environments, it's usually easier to find dead Creation Method code than it is to find dead constructor code because the search expressions on specifically named methods are easier to formulate than the search expressions on one of a group of constructors.

One liability of this refactoring is that it may introduce a nonstandard way to perform creation. If most of your classes are instantiated using new yet some are instantiated using a Creation Method, programmers will have to learn how creation gets done for each class. However, this nonstandard technique for creation may be a lesser evil than having classes with too many constructors.

After you have identified a class that has many constructors, it's best to consider applying *Extract Class* [F] or *Extract Subclass* [F] *before* you decide to apply this refactoring. *Extract Class* is a good choice if the class in question is simply doing too much work (i.e., it has too many responsibilities). *Extract Subclass* is a good choice if instances of the class use only a small portion of the class's instance variables.

Creation Methods and Factory Methods

What does our industry call a method that creates objects? Many programmers would answer "Factory Method," after the name given to a creational pattern in *Design Patterns* [DP]. But are all methods that create objects true Factory Methods? Given a broad definition of the term (i.e., a method that simply creates objects), the answer would be an emphatic "yes!" But given the way the authors of the Factory Method pattern wrote it in 1995, it's clear that not every method that creates objects offers the kind of loose coupling provided by a genuine Factory Method (e.g., see *Introduce Polymorphic Creation with Factory Method, 88*).

To help us be clear when discussing designs or refactorings related to object creation, I'm using the term Creation Method to refer to a static or nonstatic method that creates instances of a class. This means that every Factory Method is a Creation Method but not necessarily the reverse. It also means that you can substitute the term Creation Method wherever Martin Fowler uses the term "factory method" in *Refactoring* [F] and wherever Joshua Bloch uses the term "static factory method" in *Effective Java* [Bloch].

Benefits and Liabilities

+ Communicates what kinds of instances are available better than constructors.
+ Bypasses constructor limitations, such as the inability to have two constructors with the same number and type of arguments.
+ Makes it easier to find unused creation code.
− Makes creation nonstandard: some classes are instantiated using new, while others use *Creation Methods*.

Mechanics

Before beginning this refactoring, identify the *catch-all constructor*, a full-featured constructor to which other constructors delegate their work. If you don't have a catch-all constructor, create one by applying *Chain Constructors (340)*.

1. Find a client that calls a class's constructor in order to create a *kind* of instance. Apply *Extract Method* [F] on the constructor call to produce a public, static method. This new method is a *creation method*. Now apply *Move Method* [F] to move the creation method to the class containing the chosen constructor.

    ✔ Compile and test.

2. Find all callers of the chosen constructor that instantiate the same kind of instance as the creation method and update them to call the creation method.

    ✔ Compile and test.

3. If the chosen constructor is chained to another constructor, make the creation method call the chained constructor instead of the chosen constructor. You can do this by inlining the constructor, a refactoring that resembles *Inline Method* [F].

    ✔ Compile and test.

4. Repeat steps 1–3 for every constructor on the class that you'd like to turn into a Creation Method.

5. If a constructor on the class has no callers outside the class, make it non-public.

    ✔ Compile.

Example

This example is inspired from the banking domain and a certain loan risk calculator I spent several years writing, extending, and maintaining. The Loan class had numerous constructors, as shown in the following code.

```
public class Loan...
   public Loan(double commitment, int riskRating, Date maturity) {
      this(commitment, 0.00, riskRating, maturity, null);
   }

   public Loan(double commitment, int riskRating, Date maturity, Date expiry) {
      this(commitment, 0.00, riskRating, maturity, expiry);
   }
```

```java
public Loan(double commitment, double outstanding,
        int riskRating, Date maturity, Date expiry) {
  this(null, commitment, outstanding, riskRating, maturity, expiry);
}

public Loan(CapitalStrategy capitalStrategy, double commitment,
        int riskRating, Date maturity, Date expiry) {
  this(capitalStrategy, commitment, 0.00, riskRating, maturity, expiry);
}

public Loan(CapitalStrategy capitalStrategy, double commitment,
        double outstanding, int riskRating,
        Date maturity, Date expiry) {
  this.commitment = commitment;
  this.outstanding = outstanding;
  this.riskRating = riskRating;
  this.maturity = maturity;
  this.expiry = expiry;
  this.capitalStrategy = capitalStrategy;

  if (capitalStrategy == null) {
    if (expiry == null)
      this.capitalStrategy = new CapitalStrategyTermLoan();
    else if (maturity == null)
      this.capitalStrategy = new CapitalStrategyRevolver();
    else
      this.capitalStrategy = new CapitalStrategyRCTL();
  }
}
```

Loan could be used to represent seven kinds of loans. I will discuss only three of them here. A term loan is a loan that must be fully paid by its maturity date. A revolver, which is like a credit card, is a loan that signifies "revolving credit": you have a spending limit and an expiry date. A revolving credit term loan (RCTL) is a revolver that transforms into a term loan when the revolver expires.

Given that the calculator supported seven kinds of loans, you might wonder why Loan wasn't an abstract superclass with a subclass for each kind of loan. After all, that would have cut down on the number of constructors needed for Loan and its subclasses. There were two reasons why this was not a good idea.

1. What distinguishes the different kinds of loans is not so much their fields but how numbers, like capital, income, and duration, are calculated. To support three different ways to calculate capital for a term loan, we wouldn't want to create three different subclasses of Loan. It's easier to support one Loan class and have three different Strategy classes for a term loan (see the example from *Replace Conditional Logic with Strategy, 129*).

2. The application that used Loan instances needed to transform loans from one kind of loan to another. This transformation was easier to do when it involved changing a few fields on a single Loan instance, rather than completely changing one instance of a Loan subclass into another.

If you look at the Loan source code presented earlier, you'll see that it has five constructors, the last of which is its *catch-all constructor* (see *Chain Constructors, 340*). Without specialized knowledge, it is difficult to know which constructors create term loans, which ones create revolvers, and which ones create RCTLs.

I happen to know that an RCTL needs both an expiry date and a maturity date, so I know that to create an RCTL, I must call a constructor that lets me pass in both dates. Did you know that? Do you think the next programmer who reads this code will know it?

What else is embedded as implicit knowledge in the Loan constructors? Plenty. If you call the first constructor, which takes three parameters, you'll get back a term loan. But if you want a revolver, you'll need to call one of the constructors that take two dates and then supply null for the maturity date. I wonder if all users of this code will know this? Or will they just have to learn by encountering some ugly defects?

Let's see what happens when I apply the *Replace Constructors with Creation Methods* refactoring.

1. My first step is to find a client that calls one of Loan's constructors. Here is one such caller that resides in a test case:

```
public class CapitalCalculationTests...
    public void testTermLoanNoPayments() {
        ...
        Loan termLoan = new Loan(commitment, riskRating, maturity);
        ...
    }
```

In this case, a call to the above Loan constructor produces a term loan. I apply *Extract Method* [F] on that call to produce a public, static method called createTermLoan:

```
public class CapitalCalculationTests...
    public void testTermLoanNoPayments() {
        ...
        Loan termLoan = createTermLoan(commitment, riskRating, maturity);
        ...
    }
```

```
public static Loan createTermLoan(double commitment, int riskRating, Date maturity) {
    return new Loan(commitment, riskRating, maturity);
}
```

Next, I apply *Move Method* [F] on the creation method, createTermLoan, to move it to Loan. This produces the following changes:

```
public class Loan...
    public static Loan createTermLoan(double commitment, int riskRating, Date maturity) {
        return new Loan(commitment, riskRating, maturity);
    }

public class CapitalCalculationTest...
    public void testTermLoanNoPayments() {
        ...
        Loan termLoan = Loan.createTermLoan(commitment, riskRating, maturity);
        ...
    }
```

I compile and test to confirm that everything works.

2. Next, I find all callers on the constructor that createTermLoan calls, and I update them to call createTermLoan. For example:

```
public class CapitalCalculationTest...
    public void testTermLoanOnePayment() {
        ...
        Loan termLoan = new Loan(commitment, riskRating, maturity);
        Loan termLoan = Loan.createTermLoan(commitment, riskRating, maturity);
        ...
    }
```

Once again, I compile and test to confirm that everything is working.

3. The createTermLoan method is now the only caller on the constructor. Because this constructor is chained to another constructor, I can remove it by applying *Inline Method* [F] (which, in this case, is actually "inline constructor"). This leads to the following changes:

```
public class Loan...
    public Loan(double commitment, int riskRating, Date maturity) {
        this(commitment, 0.00, riskRating, maturity, null);
    }

    public static Loan createTermLoan(double commitment, int riskRating, Date maturity) {
        return new Loan(commitment, 0.00, riskRating, maturity, null);
    }
```

I compile and test to confirm that the change works.

4. Now I repeat steps 1–3 to produce additional creation methods on Loan. For example, here is some code that calls Loan's catch-all constructor:

```
public class CapitalCalculationTest...
   public void testTermLoanWithRiskAdjustedCapitalStrategy() {
      ...
      Loan termLoan = new Loan(riskAdjustedCapitalStrategy, commitment,
                          outstanding, riskRating, maturity, null);
      ...
   }
```

Notice the null value that is passed in as the last parameter to the constructor. Passing in null values to a constructor is bad practice. It reduces the code's readability. It usually happens because programmers can't find the exact constructor they need, so instead of creating yet another constructor they call a more general-purpose one.

To refactor this code to use a creation method, I'll follow steps 1 and 2. Step 1 leads to another createTermLoan method on Loan:

```
public class CapitalCalculationTest...
   public void testTermLoanWithRiskAdjustedCapitalStrategy() {
      ...
      Loan termLoan = Loan.createTermLoan(riskAdjustedCapitalStrategy, commitment,
                          outstanding, riskRating, maturity, null);
      ...
   }
```

```
public class Loan...
   public static Loan createTermLoan(double commitment, int riskRating, Date maturity) {
      return new Loan(commitment, 0.00, riskRating, maturity, null);
   }

   public static Loan createTermLoan(CapitalStrategy riskAdjustedCapitalStrategy,
      double commitment, double outstanding, int riskRating, Date maturity) {
      return new Loan(riskAdjustedCapitalStrategy, commitment,
         outstanding, riskRating, maturity, null);
   }
```

Why did I choose to overload createTermLoan(...) instead of producing a creation method with a unique name, like createTermLoanWithStrategy(...)? Because I felt that the presence of the CapitalStrategy parameter sufficiently communicated the difference between the two overloaded versions of createTermLoan(...).

Now for step 2 of the refactoring. Because the new createTermLoan(...) calls Loan's catch-all constructor, I must find other clients that call the catch-all constructor to instantiate the same kind of Loan produced by createTermLoan(...). This requires careful work because some callers of the catch-all constructor produce revolver or RCTL instances of Loan. So I update only the client code that produces term loan instances of Loan.

I don't have to perform any work for step 3 because the catch-all constructor isn't chained to any other constructors. I continue to implement step 4, which involves repeating steps 1–3. When I'm done, I end up with the following creation methods:

Loan
-Loan(capitalStrategy, commitment, outstanding, riskRating, maturity, expiry)
+createTermLoan(commitment, riskRating, maturity) : Loan
+createTermLoan(capitalStrategy, commitment, outstanding, riskRating, maturity) : Loan
+createRevolver(commitment, outstanding, riskRating, expiry) : Loan
+createRevolver(capitalStrategy, commitment, outstanding, riskRating, expiry) : Loan
+createRCTL(commitment, outstanding, riskRating, maturity, expiry) : Loan
+createRCTL(capitalStrategy, commitment, outstanding, riskRating, maturity, expiry) : Loan

5. The last step is to change the visibility of the only remaining public constructor, which happens to be Loan's catch-all constructor. Since it has no subclasses and it now has no external callers, I make it private:

```
public class Loan...
    private Loan(CapitalStrategy capitalStrategy, double commitment,
                double outstanding, int riskRating,
                Date maturity, Date expiry)...
```

I compile to confirm that everything still works. The refactoring is complete.

It's now clear how to obtain different kinds of Loan instances. The ambiguities have been revealed and the implicit knowledge has been made explicit. What's left to do? Well, because the creation methods take a fairly large number of parameters, it may make sense to apply *Introduce Parameter Object* [F].

Variations

Parameterized Creation Methods

As you consider implementing *Replace Constructors with Creation Methods*, you may calculate in your head that you'd need something on the order of 50 Creation Methods to account for every object configuration supported by your class. Writing 50 methods doesn't sound like much fun, so you may decide not to apply this refactoring. Keep in mind that there are other ways to handle this situation. First, you need not produce a Creation Method for every object

configuration: you can write Creation Methods for the most popular configurations and leave some public constructors around to handle the rest of the
cases. It also makes sense to consider using parameters to cut down on the
number of Creation Methods.

Extract Factory

Can too many Creation Methods on a class obscure its primary responsibility?
This is really a matter of taste. Some folks find that when object creation begins
to dominate the public interface of a class, the class no longer strongly communicates its main purpose. If you're working with a class that has Creation Methods on it and you find that the Creation Methods distract you from the primary
responsibilities of the class, you can refactor the related Creation Methods to a
single Factory, like so:

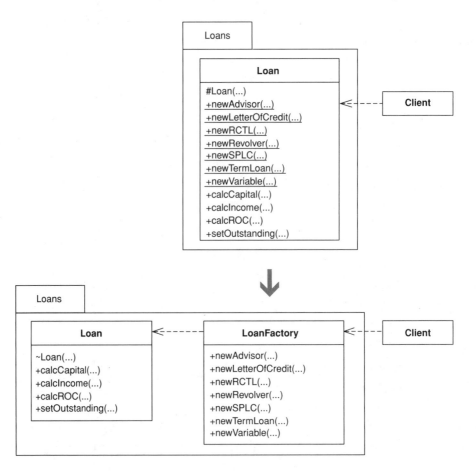

It's worth noting that LoanFactory is not an Abstract Factory [DP]. Abstract Factories can be substituted at runtime—you can define different Abstract Factory classes, each of which knows how to return a family of products, and you can outfit a system or client with a particular Abstract Factory instance. Factories tend to be less sophisticated. They are often implemented as a single class that is not part of any hierarchy.

**Move
Creation
Knowledge to
Factory**

Move Creation Knowledge to Factory

Data and code used to instantiate a class
is sprawled across numerous classes.

Move the creation knowledge into a single Factory class.

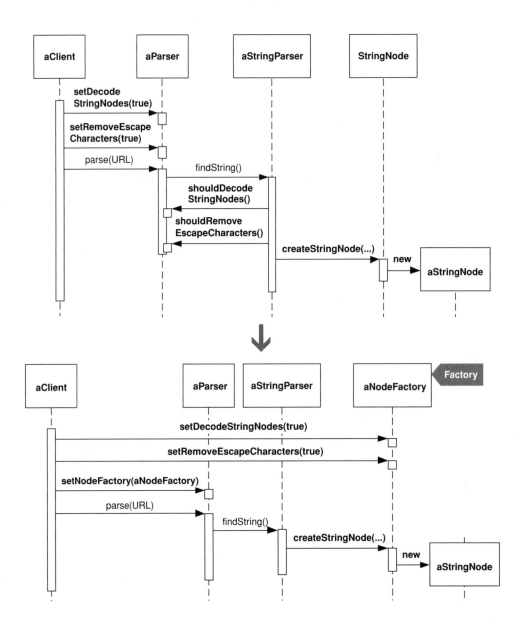

Motivation

When the knowledge for creating an object is spread out across numerous classes, you have **creation sprawl**: the placement of creational responsibilities in classes that ought not to be playing any role in an object's creation. Creation sprawl, which is a case of the *Solution Sprawl* smell (43), tends to result from an earlier design problem. For example, a client needed to configure an object based on some preferences yet lacked access to the object's creation code. If the client can't easily access the object's creation code, say, because it exists in a system layer far removed from the client, how can the client configure the object?

A typical answer is by using brute force. The client passes its configuration preferences to one object, which hands them off to another object, which holds onto them until the creation code, by means of still more objects, obtains the information for use in configuring the object. While this works, it spreads creation code and data far and wide.

The Factory pattern is helpful in this context. It uses one class to encapsulate both creation logic and a client's instantiation/configuration preferences. A client can tell a Factory instance how to instantiate/configure an object, and then the same Factory instance may be used at runtime to perform the instantiation/configuration. For example, a NodeFactory creates StringNode instances and may be configured by clients to embellish those instances with a DecodingStringNode Decorator:

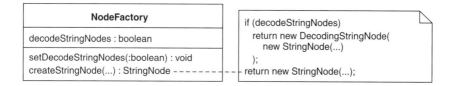

A Factory need not be implemented exclusively by a concrete class. You can use an interface to define a Factory and make an existing class implement that interface. This approach is useful when you want other areas of a system to communicate with an instance of the existing class exclusively through its Factory interface.

If the creation logic inside a Factory becomes too complex, perhaps due to supporting too many creation options, it may make sense to evolve it into an Abstract Factory [DP]. Once that's done, clients can configure a system to use a particular ConcreteFactory (i.e., a concrete implementation of an Abstract Factory) or let the system use a default ConcreteFactory. While the above NodeFactory is certainly not complicated enough to merit such an evolution, the diagram on the next page shows what it would look like as an Abstract Factory.

**Move
Creation
Knowledge to
Factory**

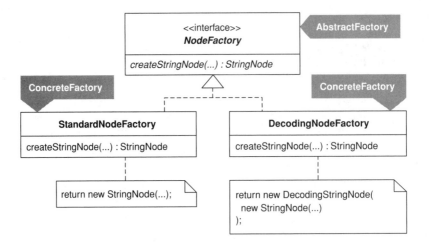

What Is a Factory?

"Factory" is one of the most overused and imprecise words in our industry. Some use the term "Factory pattern" to refer to a Factory Method [DP], some use the term to refer to an Abstract Factory [DP], some use the term to refer to both patterns, and some use the term to refer to *any* code that creates objects.

Our lack of a commonly understood definition of "Factory" limits our ability to know when a design could benefit from a Factory. So I'll offer my definition, which is both broad and bounded: A class that implements one or more Creation Methods is a Factory.

This is true if the Creation Methods are static or nonstatic; if the return type of the Creation Methods is an interface, abstract class, or concrete class; or if the class that implements the Creation Methods also implements noncreational responsibilities.

A Factory Method [DP] is a nonstatic method that returns a base class or interface type and that is implemented in a hierarchy to enable polymorphic creation (see *Introduce Polymorphic Creation with Factory Method, 88*). A Factory Method must be defined/implemented by a class and one or more subclasses of the class. The class and subclasses each act as Factories. However, we don't say that a Factory Method is a Factory.

An Abstract Factory is "an interface for creating families of related or dependent objects without specifying their concrete classes" [DP, 87]. Abstract Factories are designed to be substitutable at runtime, so a system may be configured to use a specific, concrete implementor of an Abstract Factory. Every Abstract Factory is a Factory, though not every Factory is an Abstract Factory. Classes that are Factories, not Abstract Factories, sometimes evolve into Abstract Factories when a need arises to support the creation of several families of related or dependent objects.

The next diagram, which uses bold lines to designate methods that create objects, illustrates common differences between sample Factory Method, Factory, and Abstract Factory structures.

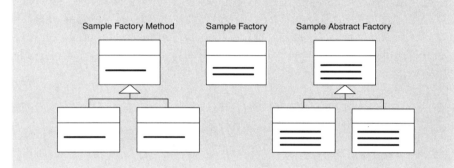

I've seen numerous systems in which the Factory pattern was overused. For example, if every object in a system is created by using a Factory, instead of direct instantiation (e.g., new StringNode(…)), the system probably has an over-abundance of Factories. Overusing this pattern often occurs when people *always* decouple client code from code that chooses between which classes to instantiate or how to instantiate them. For example, the following createQuery() method makes a choice about which of two query classes to instantiate:

```
public class Query...
   public void createQuery() throws QueryException...
      if (usingSDVersion52()) {
         query = new QuerySD52();
         ...
      } else {
         query = new QuerySD51();
         ...
      }
```

To eliminate the conditional logic in the above code, some would refactor it
to use a QueryFactory:

```
public class Query...
    public void createQuery() throws QueryException...
        query = queryFactory.createQuery();
        ...
```

QueryFactory now encapsulates the choice of what concrete query class to
instantiate. Yet does QueryFactory improve the design of this code? It certainly
doesn't consolidate creation sprawl, and if it only decouples the Query class from
the code that instantiates one of the two concrete queries, it most definitely does
not add enough value to merit its existence. This illustrates the point that it's
best not to implement a Factory unless it really improves the design of your
code or enables you to create/configure objects in a way that wasn't possible
with direct instantiation.

Benefits and Liabilities

+ Consolidates creation logic and instantiation/configuration preferences.
+ Decouples a client from creation logic.
− Complicates a design when direct instantiation would do.

Mechanics

These mechanics assume your Factory will be implemented as a class, rather
than as an interface implemented by a class. If you need a Factory interface
that is implemented by a class, you must make minor modifications to these
mechanics.

1. An *instantiator* is a class that collaborates with *other classes* to instantiate a
    product (i.e., an instance of some class). If the *instantiator* doesn't instantiate
    the *product* using a Creation Method, modify it and, if necessary, also modify
    the *product*'s class, so the instantiation occurs through a Creation Method.

    ✔ Compile and test.

2. Create a new class that will become your *factory*. Name your factory based
    on what it creates (e.g., NodeFactory, LoanFactory).

    ✔ Compile.

3. Apply *Move Method* [F] to move the Creation Method to the factory. If the Creation Method is static, you can make it nonstatic after moving it to the factory.

   ✔ Compile.

4. Update the instantiator to instantiate the factory and call the factory to obtain an instance of the class.

   ✔ Compile and test that the instantiator still functions correctly.

   Repeat this step for any instantiators that could no longer compile because of changes made during step 3.

5. Data and methods from the other classes are still being used in the instantiation. Move whatever makes sense into the factory, so it handles as much of the creation work as possible. This may involve moving where the factory gets instantiated and who instantiates it.

   ✔ Compile and test.

Example

This example comes from the HTML Parser project. As described in *Move Embellishment to Decorator (144)*, a user of the parser can instruct it to handle string parsing in different ways. If a user doesn't want parsed strings to contain encoded characters, like & (which represents an ampersand, &) or < (which represents an opening angle bracket, <), the user can call the parser's setString-NodeDecoding(shouldDecode: boolean) method, which turns the string decoding option on or off. As the sketch at the beginning of this *Move Creation Knowledge to Factory* refactoring illustrates, the parser's StringParser actually creates StringNode objects, and when it does so, it configures them to decode or not decode, based on the value of the decoding field in Parser.

While this code worked, StringNode creation knowledge was now spread across the Parser, StringParser, and StringNode classes. This problem worsened as new string parsing options were added to the Parser. Each new option required the creation of a new Parser field with corresponding getters and setters, as well as new code in the StringParser and StringNode to handle the new option. The boldface code in the diagram on the following page illustrates some of the changes made to classes that resulted from adding an escape character (e.g., \n or \r) removal option.

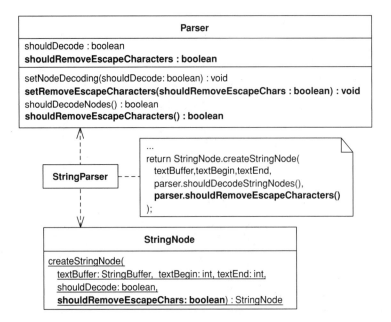

The fields, getters, and setters that were added to Parser to support different parsing options for StringNodes didn't belong on the Parser class. Why? Because Parser has the responsibility of kicking off a parsing session, not controlling how StringNodes (which represent just one of numerous Node and Tag types) ought to be parsed. In addition, the StringNode class also had no good reason to know anything about decoding or escape character removal options, which have already been modeled using the Decorator pattern (see the example for *Move Embellishment to Decorator, 144*).

Based on my earlier definition, we can say that StringNode is already a Factory because it implements a Creation Method. The trouble is, StringNode isn't helping consolidate all knowledge used in instantiating/configuring a StringNode, nor do we actually want it to because it is better to keep StringNode small and simple. A new Factory class will be better able to consolidate the instantiation/configuration, so I will refactor to one. For simplicity, the following code includes only one parsing option—the one for decoding nodes—and doesn't include the option for escape character removal.

1. StringParser instantiates StringNode objects. The first step in this *Move Creation Knowledge to Factory* refactoring is to make StringParser perform its instantiation of StringNode objects by using a Creation Method. It already does this, as the following code shows.

```
public class StringParser...
  public Node find(...) {
    ...
    return StringNode.createStringNode(
      textBuffer, textBegin, textEnd,
      parser.shouldDecodeNodes()
    );
  }

public class StringNode...
  public static Node createStringNode(
    StringBuffer textBuffer, int textBegin, int textEnd, boolean shouldDecode) {
    if (shouldDecode)
      return new DecodingStringNode(
        new StringNode(textBuffer, textBegin, textEnd)
      );
    return new StringNode(textBuffer, textBegin, textEnd);
  }
```

2. Now I create a new class that will become a factory for StringNode objects. Because a StringNode is a type of Node, I name the class NodeFactory:

```
public class NodeFactory {
}
```

3. Next, I apply *Move Method* [F] to move StringNode's Creation Method to NodeFactory. I decide to make the moved method nonstatic because I don't want client code statically bound to one Factory implementation. I also decide to delete the Creation Method in StringNode:

```
public class NodeFactory {
  public static Node createStringNode(
    StringBuffer textBuffer, int textBegin, int textEnd, boolean shouldDecode) {
    if (shouldDecode)
      return new DecodingStringNode(
        new StringNode(textBuffer, textBegin, textEnd));
    return new StringNode(textBuffer, textBegin, textEnd);
  }
}

public class StringNode...
  public static Node createStringNode(...
  }
```

After this step, StringParser and other clients that used to call the String-Node's Creation Method no longer compile. I'll fix that next.

4. Now I modify the StringParser to instantiate a NodeFactory and call it to create
    a StringNode:

```
public class StringParser...
  public Node find(...) {
    ...
    NodeFactory nodeFactory = new NodeFactory();
    return nodeFactory.createStringNode(
      textBuffer, textBegin, textEnd, parser.shouldDecodeNodes()
    );
  }
```

I perform a similar step for any other clients that no longer compile
because of work done in step 3.

5. Now comes the fun part: eliminating or reducing creation sprawl by mov-
    ing the appropriate creation code from other classes into the NodeFactory. In
    this case the other class is the Parser, which the StringParser calls to pass an
    argument to the NodeFactory during StringNode creation:

```
public class StringParser...
  public Node find(...) {
    ...
    NodeFactory nodeFactory = new NodeFactory();
    return nodeFactory.createStringNode(
      textBuffer, textBegin, textEnd, parser.shouldDecodeNodes()
    );
  }
```

I'd like to move the following Parser code to the NodeFactory:

```
public class Parser...
  private boolean shouldDecodeNodes = false;

  public void setNodeDecoding(boolean shouldDecodeNodes) {
    this.shouldDecodeNodes = shouldDecodeNodes;
  }

  public boolean shouldDecodeNodes() {
    return shouldDecodeNodes;
  }
```

However, I can't simply move this code into the NodeFactory because clients of this code are clients of the parser, which call Parser methods like
setNodeDecoding(...) to configure the parser for a given parse. Meanwhile, Node-

Factory is not even visible to parser clients: it is instantiated by StringParser, which itself is not visible to parser clients. This leads me to conclude that the NodeFactory instance must be accessible to both Parser clients and the StringParser. To make that happen, I take the following steps.

a. I first apply *Extract Class* [F] on the Parser code I want to eventually merge with the NodeFactory. This leads to the creation of the String-NodeParsingOption class:

```java
public class StringNodeParsingOption {
  private boolean decodeStringNodes;

  public boolean shouldDecodeStringNodes() {
    return decodeStringNodes;
  }

  public void setDecodeStringNodes(boolean decodeStringNodes) {
    this.decodeStringNodes = decodeStringNodes;
  }
}
```

This new class replaces the shouldDecodeNodes field, getter, and setter with a StringNodeParsingOption field and its getter and setter:

```java
public class Parser....
  private StringNodeParsingOption stringNodeParsingOption =
    new StringNodeParsingOption();

  private boolean shouldDecodeNodes = false;

  public void setNodeDecoding(boolean shouldDecodeNodes) {
    this.shouldDecodeNodes = shouldDecodeNodes;
  }

  public boolean shouldDecodeNodes() {
    return shouldDecodeNodes;
  }

  public StringNodeParsingOption getStringNodeParsingOption() {
    return stringNodeParsingOption;
  }

  public void setStringNodeParsingOption(StringNodeParsingOption option) {
    stringNodeParsingOption = option;
  }
```

**Move
Creation
Knowledge to
Factory**

Parser clients now turn StringNode decoding on by instantiating and configuring a StringNodeParsingOption instance and passing it to the parser:

```
class DecodingNodeTest...
  public void testDecodeAmpersand() {
    ...
    StringNodeParsingOption decodeNodes =
      new StringNodeParsingOption();
    decodeNodes.setDecodeStringNodes(true);
    parser.setStringNodeParsingOption(decodeNodes);
    parser.setNodeDecoding(true);
    ...
  }
```

The StringParser now obtains the state of the StringNode decoding option by means of the new class:

```
public class StringParser...
  ...
  public Node find(...) {
    NodeFactory nodeFactory = new NodeFactory();
    return nodeFactory.createStringNode(
      textBuffer,
      textBegin,
      textEnd,
      parser.getStringNodeParsingOption().shouldDecodeStringNodes()
    );
  }
```

b. Now I apply *Inline Class* [F] to merge NodeFactory with StringNodeParsing-Option. This leads to the following changes in StringParser:

```
public class StringParser...
  public Node find(...) {
    ...
    return parser.getStringNodeParsingOption().createStringNode(
      textBuffer, textBegin, textEnd,
      parser.getStringNodeParsingOption().shouldDecodeStringNodes()
    );
  }
```

And the following changes in StringNodeParsingOption:

```
public class StringNodeParsingOption...
  private boolean decodeStringNodes;
```

```
  public Node createStringNode(
    StringBuffer textBuffer, int textBegin, int textEnd, boolean shouldDecode) {
    if (decodeStringNodes)
    return new DecodingStringNode(
      new StringNode(textBuffer, textBegin, textEnd));
    return new StringNode(textBuffer, textBegin, textEnd);
  }
}
```

c. The final step is to rename the class StringNodeParsingOption to NodeFactory and then perform a similar renaming on the NodeFactory field, getter, and setter in Parser:

```
public class StringNodeParsingOption NodeFactory...

public class Parser...
  private NodeFactory nodeFactory = new NodeFactory();

  public NodeFactory getNodeFactory() {
    return nodeFactory;
  }

  public void setNodeFactory(NodeFactory nodeFactory) {
    this.nodeFactory = nodeFactory;
  }
```

And that does it. NodeFactory has helped tame creation sprawl by handling the work associated with instantiating and configuring StringNode objects.

Encapsulate Classes with Factory

Clients directly instantiate classes that reside
in one package and implement a common interface.

*Make the class constructors non-public and let clients
create instances of them using a Factory.*

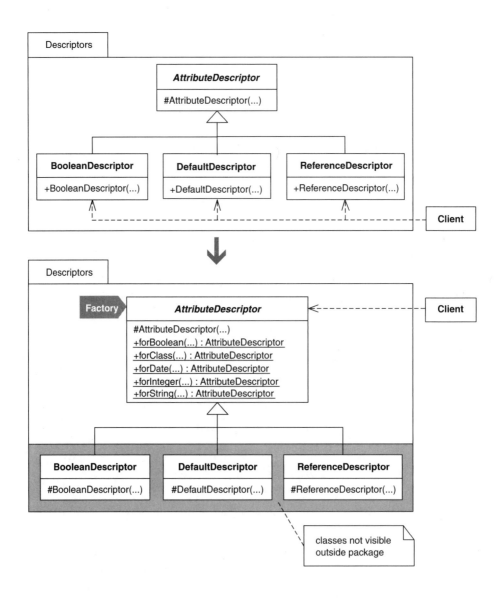

Motivation

A client's ability to directly instantiate classes is useful so long as the client needs to know about the very existence of those classes. But what if the client doesn't need that knowledge? What if the classes live in one package and implement one interface, and those conditions aren't likely to change? In that case, the classes in the package could be hidden from clients outside the package by giving a Factory the responsibility of creating and returning instances that implement a common interface.

There are several motivations for doing this. First, it provides a way to rigorously apply the mantra "program to an interface, not an implementation" [DP] by ensuring that clients interact with classes via their common interface. Second, it provides a way to reduce the "conceptual weight" [Bloch] of a package by hiding classes that don't need to be publicly visible outside their package (i.e., clients don't need to know these classes exist). And third, it simplifies the construction of available *kinds* of instances by making the set available through a Factory's intention-revealing Creation Methods.

The one major issue with this refactoring involves a dependency cycle: whenever you create a new subclass or add/modify an existing subclass constructor, you must add a new Creation Method to your Factory. If you don't often add new subclasses or add/modify constructors to existing subclasses, this is not a problem. If you do, you may wish to avoid this refactoring or transition to a design that lets clients directly instantiate whichever subclasses they like. You can also consider a hybrid approach in which you produce a Factory for the most popular kinds of instances and don't fully encapsulate all of the subclasses so that clients may instantiate classes as needed.

Programmers who make their code available to others as binary code, not source code, may also wish to avoid this refactoring because it doesn't provide clients with the ability to modify encapsulated classes or the Factory's Creation Methods.

This refactoring can yield a class that behaves as both a Factory and an implementation class (i.e., implementing non-creation-based methods). Some are comfortable with this mixture, while others aren't. If you find that such a mixtures obscures the primary responsibility of a class, consider *Extract Factory (66)*.

The sketch at the start of this refactoring gives you a glimpse of some object-to-relational database mapping code. Before the refactoring was applied, programmers (including myself) occasionally instantiated the wrong subclass or the right subclass with incorrect arguments (e.g., we called a constructor that took a primitive Java int when we really needed to call the constructor that took Java's Integer object). The refactoring reduced our defect count by encapsulating the knowledge about the subclasses and producing a single place to get a variety of well-named subclass instances.

Benefits and Liabilities

+ Simplifies the creation of kinds of instances by making the set available through intention-revealing methods.
+ Reduces the "conceptual weight" [Bloch] of a package by hiding classes that don't need to be public.
+ Helps enforce the mantra "program to an interface, not an implementation" [DP].
− Requires new/updated Creation Methods when new kinds of instances must be created.
− Limits customization when clients can only access a Factory's binary code, not its source code.

Mechanics

In general, you'll want to apply this refactoring when your classes share a common public interface, share the same superclass, and reside in the same package.

1. Find a client that calls a class's constructor in order to create a kind of instance. Apply *Extract Method* [F] on the constructor call to produce a public, static method. This new method is a *creation method*. Now apply *Move Method* [F] to move the creation method to the superclass of the class with the chosen constructor.

    ✔ Compile and test.

2. Find all callers of the chosen constructor that instantiate the same kind of instance as the creation method and update them to call the creation method.

    ✔ Compile and test.

3. Repeat steps 1 and 2 for any other kinds of instances that may be created by the class's constructor.

4. Declare the class's constructor to be non-public.

    ✔ Compile.

5. Repeat steps 1–4 for all classes you would like to encapsulate.

Example

The following example is based on object-to-relational mapping code that is used to write and read objects to and from a relational database.

1. I begin with a small hierarchy of classes that reside in a package called descriptors. These classes assist in mapping database attributes to the instance variables of objects:

```
package descriptors;

public abstract class AttributeDescriptor...
    protected AttributeDescriptor(...)

public class BooleanDescriptor extends AttributeDescriptor...
    public BooleanDescriptor(...) {
        super(...);
    }

public class DefaultDescriptor extends AttributeDescriptor...
    public DefaultDescriptor(...) {
        super(...);
    }

public class ReferenceDescriptor extends AttributeDescriptor...
    public ReferenceDescriptor(...) {
        super(...);
    }
```

The abstract AttributeDescriptor constructor is protected, and the constructors for the three subclasses are public. While I'm showing only three subclasses of AttributeDescriptor, there are actually about ten in the real code.

I'll focus on the DefaultDescriptor subclass. The first step is to identify a kind of instance that can be created by the DefaultDescriptor constructor. To do that, I look at some client code:

```
protected List createAttributeDescriptors() {
    List result = new ArrayList();
    result.add(new DefaultDescriptor("remoteId", getClass(), Integer.TYPE));
    result.add(new DefaultDescriptor("createdDate", getClass(), Date.class));
    result.add(new DefaultDescriptor("lastChangedDate", getClass(), Date.class));
    result.add(new ReferenceDescriptor("createdBy", getClass(), User.class,
        RemoteUser.class));
    result.add(new ReferenceDescriptor("lastChangedBy", getClass(), User.class,
        RemoteUser.class));
    result.add(new DefaultDescriptor("optimisticLockVersion", getClass(), Integer.TYPE));
    return result;
}
```

Here I see that DefaultDescriptor is being used to represent mappings for Integer and Date types. While it may also be used to map other types, I must focus on one kind of instance at a time. I decide to produce a creation method that will create attribute descriptors for Integer types. I begin by applying *Extract Method* [F] to produce a public, static creation method called forInteger(…):

```
protected List createAttributeDescriptors()...
   List result = new ArrayList();
   result.add(forInteger("remoteId", getClass(), Integer.TYPE));
   ...

public static DefaultDescriptor forInteger(...) {
   return new DefaultDescriptor(...);
}
```

Because forInteger(…) always creates AttributeDescriptor objects for an Integer, there is no need to pass it the value Integer.TYPE:

```
protected List createAttributeDescriptors()...
   List result = new ArrayList();
   result.add(forInteger("remoteId", getClass(), Integer.TYPE));
   ...

public static DefaultDescriptor forInteger(...) {
   return new DefaultDescriptor(..., Integer.TYPE);
}
```

I also change the forInteger(…) method's return type from DefaultDescriptor to AttributeDescriptor because I want clients to interact with all AttributeDescriptor subclasses via the AttributeDescriptor interface:

```
public static AttributeDescriptor DefaultDescriptor forInteger(...)...
```

Now I move forInteger(…) to the AttributeDescriptor class by applying *Move Method* [F]:

```
public abstract class AttributeDescriptor {
   public static AttributeDescriptor forInteger(...) {
      return new DefaultDescriptor(...);
   }
}
```

The client code now looks like this:

```
protected List createAttributeDescriptors()...
   List result = new ArrayList();
   result.add(AttributeDescriptor.forInteger(...));
   ...
```

I compile and test to confirm that everything works as expected.

2. Next, I search for all other callers to the DefaultDescriptor constructor that
    produce an AttributeDescriptor for an Integer, and I update them to call the
    new creation method:

```
protected List createAttributeDescriptors() {
    List result = new ArrayList();
    result.add(AttributeDescriptor.forInteger("remoteId", getClass()));
    ...
    result.add(AttributeDescriptor.forInteger("optimisticLockVersion", getClass()));
    return result;
}
```

    I compile and test. Everything is working.

3. Now I repeat steps 1 and 2 as I continue to produce creation methods for
    the remaining kinds of instances that the DefaultDescriptor constructor can
    create. This leads to two more creation methods:

```
public abstract class AttributeDescriptor {
    public static AttributeDescriptor forInteger(...) {
        return new DefaultDescriptor(...);
    }

    public static AttributeDescriptor forDate(...) {
        return new DefaultDescriptor(...);
    }

    public static AttributeDescriptor forString(...) {
        return new DefaultDescriptor(...);
    }
```

4. I now declare the DefaultDescriptor constructor protected:

```
public class DefaultDescriptor extends AttributeDescriptor {
    protected DefaultDescriptor(...) {
        super(...);
    }
```

    I compile and everything goes according to plan.

5. I repeat steps 1–4 for the other AttributeDescriptor subclasses. When I'm done,
    the new code

    - Gives access to AttributeDescriptor subclasses via their superclass.
    - Ensures that clients obtain subclass instances via the AttributeDescriptor
      interface.
    - Prevents clients from directly instantiating AttributeDescriptor subclasses.
    - Communicates to other programmers that AttributeDescriptor subclasses
      aren't meant to be public. Clients interact with subclass instances via
      their common interface.

Encapsulate Classes with Factory

Variations

Encapsulating Inner Classes

Java's java.util.Collections class contains a remarkable example of what encapsulating classes with Creation Methods is all about. The class's author, Joshua Bloch, needed to give programmers a way to make collections, lists, sets, and maps unmodifiable and/or synchronized. He wisely chose to implement this behavior using the protection form of the Proxy [DP] pattern. However, instead of creating public java.util Proxy classes (for handling synchronization and unmodifiabilty) and then expecting programmers to protect their own collections, he defined the proxies in the Collections class as non-public inner classes and then gave Collections a set of Creation Methods from which programmers could obtain the kinds of proxies they needed. The sketch on page 87 shows a few of the inner classes and Creation Methods specified by the Collections class.

Notice that java.util.Collections even contains small hierarchies of inner classes, all of which are non-public. Each inner class has a corresponding method that receives a collection, protects it, and then returns the protected instance, using a commonly defined interface type (such as List or Set). This solution reduced the number of classes programmers needed to know about, while providing the necessary functionality. The java.util.Collections class is also an example of a Factory.

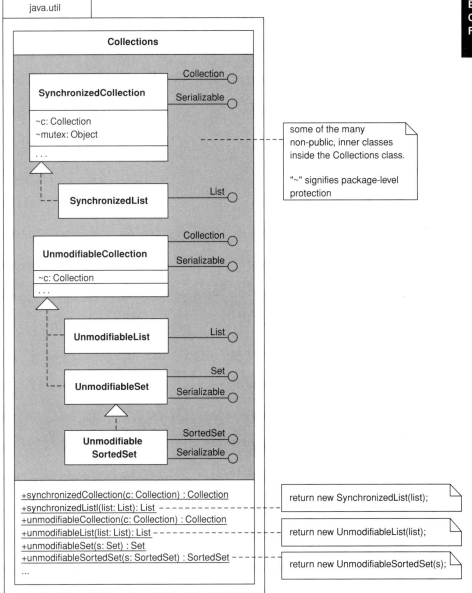

some of the many
non-public, inner classes
inside the Collections class.

"~" signifies package-level
protection

return new SynchronizedList(list);

return new UnmodifiableList(list);

return new UnmodifiableSortedSet(s);

Introduce Polymorphic Creation with Factory Method

Classes in a hierarchy implement a method similarly,
except for an object creation step.

*Make a single superclass version of the method that
calls a Factory Method to handle the instantiation.*

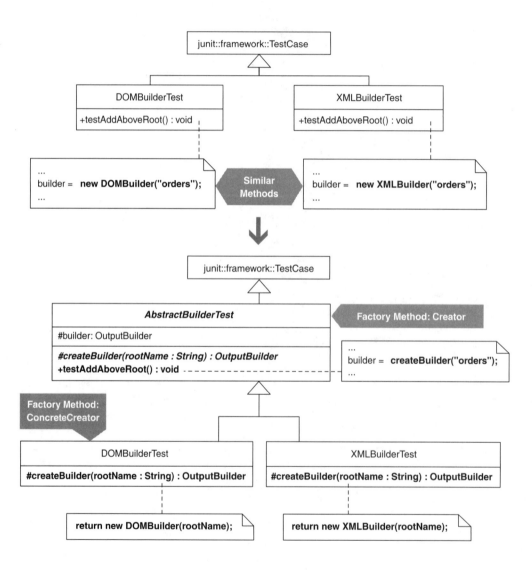

Motivation

To form a Creation Method (see *Replace Constructors with Creation Methods*, 57), a class must implement a static or nonstatic method that instantiates and returns an object. On the other hand, if you wish to form a Factory Method [DP], you need the following:

- A type (defined by an interface, abstract class, or class) to identify the set of classes that Factory Method implementors may instantiate and return

- The set of classes that implement that type

- Several classes that implement the Factory Method, making local decisions about which of the set of classes to instantiate, initialize, and return

While that may sound like a tall order, Factory Methods are most common in object-oriented programs because they provide a way to make object creation polymorphic.

In practice, Factory Methods are usually implemented within a class hierarchy, though they may be implemented by classes that simply share a common interface. It is common for an abstract class to either declare a Factory Method and force subclasses to override it or to provide a default Factory Method implementation and let subclasses inherit or override that implementation.

Factory Methods are often designed into framework classes to make it easy for programmers to extend a framework's functionality. Such extensions are commonly implemented by subclassing a framework class and overriding a Factory Method to return a specific object.

Because the signature of a Factory Method must be the same for all implementers of the Factory Method, you may be forced to pass unnecessary parameters to some Factory Method implementers. For example, if one subclass requires an int and a double to create an object, while another subclass requires only an int to create an object, a Factory Method implemented by both subclasses will need to accept both an int and a double. Since the double will be unnecessary for one subclass, looking at the code may be a bit confusing.

Factory Methods are often called by Template Methods [DP]. The collaboration of these two patterns frequently evolves into a class hierarchy as a result of refactoring to rid the hierarchy of duplicate code. For example, imagine that you find a method either in a superclass and overridden by a subclass or in several subclasses, and this method is implemented nearly identically in these places except for an object creation step. You see how you could replace all versions of this method with a single superclass Template Method, provided that

Introduce
Polymorphic
Creation with
Factory Method

the Template Method can issue one object creation call without knowing the class of object that the superclass and/or subclasses will instantiate, initialize, and return. No pattern is better suited to that task than Factory Method.

Is using a Factory Method simpler than calling new or calling a Creation Method? The pattern certainly isn't simpler to implement. However, the resulting code that uses a Factory Method tends to be simpler than code that duplicates a method in several classes just to perform custom object creation.

Benefits and Liabilities

+ Reduces duplication resulting from a custom object creation step.
+ Effectively communicates where creation occurs and how it may be overridden.
+ Enforces what type a class must implement to be used by a Factory Method.
− May require you to pass unnecessary parameters to some Factory Method implementers.

Mechanics

This refactoring is most commonly used in the following situations:

- When sibling subclasses implement a method similarly, except for an object creation step

- When a superclass and subclass implement a method similarly, except for an object creation step

The mechanics presented in this subsection handle the sibling subclasses scenario and can easily be adapted for the superclass and subclass scenario. For the purposes of these mechanics, a method that is implemented similarly in a hierarchy, except for an object creation step, will be called a *similar method*.

1. In a subclass that contains a similar method, modify the method so the custom object creation occurs in what these steps will call an *instantiation method*. You'll usually do this by applying *Extract Method* [F] on the creation code or by refactoring the creation code to call a previously extracted instantiation method.

Use a generic name for the instantiation method (e.g., `createBuilder`, `new-Product`) because the same method name will need to be used in the sibling subclass's similar methods. Make the return type for the instantiation method be the type that is common for the custom instantiation logic in the sibling subclass's similar methods.

✔ Compile and test.

2. Repeat step 1 for the similar method in the sibling subclasses. This should yield one instantiation method for each of the sibling's subclasses, and the instantiation method's signature should be the same in every sibling subclass.

✔ Compile and test.

3. Next, modify the superclass of the sibling subclasses. If you can't modify that class or would rather not do so, apply *Extract Superclass* [F] to produce a superclass that inherits from the superclass of the sibling subclasses and makes the sibling subclasses inherit from the new superclass.

    The participant name for the superclass of the sibling subclasses is Factory Method: Creator [DP].

✔ Compile and test.

4. Apply *Form Template Method* [F] on the similar method. This will involve applying *Pull Up Method* [F]. When you apply that refactoring, be sure to implement the following advice, which comes from a note in the mechanics for *Pull Up Method* [F]:

    > If you are in a strongly typed language and the [method you want to pull up] calls another method that is present on both subclasses but not the superclass, declare an abstract method on the superclass. [F, 323]

    One such abstract method you'll declare on the superclass will be for your instantiation method. Having declared that abstract method, you will have implemented a *factory method*. Each of the sibling subclasses is now a Factory Method: ConcreteCreator [DP].

✔ Compile and test.

5. Repeat steps 1–4 if you have additional similar methods in the sibling subclasses that could benefit from calling the previously created factory method.

6. If the factory method in a majority of ConcreteCreators contains the same instantiation code, move that code to the superclass by transforming the

factory method declaration in the superclass into a concrete factory method that performs the default ("majority case") instantiation behavior.

✔ Compile and test.

Example

In one of my projects, I had used test-driven development to produce an XML-Builder—a Builder [DP] that allowed clients to easily produce XML. Then I found that I needed to create a DOMBuilder, a class that would behave like the XML-Builder, only it would internally produce XML by creating a Document Object Model (DOM) and give clients access to that DOM.

To produce the DOMBuilder, I used the same tests I'd already written to produce the XMLBuilder. I needed to make only one modification to each test: instantiation of a DOMBuilder instead of an XMLBuilder:

```
public class DOMBuilderTest extends TestCase...
  private OutputBuilder builder;

  public void testAddAboveRoot() {
   String invalidResult =
   "<orders>" +
     "<order>" +
     "</order>" +
   "</orders>" +
   "<customer>" +
   "</customer>";
   builder = new DOMBuilder("orders");  // used to be new XMLBuilder("orders")
   builder.addBelow("order");
   try {
     builder.addAbove("customer");
     fail("expecting java.lang.RuntimeException");
   } catch (RuntimeException ignored) {}
  }
```

A key design goal for DOMBuilder was to make it and XMLBuilder share the same type: OutputBuilder, as shown in the following diagram.

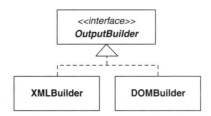

After writing the DOMBuilder-, I had nine test methods that were nearly identical on the XMLBuilderTest and DOMBuilderTest. In addition, DOMBuilderTest had its own unique tests, which tested access to and contents of a DOM. I wasn't happy with all the test-code duplication, because if I made a change to an XMLBuilder-Test, I needed to make the same change to the corresponding DOMBuilderTest. I knew it was time to refactor to the Factory Method. Here's how I went about doing that work.

1. The similar method I first identify is the test method, testAddAboveRoot(). I extract its instantiation logic into an instantiation method like so:

```
public class DOMBuilderTest extends TestCase...
  private OutputBuilder createBuilder(String rootName) {
    return new DOMBuilder(rootName);
  }

  public void testAddAboveRoot() {
    String invalidResult =
    "<orders>" +
      "<order>" +
      "</order>" +
    "</orders>" +
    "<customer>" +
    "</customer>";
    builder = createBuilder("orders");
    builder.addBelow("order");
    try {
      builder.addAbove("customer");
      fail("expecting java.lang.RuntimeException");
    } catch (RuntimeException ignored) {}
  }
```

Notice that the return type for the new createBuilder(…) method is an OutputBuilder. I use that return type because the sibling subclass, XMLBuilderTest, will need to define its own createBuilder(…) method (in step 2) and I want the instantiation method's signature to be the same for both classes.

I compile and run my tests to ensure that everything's still working.

2. Now I repeat step 1 for all other sibling subclasses, which in this case is just XMLBuilderTest:

```
public class XMLBuilderTest extends TestCase...
  private OutputBuilder createBuilder(String rootName) {
    return new XMLBuilder(rootName);
  }

  public void testAddAboveRoot() {
    String invalidResult =
```

```
    "<orders>" +
      "<order>" +
      "</order>" +
    "</orders>" +
    "<customer>" +
    "</customer>";
    builder = createBuilder("orders");
    builder.addBelow("order");
    try {
      builder.addAbove("customer");
      fail("expecting java.lang.RuntimeException");
    } catch (RuntimeException ignored) {}
  }
```

I compile and test to make sure the tests still work.

3. I'm now about to modify the superclass of my tests. But that superclass is TestCase, which is part of the JUnit framework. I don't want to modify that superclass, so I apply *Extract Superclass* [F] to produce AbstractBuilderTest, a new superclass for my test classes:

```
public class AbstractBuilderTest extends TestCase {
}
```

```
public class XMLBuilderTest extends AbstractBuilderTest...
```

```
public class DOMBuilderTest extends AbstractBuilderTest...
```

4. I can now apply *Form Template Method (205)*. Because the similar method is now identical in XMLBuilderTest and DOMBuilderTest, the *Form Template Method* mechanics I must follow instruct me to use *Pull Up Method* [F] on testAdd-AboveRoot(). Those mechanics first lead me to apply *Pull Up Field* [F] on the builder field:

```
public class AbstractBuilderTest extends TestCase {
  protected OutputBuilder builder;
}
```

```
public class XMLBuilderTest extends AbstractBuilderTest...
  private OutputBuilder builder;
```

```
public class DOMBuilderTest extends AbstractBuilderTest...
  private OutputBuilder builder;
```

Continuing with the *Pull Up Method* [F] mechanics for testAddAboveRoot(), I now find that I must declare an abstract method on the superclass for any method that is called by testAddAboveRoot() and present in the XMLBuilderTest and DOMBuilderTest. The method, createBuilder(…), is such a method, so I pull up an abstract method declaration of it:

```java
public abstract class AbstractBuilderTest extends TestCase {
  protected OutputBuilder builder;

  protected abstract OutputBuilder createBuilder(String rootName);
}
```

I can now proceed with pulling up testAddAboveRoot() to AbstractBuilderTest:

```java
public abstract class AbstractBuilderTest extends TestCase...
  public void testAddAboveRoot() {
    String invalidResult =
    "<orders>" +
      "<order>" +
      "</order>" +
    "</orders>" +
    "<customer>" +
    "</customer>";
    builder = createBuilder("orders");
    builder.addBelow("order");
    try {
      builder.addAbove("customer");
      fail("expecting java.lang.RuntimeException");
    } catch (RuntimeException ignored) {}
  }
```

That step removed testAddAboveRoot() from XMLBuilderTest and DOMBuilder-Test. The createBuilder(…) method, which is now declared in AbstractBuilderTest and implemented in XMLBuilderTest and DOMBuilderTest, now implements the Factory Method [DP] pattern.

As always, I compile and test my tests to make sure that they still work.

5. Since there are additional similar methods between XMLBuilderTest and DOM-BuilderTest, I repeat steps 1–4 for each similar method.

6. At this point I consider creating a default implementation of createBuilder(…) in AbstractBuilderTest. I would only do this if it would help reduce duplication in the multiple subclass implementations of createBuilder(…). In this case, I don't have such a need because XMLBuilderTest and DOMBuilderTest each instantiate their own kind of OutputBuilder. So that brings me to the end of the refactoring.

Encapsulate Composite with Builder

Building a Composite is repetitive, complicated,
or error-prone.

Simplify the build by letting a Builder handle the details.

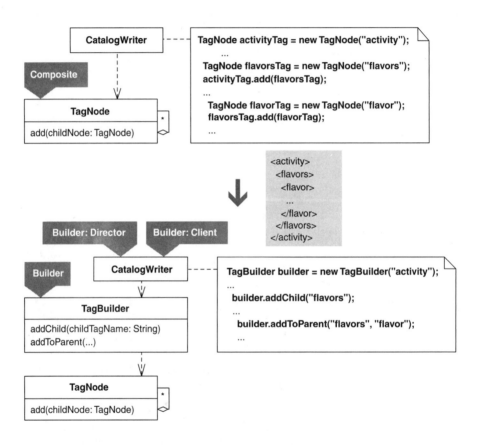

A Builder [DP] performs burdensome or complicated construction steps on behalf of a client. A common motivation for refactoring to a Builder is to simplify client code that creates complex objects. When difficult or tedious parts of creation are implemented by a Builder, a client can direct the Builder's creation work without having to know how that work is accomplished.

Builders often encapsulate Composites [DP] because the construction of Composites can frequently be repetitive, complicated, or error-prone. For example, to add a child node to a parent node, a client must do the following:

- Instantiate a new node

- Initialize the new node

- Correctly add the new node to the right parent node

This process is error-prone because you can either forget to add a new node to a parent or you can add the new node to the wrong parent. The process is repetitive because it requires performing the same batch of construction steps over and over again. It's well worth refactoring to any Builder that can reduce errors or minimize and simplify creation steps.

Another motivation for encapsulating a Composite with a Builder is to decouple client code from Composite code. For example, in the client code shown in the following diagram, notice how the creation of the DOM Composite, orderTag, is tightly coupled to the DOM's Document, DocumentImpl, Element, and Text interfaces and classes.

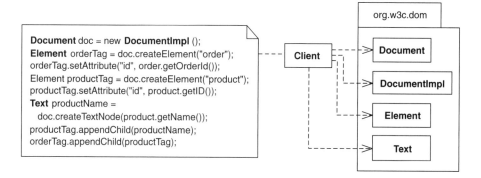

Such tight coupling makes it difficult to change Composite implementations. On one project, we needed to upgrade our system to use a newer version of the DOM, which happened to have several differences from the DOM 1.0 version we had been using. This painful upgrade involved changing many lines of Composite-construction code that were spread across the system. As part of the upgrade, we encapsulated the new DOM code within a DOMBuilder, as shown in the diagram on the following page.

Encapsulate Composite with Builder

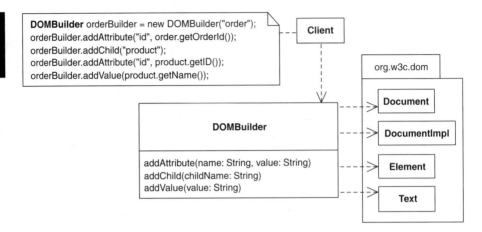

All of the methods on DOMBuilder accept strings as arguments and return void. There is no mention of DOM interfaces or classes in DOMBuilder's interface, yet DOMBuilder internally assembles DOM objects at runtime. Client code that uses a DOMBuilder is loosely coupled to DOM code. That's good, for when future versions of the DOM are released or when we decide to use JDOM or our own TagNode objects, we can easily produce new Builders that feature the identical interface as DOMBuilder. Having one generic Builder interface also enables us to configure our system to use whatever Builder implementation is needed in a given context.

The authors of *Design Patterns* describe the intent of the Builder pattern as follows: "Separate the construction of a complex object from its internal representation so that the same construction process can create different representations" [DP, 97].

While "creat[ing] different representations" of a complex object is a useful service, it isn't the only service a Builder provides. As mentioned earlier, simplifying construction or decoupling client code from a complex object are also equally good reasons for using a Builder.

A Builder's interface ought to reveal its intentions so clearly that anyone who looks at it will instantly know what it does. In practice, a Builder's interface, or a portion of it, may not be so clear because Builders do a lot of work behind the scenes to make construction simple. This means that you may need to look at a Builder's implementation or read its test code or documentation to fully understand the features it provides.

Benefits and Liabilities

+ Simplifies a client's code for constructing a Composite.
+ Reduces the repetitive and error-prone nature of Composite creation.
+ Creates a loose coupling between client and Composite.
+ Allows for different representations of the encapsulated Composite or complex object.
− May not have the most intention-revealing interface.

Mechanics

Because there are numerous ways to write a Builder that builds a Composite, there cannot be one set of mechanics for this refactoring. Instead, I'll offer general steps that you can implement as you see fit. Whatever design you choose for your Builder, I suggest that you use test-driven development [Beck, TDD] to produce it.

The following mechanics assume you already have Composite-construction code and you'd like to encapsulate this code with a Builder.

1. Create a *builder*, a new class that will become a Builder [DP] by the end of this refactoring. Make it possible for your builder to produce a one-node Composite [DP]. Add a method to the builder to obtain the result of its build.

   ✔ Compile and test.

2. Make the builder capable of building children. This often involves creating multiple methods for allowing clients to easily direct the creation and positioning of children.

   ✔ Compile and test.

3. If the Composite-construction code you're replacing sets attributes or values on nodes, make the builder capable of setting those attributes and values.

   ✔ Compile and test.

4. Reflect on how simple your builder is for clients to use, and then make it simpler.

Encapsulate Composite with Builder

5. Refactor your Composite-construction code to use the new builder. This involves making your client code what is known in *Design Patterns* as a Builder: Client and Builder: Director.

   ✔ Compile and test.

Example

The Composite I'd like to encapsulate with a Builder is called TagNode. This class is featured in the refactoring *Replace Implicit Tree with Composite (178)*. TagNode facilitates the creation of XML. It plays all three Composite roles because the TagNode class is a Component, which can be either a Leaf or a Composite at runtime, as shown in the following diagram.

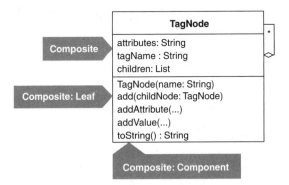

TagNode's toString() method outputs an XML representation of all TagNode objects it contains. A TagBuilder will encapsulate TagNode, providing clients with a less repetitive and error-prone way to create a Composite of TagNode objects.

1. My first step is to create a builder that can successfully build one node. In this case, I want to create a TagBuilder that produces the correct XML for a tree containing a single TagNode. I begin by writing a failing test that uses assertXmlEquals, a method I wrote for comparing two pieces of XML:

```
public class TagBuilderTest...
  public void testBuildOneNode() {
    String expectedXml =
      "<flavors/>";
    String actualXml = new TagBuilder("flavors").toXml();
    assertXmlEquals(expectedXml, actualXml);
  }
```

Passing that test is easy. Here's the code I write:

```
public class TagBuilder {
  private TagNode rootNode;

  public TagBuilder(String rootTagName) {
    rootNode = new TagNode(rootTagName);
  }

  public String toXml() {
    return rootNode.toString();
  }
}
```

The compiler and test code are happy with this new code.

2. Now I'll make TagBuilder capable of handling children. I want to deal with numerous scenarios, each of which causes me to write a different TagBuilder method.

I start with the scenario of adding a child to a root node. Because I want TagBuilder to both create a child node and position it correctly within the encapsulated Composite, I decide to produce one method for doing just that, called addChild(). The following test uses this method:

```
public class TagBuilderTest...
  public void testBuildOneChild() {
    String expectedXml =
      "<flavors>"+
        "<flavor/>" +
      "</flavors>";

    TagBuilder builder = new TagBuilder("flavors");
    builder.addChild("flavor");
    String actualXml = builder.toXml();

    assertXmlEquals(expectedXml, actualXml);
  }
```

Here are the changes I make to pass this test:

```
public class TagBuilder {
  private TagNode rootNode;
  private TagNode currentNode;

  public TagBuilder(String rootTagName) {
    rootNode = new TagNode(rootTagName);
    currentNode = rootNode;
  }
```

```
public void addChild(String childTagName) {
  TagNode parentNode = currentNode;
  currentNode = new TagNode(childTagName);
  parentNode.add(currentNode);
}

public String toXml() {
  return rootNode.toString();
}
}
```

That was easy. To fully test that the new code works, I make an even harder test and see if it runs successfully:

```
public class TagBuilderTest...
  public void testBuildChildrenOfChildren() {
    String expectedXml =
      "<flavors>"+
        "<flavor>" +
          "<requirements>" +
            "<requirement/>" +
          "</requirements>" +
        "</flavor>" +
      "</flavors>";

    TagBuilder builder = new TagBuilder("flavors");
    builder.addChild("flavor");
      builder.addChild("requirements");
        builder.addChild("requirement");
    String actualXml = builder.toXml();

    assertXmlEquals(expectedXml, actualXml);
  }
```

The code passes this test as well. It's now time to handle another scenario—adding a sibling. Again, I write a failing test:

```
public class TagBuilderTest...
  public void testBuildSibling() {
    String expectedXml =
      "<flavors>"+
        "<flavor1/>" +
        "<flavor2/>" +
      "</flavors>";

    TagBuilder builder = new TagBuilder("flavors");
    builder.addChild("flavor1");
    builder.addSibling("flavor2");
    String actualXml = builder.toXml();

    assertXmlEquals(expectedXml, actualXml);
  }
```

Adding a sibling for an existing child implies that there is a way for Tag-Builder to know who the common parent is for the child and its new sibling. There is currently no way to know this, as each TagNode instance doesn't store a reference to its parent. So I write the following failing test to drive the creation of this needed behavior:

```
public class TagNodeTest...
  public void testParents() {
    TagNode root = new TagNode("root");
    assertNull(root.getParent());

    TagNode childNode = new TagNode("child");
    root.add(childNode);
    assertEquals(root, childNode.getParent());
    assertEquals("root", childNode.getParent().getName());
  }
```

To pass this test, I add the following code to TagNode:

```
public class TagNode...
  private TagNode parent;

  public void add(TagNode childNode) {
    childNode.setParent(this);
    children().add(childNode);
  }

  private void setParent(TagNode parent) {
    this.parent = parent;
  }

  public TagNode getParent() {
    return parent;
  }
```

With the new functionality in place, I can refocus on writing code to pass the testBuildSibling() test, listed earlier. Here's the new code I write:

```
public class TagBuilder...
  public void addChild(String childTagName) {
    addTo(currentNode, childTagName);
  }

  public void addSibling(String siblingTagName) {
    addTo(currentNode.getParent(), siblingTagName);
  }

  private void addTo(TagNode parentNode, String tagName) {
    currentNode = new TagNode(tagName);
    parentNode.add(currentNode);
  }
```

Once again, the compiler and tests are happy with the new code. I write additional tests to confirm that sibling and child behavior works under various conditions.

Now I need to handle a final child-building scenario: the case when add-Child() or addSibling() won't work because a child must be added to a specific parent. The test below indicates the problem:

```java
public class TagBuilderTest...
  public void testRepeatingChildrenAndGrandchildren() {
    String expectedXml =
      "<flavors>"+
        "<flavor>" +
          "<requirements>" +
            "<requirement/>" +
          "</requirements>" +
        "</flavor>" +
        "<flavor>" +
          "<requirements>" +
            "<requirement/>" +
          "</requirements>" +
        "</flavor>" +
      "</flavors>";

    TagBuilder builder = new TagBuilder("flavors");
    for (int i=0; i<2; i++) {
      builder.addChild("flavor");
        builder.addChild("requirements");
          builder.addChild("requirement");
    }

    assertXmlEquals(expectedXml, builder.toString());
  }
```

The preceding test won't pass because it doesn't build what is expected. When the loop runs for the second time, the call to the builder's addChild() method picks up where it left off, meaning that it adds a child to the last added node, which produces the following incorrect result:

```
<flavors>
  <flavor>
    <requirements>
      <requirement/>
        <flavor>    ← Error: misplaced tags
          <requirements>
            <requirement/>
          </requirements>
        </flavor>
    </requirements>
  </flavor>
<flavors>
```

To fix this problem, I change the test to refer to a method I call addTo-Parent(), which enables a client to add a new node to a specific parent:

```
public class TagBuilderTest...
  public void testRepeatingChildrenAndGrandchildren()...
    ...
    TagBuilder builder = new TagBuilder("flavors");
    for (int i=0; i<2; i++) {
      builder.addToParent("flavors", "flavor");
        builder.addChild("requirements");
          builder.addChild("requirement");
    }
    assertXmlEquals(expectedXml, builder.toXml());
```

This test won't compile or run until I implement addToParent(). The idea behind addToParent() is that it will ask the TagBuilder's currentNode if its name matches the supplied parent name (passed via a parameter). If the name matches, the method will add a new child node to currentNode, or if the name doesn't match, the method will ask for currentNode's parent and continue the process until either a match is found or a null parent is encountered. The pattern name for this behavior is Chain of Responsibility [DP].

To implement the Chain of Responsibility, I write the following new code in TagBuilder:

```
public class TagBuilder...
  public void addToParent(String parentTagName, String childTagName) {
    addTo(findParentBy(parentTagName), childTagName);
  }

  private void addTo(TagNode parentNode, String tagName) {
    currentNode = new TagNode(tagName);
    parentNode.add(currentNode);
  }

  private TagNode findParentBy(String parentName) {
    TagNode parentNode = currentNode;
    while (parentNode != null) {
      if (parentName.equals(parentNode.getName()))
        return parentNode;
      parentNode = parentNode.getParent();
    }
    return null;
  }
```

The test passes. Before I move on, I want addToParent() to deal with the case where the name supplied for a parent node does not exist. So I write the following test:

```
public class TagBuilderTest...
  public void testParentNameNotFound() {
    TagBuilder builder = new TagBuilder("flavors");
    try {
      for (int i=0; i<2; i++) {
        builder.addToParent("favors", "flavor");   ← should be "flavors" not "favors"
        builder.addChild("requirements");
        builder.addChild("requirement");
      }
      fail("should not allow adding to parent that doesn't exist.");
    } catch (RuntimeException runtimeException) {
      String expectedErrorMessage = "missing parent tag: favors";
      assertEquals(expectedErrorMessage, runtimeException.getMessage());
    }
  }
}
```

I make this test pass by making the following modifications to TagBuilder:

```
public class TagBuilder...
  public void addToParent(String parentTagName, String childTagName) {
    TagNode parentNode = findParentBy(parentTagName);
    if (parentNode == null)
      throw new RuntimeException("missing parent tag: " + parentTagName);
    addTo(parentNode, childTagName);
  }
```

3. Now I make TagBuilder capable of adding attributes and values to nodes. This is an easy step because the encapsulated TagNode already handles attributes and values. Here's a test that checks to see whether both attributes and values are handled correctly:

```
public class TagBuilderTest...
  public void testAttributesAndValues() {
    String expectedXml =
      "<flavor name='Test-Driven Development'>" +      ← tag with attribute
        "<requirements>" +
          "<requirement type='hardware'>" +
            "1 computer for every 2 participants" +    ← tag with value
          "</requirement>" +
          "<requirement type='software'>" +
            "IDE" +
          "</requirement>" +
        "</requirements>" +
      "</flavor>";
```

```
    TagBuilder builder = new TagBuilder("flavor");
    builder.addAttribute("name", "Test-Driven Development");
      builder.addChild("requirements");
        builder.addToParent("requirements", "requirement");
        builder.addAttribute("type", "hardware");
        builder.addValue("1 computer for every 2 participants");
        builder.addToParent("requirements", "requirement");
        builder.addAttribute("type", "software");
        builder.addValue("IDE");

    assertXmlEquals(expectedXml, builder.toXml());
  }
```

The following new methods make the test pass:

```
public class TagBuilder...
  public void addAttribute(String name, String value) {
    currentNode.addAttribute(name, value);
  }

  public void addValue(String value) {
    currentNode.addValue(value);
  }
```

4. Now it's time to reflect on how simple TagBuilder is and how easy it is for clients to use. Is there a simpler way to produce XML? This is not the kind of question you can normally answer right away. Experiments and hours, days, or weeks of reflection can sometimes yield a simpler idea. I'll discuss a simpler implementation in the Variations section below. For now, I move on to the last step.

5. I conclude the refactoring by replacing Composite-construction code with code that uses the TagBuilder. I'm not aware of any easy way to do this; Composite-construction code can span large parts of a system. Hopefully you have test code to catch you if you make any mistakes during the transformation. Here's a method on a class called CatalogWriter that must be changed from using TagNode to using TagBuilder:

```
public class CatalogWriter...
  public String catalogXmlFor(Activity activity) {
    TagNode activityTag = new TagNode("activity");
    ...
    TagNode flavorsTag = new TagNode("flavors");
    activityTag.add(flavorsTag);
    for (int i=0; i < activity.getFlavorCount(); i++) {
      TagNode flavorTag = new TagNode("flavor");
```

Encapsulate
Composite
with Builder

```
    flavorsTag.add(flavorTag);
    Flavor flavor = activity.getFlavor(i);
    ...
    int requirementsCount = flavor.getRequirements().length;
    if (requirementsCount > 0) {
      TagNode requirementsTag = new TagNode("requirements");
      flavorTag.add(requirementsTag);
      for (int r=0; r < requirementsCount; r++) {
        Requirement requirement = flavor.getRequirements()[r];
        TagNode requirementTag = new TagNode("requirement");
        ...
        requirementsTag.add(requirementTag);
      }
    }
  }
  return activityTag.toString();
}
```

This code works with the domain objects Activity, Flavor, and Requirement, as shown in the following diagram.

You may wonder why this code creates a Composite of TagNode objects just to render Activity data into XML, rather than simply asking Activity, Flavor, and Requirement instances to render themselves into XML via their own toXml() method. That's a fine question to ask, for if domain objects already form a Composite structure, it may not make any sense to form another Composite structure, like activityTag, just to render the domain objects into XML. In this case, however, producing the XML externally from the domain objects makes sense because the system that uses these domain objects must produce several XML representations of them, all of which are quite different. A single toXml() method for every domain object wouldn't work well here—each implementation of the method would need to produce too many different XML representations of the domain object.

After transforming the catalogXmlFor(…) method to use a TagBuilder, it looks like this:

```
public class CatalogWriter...
  private String catalogXmlFor(Activity activity) {
    TagBuilder builder = new TagBuilder("activity");
    ...
    builder.addChild("flavors");
```

```
    for (int i=0; i < activity.getFlavorCount(); i++) {
      builder.addToParent("flavors", "flavor");
      Flavor flavor = activity.getFlavor(i);
      ...
      int requirementsCount = flavor.getRequirements().length;
      if (requirementsCount > 0) {
        builder.addChild("requirements");
        for (int r=0; r < requirementsCount; r++) {
          Requirement requirement = flavor.getRequirements()[r];
          builder.addToParent("requirements", "requirement");
          ...
        }
      }
    }
    return builder.toXml();
  }
```

And that does it for this refactoring! TagNode is now fully encapsulated by TagBuilder.

Improving a Builder

I could not resist telling you about a performance improvement made to the Tag-Builder because it reveals the elegance and simplicity of the Builder pattern. Some of my colleagues at a company called Evant had done some profiling of our system, and they'd found that a StringBuffer used by the TagBuilder's encapsulated TagNode was causing performance problems. This StringBuffer is used as a Collecting Parameter—it is created and then passed to every node in a composite of Tag-Node objects in order to produce the results returned from calling TagNode's toXml() method. To see how this works, see the example in *Move Accumulation to Collecting Parameter (313)*.

The StringBuffer that was being used in this operation was not instantiated with any particular size, which meant that as more and more XML was added to the StringBuffer, it needed to automatically grow when it could no longer hold all its data. That's fine; the StringBuffer class is designed to automatically grow when needed. But there's a performance penalty because StringBuffer must work to transparently increase its size and shift data around. That performance penalty was not acceptable on the Evant system.

The solution lay in knowing the exact size the StringBuffer needs to be before instantiating it. How could we compute the appropriate size? Easy. As each node, attribute, or value is added to the TagBuilder, it can increment a buffer size based on the size of what is being added. The final computed buffer size can then be used to instantiate a StringBuffer that never needs to grow in size.

To implement this performance improvement, we started as usual by writing a failing test. The following test builds an XML tree by making calls to a TagBuilder, then obtains the size of the resulting XML string returned by the builder, and finally compares the size of that string with the computed buffer size:

```
public class TagBuilderTest...
  public void testToStringBufferSize() {
    String expected =
    "<requirements>" +
      "<requirement type='software'>" +
        "IDE" +
      "</requirement>" +
    "</requirements>";

    TagBuilder builder = new TagBuilder("requirements");
    builder.addChild("requirement");
    builder.addAttribute("type", "software");
    builder.addValue("IDE");

    int stringSize = builder.toXml().length();
    int computedSize = builder.bufferSize();
    assertEquals("buffer size", stringSize, computedSize);
  }
```

To pass this test and others like it, we altered TagBuilder as follows:

```
public class TagBuilder...
  private int outputBufferSize;
  private static int TAG_CHARS_SIZE = 5;
  private static int ATTRIBUTE_CHARS_SIZE = 4;

  public TagBuilder(String rootTagName) {
    ...
    incrementBufferSizeByTagLength(rootTagName);
  }

  private void addTo(TagNode parentNode, String tagName) {
    ...
    incrementBufferSizeByTagLength(tagName);
  }

  public void addAttribute(String name, String value) {
    ...
    incrementBufferSizeByAttributeLength(name, value);
  }

  public void addValue(String value) {
    ...
    incrementBufferSizeByValueLength(value);
  }

  public int bufferSize() {
    return outputBufferSize;
  }
```

```
private void incrementBufferSizeByAttributeLength(String name, String value) {
  outputBufferSize += (name.length() + value.length() + ATTRIBUTE_CHARS_SIZE);
}

private void incrementBufferSizeByTagLength(String tag) {
  int sizeOfOpenAndCloseTags = tag.length() * 2;
  outputBufferSize += (sizeOfOpenAndCloseTags + TAG_CHARS_SIZE);
}

private void incrementBufferSizeByValueLength(String value) {
  outputBufferSize += value.length();
}
```

These changes to TagBuilder are transparent to users of TagBuilder because it encapsulates the new performance logic. The only additional change needed to be made to TagBuilder's toXml() method, so that it could instantiate a StringBuffer of the correct size and pass it to the root TagNode, which accumulates the XML contents. To make that happen, we changed the toXml() method from

```
public class TagBuilder...
  public String toXml() {
    return rootNode.toString();
  }
```

to

```
public class TagBuilder...
  public String toXml() {
    StringBuffer xmlResult = new StringBuffer(outputBufferSize);
    rootNode.appendContentsTo(xmlResult);
    return xmlResult.toString();
  }
```

That was it. The test passed, and TagBuilder ran significantly faster.

Variations

A Schema-Based Builder

TagBuilder contains three methods for adding nodes to a Composite:

- addChild(String childTagName)
- addSibling(String siblingTagName)
- addToParent(String parentTagName, String childTagName)

Each of these methods is involved in creating and positioning new tag nodes within an encapsulated Composite. I wondered if I could write a Builder that would use only a single method, called add(String tagName). To do that, the Builder

Encapsulate Composite with Builder

would need to know where to position tags added by clients. I decided to experiment with this idea. I called the result a SchemaBasedTreeBuilder. Here's a test that shows how it works:

```
public class SchemaBasedTagBuilderTest...
  public void testTwoSetsOfGreatGrandchildren() {
    TreeSchema schema = new TreeSchema(
      "orders" +
      "  order" +
      "    item" +
      "      apple" +
      "      orange"
    );

    String expected =
      "<orders>" +
        "<order>" +
          "<item>" +
            "<apple/>" +
            "<orange/>" +
          "</item>" +
          "<item>" +
            "<apple/>" +
            "<orange/>" +
          "</item>" +
        "</order>" +
      "</orders>";

    SchemaBasedTagBuilder builder = new SchemaBasedTagBuilder(schema);
    builder.add("orders");
      builder.add("order");
      for (int i=0; i<2; i++) {
        builder.add("item");
          builder.add("apple");
          builder.add("orange");
      }
    assertXmlEquals(expected, builder.toString());
  }
```

The SchemaBasedTreeBuilder learns where it needs to position tags by means of a TreeSchema instance. TreeSchema is a class that accepts a tab-delimited string, which defines a tree of tag names:

```
"orders" +
"  order" +
"    item" +
"      apple" +
"      orange"
```

TreeSchema takes this string and converts it into the following Map:

Child	Parent
orders	null
order	orders
item	order
apple	item
orange	item

At runtime, the SchemaBasedTagBuilder uses a TreeSchema's map to figure out where to position a new tag. For example, if I write builder.add("orange"), the builder learns from its treeSchema instance that the parent of an "orange" tag is an "item" tag and then proceeds to add a new "orange" tag to the closest "item" tag.

This approach works well until you have two tags with the same name:

```
"organization" +
"  name" +
"  departments" +
"    department" +
"      name"
```

In this case, a TreeSchema's map must list two parents for the "name" tag:

Child	Parent
…	…
name	organization, department
…	…

At runtime, the SchemaBasedTagBuilder will look up a new tag's parent names, find the closest parent tag, and add the new tag to the closest parent tag. If a client wants to specify exactly which parent to add a new tag to, rather than relying on the closest tag behavior, the client can call an add() method that makes the connection explicit:

```
builder.add("department","name");  // tell builder exactly where to add "name"
```

So that's the SchemaBasedTagBuilder. It accomplishes the same work as TagBuilder but in a different way. I normally use a TagBuilder for building XML; however, given a large XML document to create, I would consider using a SchemaBasedTag-Builder because it would remove the need to worry about where to place tags. In addition, if the large XML document had an XML schema associated with it, I'd likely write code to transform that XML schema into a TreeSchema for use by the SchemaBasedTagBuilder.

**Inline
Singleton**

Inline Singleton

Code needs access to an object but
doesn't need a global point of access to it.

*Move the Singleton's features to a class that stores and
provides access to the object. Delete the Singleton.*

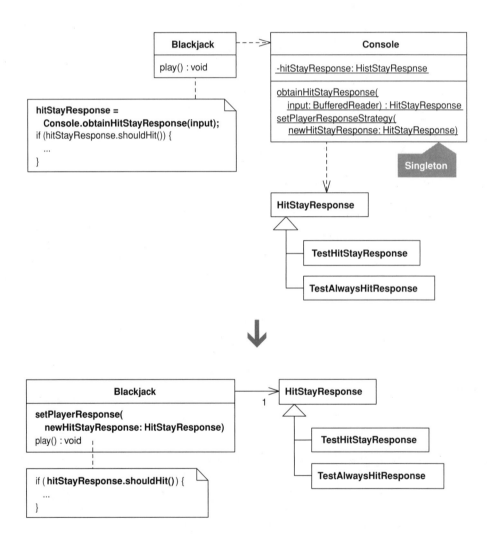

Motivation

Singletonitis, a term I coined, means "addiction to the Singleton pattern." The intent of a Singleton is to "ensure a class only has one instance, and provide a global point of access to it" [DP, 127]. You're infected with Singletonitis when the Singleton pattern fixes itself so deeply into your skull that it begins lording it over other patterns and simpler design ideas, causing you to produce way too many Singletons.

I've rid myself of Singletonitis and am now considering starting "Singletons Anonymous," a place where recovering Singleton abusers can support each other on the slow journey back to using simple, nonglobal objects. The *Inline Singleton* refactoring is a useful step on that journey. It helps rid your systems of unnecessary Singletons. This leads to the obvious question: When is a Singleton unnecessary?

Short answer: Most of the time.

Long answer: A Singleton is unnecessary when it's simpler to pass an object resource as a reference to the objects that need it, rather than letting objects access the resource globally. A Singleton is unnecessary when it's used to obtain insignificant memory or performance improvements. A Singleton isn't necessary when code deep down in a layer of a system needs to access a resource but the code doesn't belong in that layer to begin with. I could go on. The point is that Singletons aren't necessary when you can design or redesign to avoid using them.

When writing this refactoring, I decided to ask Ward Cunningham and Kent Beck to comment on the Singleton pattern.

Ward Cunningham on Singletons

So much of the Singleton pattern is about coaxing language protection mechanisms into protecting this one aspect: singularity. I guess it is important, but it seems to have grown out of proportion.

There is a proper context for every computation. So much of object-oriented programming is about establishing context, about balancing the lifetimes of variables, causing them to live the right length of time and then die gracefully. I'm not afraid of a few globals. They provide the global context that everyone must understand. There shouldn't be many though. Too many would scare me.

Kent Beck on Singletons

The real problem with Singletons is that they give you such a good excuse not to think carefully about the appropriate visibility of an object. Finding the right balance of exposure and protection for an object is critical for maintaining flexibility.

Massimo Arnoldi and I once worked on a system that had a Singleton for storing exchange rates. Every time we wrote a test that handled multiple currencies, we had to make sure to save the old exchange rates, store some new ones, run the test, then restore the old exchange rates. One day we got fed up with test mistakes that were caused by using the wrong exchange rates.

"But the exchange rates are used all over the system!" we whined. A good idea is a good idea, though, so we looked at all the places where the exchange rates were used. We added parameters as necessary to pass the exchange rates explicitly. We thought it would be a huge amount of work, but it only took us half an hour. Sometimes it was a little difficult to get the exchange rates to where they were needed, but it was obvious how to refactor to make it easy. These refactorings also resolved several chronic design problems that had bothered us but we hadn't known how to tackle.

The result of the half hour:

- Cleaner, more flexible overall design

- Stable tests

- A deep sense of relief

Martin Fowler also acknowledges the need for a few globals, though he uses them only as a last resort. His Registry pattern, from *Patterns of Enterprise Application Architecture*, is a slight variation on Singleton. Martin describes a Registry as "a well-known object that other objects can use to find common objects and services" [Fowler, PEAA, 480]. Regarding when to use this pattern, he writes:

There are alternatives to using a *Registry*. One is to pass around any widely needed data in parameters. The problem with this is that parameters are added to method calls when they aren't needed by the called method but only by some other method that's called several layers deep in the call tree. Passing a parameter around when it's not needed 90 percent of the time is what leads me to use a *Registry* instead. . . .

So there are times when it is right to use a *Registry*, but remember that any global data is always guilty until proven innocent. [Fowler, PEAA, 482–483]

My rather close reading of *Design Patterns* [DP] infected me with Singletonitis. Every pattern in that book contains a Related Patterns section, and in many of those sections you'll find sentences that mention Singleton. For example, in the section on the State pattern, the authors write, "State objects are often Singletons" [DP, 313], and in the section on the Abstract Factory pattern, they write, "A concrete factory is often a Singleton" [DP, 95]. In defense of the authors, these sentences simply observe that State and Abstract Factory classes *often* are Singletons. The book doesn't say they have to be. If there is a good reason to make a class a Singleton or Registry, do so. The refactoring *Limit Instantiation with Singleton (296)* describes a good reason to refactor to a Singleton: real performance improvement. It also cautions against premature optimization.

One thing is certain: you need to think and explore *really hard* before you implement a Singleton. And if you encounter a Singleton that shouldn't be a Singleton, by all means *inline it*!

Benefits and Liabilities

+ Makes object collaborations more visible and explicit.
+ Requires no special code to protect a single instance.
− Complicates a design when passing an object instance through many layers is awkward or difficult.

Mechanics

This refactoring's mechanics are identical to those of *Inline Class* [F]. In the following steps, an *absorbing class* is one that will take on the responsibilities of the inlined Singleton.

1. Declare the Singleton's public methods on your absorbing class. Make the new methods delegate back to the Singleton, and remove any "static" designations they may have (in the absorbing class).

    If your absorbing class is itself a Singleton, you'll want to keep the "static" designations for the methods.

2. Change all client code references to the Singleton to references to the absorbing class.

    ✔ Compile and test.

3. Use *Move Method* [F] and *Move Field* [F] to move features from the Singleton to the absorbing class until there is nothing left.

    As in step 1, if your absorbing class is not a Singleton itself, remove any "static" designations from the methods and fields you move.

    ✔ Compile and test.

4. Delete the Singleton.

Example

The code for this example comes from an early evolution of a simple, console-based blackjack game. The game is played on a console by displaying a player's cards, repeatedly prompting a player to hit or stay, and then displaying the player's hand and the dealer's hand to reveal who won. Test code can run this game and simulate user input, such as hitting and staying during game play.

A player's simulated input is specified and obtained at runtime from a Singleton called Console, which holds on to one instance of HitStayResponse or one of its subclasses:

```
public class Console {
  static private HitStayResponse hitStayResponse =
    new HitStayResponse();

  private Console() {
    super();
  }

  public static HitStayResponse obtainHitStayResponse(BufferedReader input) {
    hitStayResponse.readFrom(input);
    return hitStayResponse;
  }

  public static void setPlayerResponse(HitStayResponse newHitStayResponse) {
    hitStayResponse = newHitStayResponse;
  }
}
```

Prior to starting game play, a particular HitStayResponse is registered with the Console. For example, here's some test code that registers a TestAlwaysHitResponse instance with the Console:

```
public class ScenarioTest extends TestCase...
  public void testDealerStandsWhenPlayerBusts() {
    Console.setPlayerResponse(new TestAlwaysHitResponse());
    int[] deck = { 10, 9, 7, 2, 6 };
    Blackjack blackjack = new Blackjack(deck);
    blackjack.play();
    assertTrue("dealer wins", blackjack.didDealerWin());
    assertTrue("player loses", !blackjack.didPlayerWin());
    assertEquals("dealer total", 11, blackjack.getDealerTotal());
    assertEquals("player total", 23, blackjack.getPlayerTotal());
  }
```

The Blackjack code that calls the Console to obtain the registered HitStayResponse instance isn't complicated code. Here's how it looks:

```
public class Blackjack...
  public void play() {
    deal();
    writeln(player.getHandAsString());
    writeln(dealer.getHandAsStringWithFirstCardDown());
    HitStayResponse hitStayResponse;
    do {
      write("H)it or S)tay: ");
      hitStayResponse = Console.obtainHitStayResponse(input);
      write(hitStayResponse.toString());
      if (hitStayResponse.shouldHit()) {
        dealCardTo(player);
        writeln(player.getHandAsString());
      }
    }
    while (canPlayerHit(hitStayResponse));
    // ...
  }
```

The above code doesn't live in an application layer that's surrounded by other application layers, thereby making it hard to pass one HitStayResponse instance all the way to a layer that needs it. All of the code to access a HitStay-Response instance lives within Blackjack itself. So why should Blackjack have to go through a Console just to get to a HitStayResponse? It shouldn't! It's yet another Singleton that doesn't need to be a Singleton. Time to refactor.

1. The first step is to declare the public methods of Console, the Singleton, on Blackjack, the absorbing class. When I do this, I make each method delegate back to the Console, and I remove the "static" designation for each method:

    ```
    public class Blackjack...
      public static HitStayResponse obtainHitStayResponse(BufferedReader input) {
        return Console.obtainHitStayResponse(input);
      }
    ```

```
public static void setPlayerResponse(HitStayResponse newHitStayResponse) {
  Console.setPlayerResponse(newHitStayResponse);
}
```

2. Now I change all callers to Console methods to be callers to Blackjack's versions of the methods. Here are a few such changes:

```
public class ScenarioTest extends TestCase...
  public void testDealerStandsWhenPlayerBusts() {
    Console.setPlayerResponse(new TestAlwaysHitResponse());
    int[] deck = { 10, 9, 7, 2, 6 };
    Blackjack blackjack = new Blackjack(deck);
    blackjack.setPlayerResponse(new TestAlwaysHitResponse());
    blackjack.play();
    assertTrue("dealer wins", blackjack.didDealerWin());
    assertTrue("player loses", !blackjack.didPlayerWin());
    assertEquals("dealer total", 11, blackjack.getDealerTotal());
    assertEquals("player total", 23, blackjack.getPlayerTotal());
  }
```

and

```
public class Blackjack...
  public void play() {
    deal();
    writeln(player.getHandAsString());
    writeln(dealer.getHandAsStringWithFirstCardDown());
    HitStayResponse hitStayResponse;
    do {
      write("(H)it or S)tay: ");
      hitStayResponse = Console.obtainHitStayResponse(input);
      write(hitStayResponse.toString());
      if (hitStayResponse.shouldHit()) {
        dealCardTo(player);
        writeln(player.getHandAsString());
      }
    }
    while (canPlayerHit(hitStayResponse));
    // ...
  }
```

At this point I compile, run my automated tests, and play the game on the console to confirm that everything is working correctly.

3. I can now apply *Move Method* [F] and *Move Field* [F] to get all of Console's features onto Blackjack. When I'm done, I compile and test to make sure that Blackjack still works.

4. Now I delete Console and, as Martin recommends in his *Inline Class* [F] refactoring, I hold a very short but moving memorial service for another ill-fated Singleton.

Chapter 7

Simplification

Much of the code we write doesn't start out being simple. To make it simple, we must reflect on what isn't simple about it and continually ask, "How could it be simpler?" We can often simplify code by considering a completely different solution. The refactorings in this chapter present different solutions for simplifying methods, state transitions, and tree structures.

Compose Method (123) is about producing methods that efficiently communicate what they do and how they do what they do. A Composed Method [Beck, SBPP] consists of calls to well-named methods that are all at the same level of detail. If you want to keep your system simple, endeavor to apply *Compose Method (123)* everywhere.

Algorithms often become complex as they begin to support many variations. *Replace Conditional Logic with Strategy (129)* shows how to simplify algorithms by breaking them up into separate classes. Of course, if your algorithm isn't sufficiently complicated to justify a Strategy [DP], refactoring to one will only complicate your design.

You probably won't refactor to a Decorator [DP] frequently. Yet it is a great simplification tool for a certain situation: when you have too much special-case or embellishment logic in a class. *Move Embellishment to Decorator (144)* describes how to identify when you really need a Decorator and then shows how to separate embellishments from the core responsibility of a class.

Logic for controlling state transitions is notorious for becoming complex. This is especially true as you add more and more state transitions to a class. The refactoring *Replace State-Altering Conditionals with State (166)* describes how to drastically simplify complex state transition logic and helps you determine whether your logic is complex enough to require a State [DP] implementation.

Replace Implicit Tree with Composite (178) is a refactoring that targets the complexity of building and working with tree structures. It shows how a

121

Composite [DP] can simplify a client's creation and interaction with a tree structure.

The Command pattern [DP] is useful for simplifying certain types of code. The refactoring *Replace Conditional Dispatcher with Command (191)* shows how this pattern can completely simplify a switch statement that controls which chunk of behavior to execute.

Compose Method

You can't rapidly understand a method's logic.

Transform the logic into a small number of intention-revealing steps at the same level of detail.

```
public void add(Object element) {
    if (!readOnly) {
        int newSize = size + 1;
        if (newSize > elements.length) {
            Object[] newElements =
                new Object[elements.length + 10];
            for (int i = 0; i < size; i++)
                newElements[i] = elements[i];
            elements = newElements;
        }
        elements[size++] = element;
    }
}
```

```
public void add(Object element) {
    if (readOnly)
        return;
    if (atCapacity())
        grow();
    addElement(element);
}
```

Motivation

Kent Beck once said that some of his best patterns are those that he thought someone would laugh at him for writing. *Composed Method* [Beck, SBPP] may be such a pattern. A Composed Method is a small, simple method that you can understand in seconds. Do you write a lot of Composed Methods? I like to think I do, but I often find that I don't, at first. So I have to go back and refactor to this pattern. When my code has many Composed Methods, it tends to be easy to use, read, and extend.

A Composed Method is composed of calls to other methods. Good Composed Methods have code at the same level of detail. For example, the code set in bold in the following listing is not at the same level of detail as the nonbold code:

**Compose
Method**

```
private void paintCard(Graphics g) {
   Image image = null;
   if (card.getType().equals("Problem")) {
     image = explanations.getGameUI().problem;
   } else if (card.getType().equals("Solution")) {
     image = explanations.getGameUI().solution;
   } else if (card.getType().equals("Value")) {
     image = explanations.getGameUI().value;
   }
   g.drawImage(image,0,0,explanations.getGameUI());

   if (shouldHighlight())
     paintCardHighlight(g);
   paintCardText(g);
}
```

By refactoring to a Composed Method, all of the methods called within the paintCard() method are now at the same level of detail:

```
private void paintCard(Graphics g) {
   paintCardImage(g);
   if (shouldHighlight())
     paintCardHighlight(g);
   paintCardText(g);
}
```

Most refactorings to Composed Method involve applying *Extract Method* [F] several times until the Composed Method does most (if not all) of its work via calls to other methods. The most difficult part is deciding what code to include or not include in an extracted method. If you extract too much code into a method, you'll have a hard time naming the method to adequately describe what it does. In that case, just apply *Inline Method* [F] to get the code back into the original method, and then explore other ways to break it up.

Once you finish this refactoring, you will likely have numerous small, private methods that are called by your Composed Method. Some may consider such small methods to be a performance problem. They are only a performance problem when a profiler says they are. I rarely find that my worst performance problems relate to Composed Methods; they almost always relate to other coding problems.

If you apply this refactoring on numerous methods within the same class, you may find that the class has an overabundance of small, private methods. In that case, you may see an opportunity to apply *Extract Class* [F].

Another possible downside of this refactoring involves debugging. If you debug a Composed Method, it can become difficult to find where the actual work gets done because the logic is spread out across many small methods.

A Composed Method's name communicates *what* it does, while its body communicates *how* it does what it does. This allows you to rapidly comprehend the code in a Composed Method. When you add up all the time you and your team spend trying to understand a system's code, you can just imagine how much more efficient and effective you'll be if the system is composed of many Composed Methods.

Benefits and Liabilities

+ Efficiently communicates what a method does and how it does what it does.
+ Simplifies a method by breaking it up into well-named chunks of behavior at the same level of detail.
− Can lead to an overabundance of small methods.
− Can make debugging difficult because logic is spread out across many small methods.

Mechanics

This is one of the most important refactorings I know. Conceptually, it is also one of the simplest—so you'd think that this refactoring would lead to a simple set of mechanics. In fact, it's just the opposite. While the steps themselves aren't complex, there is no simple, repeatable set of steps. Instead, there are guidelines for refactoring to Composed Method, some of which include the following.

- *Think small:* Composed Methods are rarely more than ten lines of code and are usually about five lines.

- *Remove duplication and dead code:* Reduce the amount of code in the method by getting rid of blatant and/or subtle code duplication or code that isn't being used.

- *Communicate intention:* Name your variables, methods, and parameters clearly so they communicate their purposes (e.g., `public void addChildTo(Node parent)`).

**Compose
Method**

- *Simplify:* Transform your code so it's as simple as possible. Do this by questioning how you've coded something and by experimenting with alternatives.

- *Use the same level of detail:* When you break up one method into chunks of behavior, make the chunks operate at similar levels of detail. For example, if you have a piece of detailed conditional logic mixed in with some high-level method calls, you have code at different levels of detail. Push the detail down into a well-named method, at the same level of detail as the other methods in the Composed Method.

Example

This example comes from a custom-written collections library. A List class contains an add(...) method by which a user can add an object to a List instance:

```
public class List...
    public void add(Object element) {
        if (!readOnly) {
            int newSize = size + 1;
            if (newSize > elements.length) {
                Object[] newElements =
                    new Object[elements.length + 10];
                for (int i = 0; i < size; i++)
                    newElements[i] = elements[i];
                elements = newElements;
            }
            elements[size++] = element;
        }
    }
```

The first thing I want to change about this 11-line method is its first conditional statement. Instead of using a conditional to wrap all of the method's code, I'd rather see the condition used as a guard clause, by which we can make an early exit from the method:

```
public class List...
    public void add(Object element) {
        if (readOnly)
            return;
        int newSize = size + 1;
        if (newSize > elements.length) {
            Object[] newElements =
                new Object[elements.length + 10];
            for (int i = 0; i < size; i++)
                newElements[i] = elements[i];
            elements = newElements;
```

```
    }
    elements[size++] = element;
}
```

Next, I study the code in the middle of the method. This code checks to see whether the size of the elements array will exceed capacity if a new object is added. If capacity will be exceeded, the elements array is expanded by a factor of 10. The magic number 10 doesn't communicate very well at all. I change it to be a constant:

```
public class List...
    private final static int GROWTH_INCREMENT = 10;

    public void add(Object element)...
        ...
        Object[] newElements =
            new Object[elements.length + GROWTH_INCREMENT];
        ...
```

Next, I apply *Extract Method* [F] on the code that checks whether the elements array is at capacity and needs to grow. This leads to the following code:

```
public class List...
    public void add(Object element) {
        if (readOnly)
            return;
        if (atCapacity()) {
            Object[] newElements =
                new Object[elements.length + GROWTH_INCREMENT];
            for (int i = 0; i < size; i++)
                newElements[i] = elements[i];
            elements = newElements;
        }
        elements[size++] = element;
    }

    private boolean atCapacity() {
        return (size + 1) > elements.length;
    }
```

Next, I apply *Extract Method* [F] on the code that grows the size of the elements array:

```
public class List...
    public void add(Object element) {
        if (readOnly)
            return;
        if (atCapacity())
            grow();
        elements[size++] = element;
    }
```

```
private void grow() {
  Object[] newElements =
    new Object[elements.length + GROWTH_INCREMENT];
  for (int i = 0; i < size; i++)
    newElements[i] = elements[i];
  elements = newElements;
}
```

Compose Method

Finally, I focus on the last line of the method:

```
elements[size++] = element;
```

Although this is one line of code, it is not at the same level of detail as the rest of the method. I fix this by extracting this code into its own method:

```
public class List...
  public void add(Object element) {
    if (readOnly)
      return;
    if (atCapacity())
      grow();
    addElement(element);
  }

  private void addElement(Object element) {
    elements[size++] = element;
  }
```

The add(…) method now contains only five lines of code. Before this refactoring, it would take a little time to understand what the method was doing. After this refactoring, I can rapidly understand what the method does in one second. This is a typical result of applying *Compose Method*.

Replace Conditional Logic with Strategy

Conditional logic in a method controls which
of several variants of a calculation are executed.

*Create a Strategy for each variant and make the method
delegate the calculation to a Strategy instance.*

Replace
Conditional
Logic with
Strategy

Loan

double capital() : double

```
capital() {
    if (expiry == null && maturity != null)
        return commitment * duration() * riskFactor();
    if (expiry != null && maturity == null) {
        if (getUnusedPercentage() != 1.0)
            return commitment * getUnusedPercentage()
                      * duration() * riskFactor();
        else
            return (outstandingRiskAmount() * duration() * riskFactor())
            + (unusedRiskAmount() * duration() * unusedRiskFactor());
    }
    return 0.0;
}
```

Loan

double capital() : double

```
capital() {
    return capitalStrategy.capital(this);
}
```

Strategy: Context

1

CapitalStrategy

capital(loan: Loan) : double

Strategy

**Strategy:
ConcreteStrategy**

CapitalStrategyAdvisedLine	**CapitalStrategyRevolver**	**CapitalStrategyTermLoan**
capital(loan: Loan) : double	capital(loan: Loan) : double	capital(loan: Loan) : double

```
capital(Loan loan) {
    return loan.getCommitment() * duration(loan) * riskFactorFor(loan);
}
```

Motivation

"Simplifying Conditional Expressions" is a chapter in *Refactoring* [F] that contains over a half-dozen highly useful refactorings devoted to cleaning up conditional complexity. About *Decompose Conditional* [F], Martin Fowler writes, "One of the most common areas of complexity in a program lies in complex conditional logic" [F, 238]. We often find such logic in algorithms because they tend to grow, becoming more sophisticated over time. The Strategy pattern [DP] helps manage the complexity that results from having numerous variations of an algorithm.

Conditional logic is often used to decide which variation of an algorithm to use. Refactorings like *Decompose Conditional* [F] or *Compose Method (123)* can simplify such code. On the other hand, they can also overrun your host class with small methods that apply only to specific variations of the algorithm, thereby complicating the host class. In such a situation, it may be better to move each algorithm variation to new classes or to subclasses of the host class. This essentially involves choosing between object composition and inheritance.

Replace Conditional Logic with Strategy (129) involves object composition: you produce a family of classes for each variation of the algorithm and outfit the host class with one Strategy instance to which the host delegates at runtime. An inheritance-based solution can be achieved by applying *Replace Conditional with Polymorphism* [F]. The prerequisite for that refactoring is an inheritance structure (i.e., the algorithm's host class must have subclasses). If subclasses exist and each variation of the algorithm maps easily to specific subclasses, this is probably your preferred refactoring. If you must first create the subclasses, you'll have to decide whether it would be easier to use an object-compositional approach, like refactoring to Strategy. If the conditionals in the algorithm are controlled by one type code, it may be easy to create subclasses of the algorithm's host class, one for each type code (see *Replace Type Code with Subclasses* [F]). If there is no such type code, you'll likely be better off refactoring to Strategy. Finally, if clients need to swap one calculation type for another at runtime, you'd better avoid an inheritance-based approach because this means changing the type of object a client is working with rather than simply substituting one Strategy instance for another.

When deciding whether to refactor to or towards a Strategy, you have to consider how the algorithm embedded in each Strategy will access the data it needs to do its job. As the Mechanics section points out, there are two ways to do this: pass the host class (called the *context*) to the Strategy so it can call back on methods to get its data, or just pass the data directly to the Strategy via parameters. Both of these approaches have upsides and downsides, which are discussed in the Mechanics section.

The Strategy and Decorator patterns offer alternative ways to eliminate conditional logic associated with special-case or alternative behavior. The sidebar Decorator vs. Strategy in the Motivation section of *Move Embellishment to Decorator (144)* offers a look at how these two patterns differ.

When implementing a Strategy-based design, you'll want to consider how your context class will obtain its Strategy. If you don't have many combinations of Strategies and context classes, it's good practice to shield client code from having to worry about both instantiating a Strategy instance and outfitting a context with a Strategy instance. *Encapsulate Classes with Factory (80)* can help with this: just define one or more methods that return a context instance, properly outfitted with the appropriate Strategy instance.

Replace Conditional Logic with Strategy

Benefits and Liabilities

+ Clarifies algorithms by decreasing or removing conditional logic.
+ Simplifies a class by moving variations on an algorithm to a hierarchy.
+ Enables one algorithm to be swapped for another at runtime.
− Complicates a design when an inheritance-based solution or a refactoring from "Simplifying Conditional Expressions" [F] is simpler.
− Complicates how algorithms obtain or receive data from their context class.

Mechanics

Identify the *context*, a class with a calculation method that contains a lot of conditional logic.

1. Create a *strategy*, a concrete class (known as Strategy:ConcreteStrategy in *Design Patterns* [DP]) that will become a genuine ConcreteStrategy by the end of this refactoring. Name your strategy after the behavior performed by the calculation method. You can append the word "Strategy" to the class name if you find it helps communicate the purpose of this new type.

2. Apply *Move Method* [F] to move the calculation method to the strategy. When you perform this step, retain a version of the calculation method on the context that delegates to the strategy's calculation method. Implementing

this delegation will involve defining and instantiating a *delegate*, a field in context that holds a reference to a strategy.

Since most strategies require data in order to do their calculations, you'll need to determine how to make that data available to the strategy. Here are two common approaches.

a. Pass the context as a parameter to the strategy's constructor or calculation method. This may involve making context methods `public` so the strategy can obtain the information it needs. A downside of this approach is that it often breaks "information hiding" (i.e., data that was visible only to the context now must be made visible to other classes, such as the strategy). An upside to this approach is that when you add new public methods to your context, they will be immediately available to all concrete strategies without a lot of code changes. If you take this approach, consider giving the least public access to context data—for example, in Java, consider giving your strategies package protection access to context data.

b. Pass the necessary data from the context to the strategy via calculation method parameters. A downside of this approach is that data will be passed to every concrete strategy regardless of whether particular strategies need that data. An upside to this approach is that it involves the least coupling between the context and the strategy.

    A challenge of following this approach relates to the amount of data you'll need to pass to the strategy. If you have to pass ten parameters to your strategy, it may be better to pass the entire context as a reference to the strategy. On the other hand, you may be able to apply *Introduce Parameter Object* [F] to cut down the number of parameters you must pass to your strategy, thereby making data-passing an acceptable approach. Furthermore, if some parameters are passed to the strategy solely to handle the needs of a specific concrete strategy, you can remove that data from the parameter list and pass it to the concrete strategy via a constructor or initialization method.

There may be helper methods in the context that really belong in the strategy because they are referenced only by the calculation method that's now in the strategy. Move such helper methods from the context to the strategy by implementing whatever accessors are necessary.

✔ Compile and test.

3. Let clients outfit a context with an instance of the strategy by applying *Extract Parameter (346)* on the context code that instantiates a concrete strategy and assigns it to the delegate.

    ✔ Compile and test.

4. Apply *Replace Conditional with Polymorphism* [F] on the strategy's calculation method. To apply that refactoring, you'll first be given a choice to use *Replace Type Code with Subclasses* [F] or *Replace Type Code with State/Strategy* [F]. Choose the former. You'll need to implement *Replace Type Code with Subclasses* [F] whether you have an explicit type code or not. If conditional logic in the calculation method identifies particular types of the calculation, use that conditional logic in place of explicit types as you work through the mechanics for *Replace Type Code with Subclasses* [F].

    Focus on producing one subclass at a time. Upon completion of this step, you'll have substantially reduced the conditional logic in the strategy and you'll have concrete strategies for each variety of the original calculation method. If possible, make the strategy an abstract class.

    ✔ Compile and test with combinations of context instances and concrete strategy instances.

Example

The example in the code sketch presented in the introduction to this refactoring deals with calculating capital for three different kinds of bank loans: a term loan, a revolver, and an advised line. It contains a fair amount of conditional logic used in performing the capital calculation, though it's less complicated and contains less conditional logic than was present in the original code, which handled capital calculations for seven distinct loan types.

In this example, we'll see how Loan's method for calculating capital can be *strategized* (i.e., delegated to a Strategy object). As you study the example, you may wonder why Loan wasn't simply subclassed to support the different styles of capital calculations. That would not have been a good design choice because the application that used Loan needed to accomplish the following.

*   Calculate capital for loans in a variety of ways. Had there been one Loan subclass for each type of capital calculation, the Loan hierarchy would have been overburdened with subclasses, as shown in the diagram on the following page.

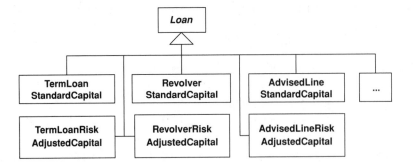

- Change a loan's capital calculation at runtime, without changing the class type of the Loan instance. This is easier to do when it involves exchanging a Loan object's Strategy instance for another Strategy instance, rather than changing the whole Loan object from one subclass of Loan into another.

Now let's look at some code. The Loan class, which plays the role of the context (as defined in the Mechanics section), contains a calculation method called capital():

```
public class Loan...
    public double capital() {
        if (expiry == null && maturity != null)
            return commitment * duration() * riskFactor();
        if (expiry != null && maturity == null) {
            if (getUnusedPercentage() != 1.0)
                return commitment * getUnusedPercentage() * duration() * riskFactor();
            else
                return (outstandingRiskAmount() * duration() * riskFactor())
                    + (unusedRiskAmount() * duration() * unusedRiskFactor());
        }
        return 0.0;
    }
}
```

Much of the conditional logic deals with figuring out whether the loan is a term loan, a revolver, or an advised line. For example, a null expiry date and a non-null maturity date indicate a term loan. That code doesn't reveal its intentions well, does it? Once the code figures out what type of loan it has, a specific capital calculation can be performed. There are three such capital calculations, one for each loan type. All three of these calculations rely on the following helper methods:

```
public class Loan...
    private double outstandingRiskAmount() {
        return outstanding;
    }
```

```
    private double unusedRiskAmount() {
        return (commitment - outstanding);
    }

    public double duration() {
        if (expiry == null && maturity != null)
            return weightedAverageDuration();
        else if (expiry != null && maturity == null)
            return yearsTo(expiry);
        return 0.0;
    }

    private double weightedAverageDuration() {
        double duration = 0.0;
        double weightedAverage = 0.0;
        double sumOfPayments = 0.0;
        Iterator loanPayments = payments.iterator();
        while (loanPayments.hasNext()) {
            Payment payment = (Payment)loanPayments.next();
            sumOfPayments += payment.amount();
            weightedAverage += yearsTo(payment.date()) * payment.amount();
        }
        if (commitment != 0.0)
            duration = weightedAverage / sumOfPayments;
        return duration;
    }

    private double yearsTo(Date endDate) {
        Date beginDate = (today == null ? start : today);
        return ((endDate.getTime() - beginDate.getTime()) / MILLIS_PER_DAY) / DAYS_PER_YEAR;
    }

    private double riskFactor() {
        return RiskFactor.getFactors().forRating(riskRating);
    }

    private double unusedRiskFactor() {
        return UnusedRiskFactors.getFactors().forRating(riskRating);
    }
```

The Loan class can be simplified by extracting specific calculation logic into individual strategy classes, one for each loan type. For example, the method weightedAverageDuration() is used only to calculate capital for a term loan.

I'll now proceed with the refactoring to Strategy.

1. Since the strategy I'd like to create will handle the calculation of a loan's capital, I create a class called CapitalStrategy.

    ```
    public class CapitalStrategy {
    }
    ```

2. Now I apply *Move Method* [F] to move the capital() calculation to Capital-Strategy. This step involves leaving a simple version of capital() on Loan, which will delegate to an instance of CapitalStrategy.

    The first step is to declare capital() in CapitalStrategy:

```
public class CapitalStrategy {
  public double capital() {
    return 0.0;
  }
}
```

Now I need to copy code from Loan to CapitalStrategy. Of course, this will involve copying the capital() method. The mechanics for *Move Method* [F] encourage me to move whatever features (data or methods) are used solely by capital(). I begin by copying the capital() method and then see what else I can easily move from Loan to CapitalStrategy. I end up with the following code, which doesn't compile at the moment:

```
public class CapitalStrategy...
  public double capital() {   // copied from Loan
    if (expiry == null && maturity != null)
      return commitment * duration() * riskFactor();
    if (expiry != null && maturity == null) {
      if (getUnusedPercentage() != 1.0)
        return commitment * getUnusedPercentage() * duration() * riskFactor();
      else
        return (outstandingRiskAmount() * duration() * riskFactor())
            + (unusedRiskAmount() * duration() * unusedRiskFactor());
    }
    return 0.0;
  }

  private double riskFactor() {        // moved from Loan
    return RiskFactor.getFactors().forRating(riskRating);
  }

  private double unusedRiskFactor() {    // moved from Loan
    return UnusedRiskFactors.getFactors().forRating(riskRating);
  }
```

I find that I cannot move the duration() method from Loan to CapitalStrategy because the weightedAverageDuration() method relies on Loan's payment information. Once I make that payment information accessible to CapitalStrategy, I'll be able to move duration() and its helper methods to CapitalStrategy. I'll do that soon. For now, I need to make the code I copied into CapitalStrategy compile. To do that, I must decide whether to pass a Loan reference as a parameter to capital() and its two helper methods or pass data as parameters to capital(), which it can use and pass to its helper methods. I determine that capital() needs the following information from a Loan instance:

Replace
Conditional
Logic with
Strategy

- Expiry date

- Maturity date

- Duration

- Commitment amount

- Risk rating

- Unused percentage

- Outstanding risk amount

- Unused risk amount

If I can make that list smaller, I could go with a data-passing approach. So I speculate that I could create a LoanRange class to store dates associated with Loan instances (e.g., expiry and maturity dates). I might also be able to group the commitment amount, outstanding risk amount, and unused risk amount into a LoanRisk class or something with a better name.

Yet I quickly abandon these ideas when I realize that I have other methods to move from Loan to CapitalStrategy (such as duration()), which require that I pass even more information (such as payments) to CapitalStrategy. I decide to simply pass a Loan reference to CapitalStrategy and make the necessary changes on Loan to make all the code compile:

```
public class CapitalStrategy...
    public double capital(Loan loan) {
        if (loan.getExpiry() == null && loan.getMaturity() != null)
            return loan.getCommitment() * loan.duration() * riskFactorFor(loan);
        if (loan.getExpiry() != null && loan.getMaturity() == null) {
            if (loan.getUnusedPercentage() != 1.0)
                return loan.getCommitment() * loan.getUnusedPercentage()
                * loan.duration() * riskFactorFor(loan);
            else
                return
                    (loan.outstandingRiskAmount() * loan.duration() * riskFactorFor(loan))
                + (loan.unusedRiskAmount() * loan.duration() * unusedRiskFactorFor(loan));
        }
        return 0.0;
    }
```

```
private double riskFactorFor(Loan loan) {
    return RiskFactor.getFactors().forRating(loan.getRiskRating());
}

private double unusedRiskFactorFor(Loan loan) {
    return UnusedRiskFactors.getFactors().forRating(loan.getRiskRating());
}
```

**Replace
Conditional
Logic with
Strategy**

The changes I make to Loan all involve creating new methods that make
Loan data accessible. Since CapitalStrategy lives in the same package as Loan, I
can limit the visibility of this data by using Java's "package protection" feature. I do this by not assigning an explicit visibility (public, private, or protected) to each method:

```
public class Loan...
    Date getExpiry() {
        return expiry;
    }

    Date getMaturity() {
        return maturity;
    }

    double getCommitment() {
        return commitment;
    }

    double getUnusedPercentage() {
        return unusedPercentage;
    }

    private double outstandingRiskAmount() {
        return outstanding;
    }

    private double unusedRiskAmount() {
        return (commitment - outstanding);
    }
```

Now all the code in CapitalStrategy compiles. The next step in *Move Method*
[F] is to make Loan delegate to CapitalStrategy for the capital calculation:

```
public class Loan...
    public double capital() {
        return new CapitalStrategy().capital(this);
    }
```

Now everything compiles. I run my tests, such as the one below, to see that everything still works:

```
public class CapitalCalculationTests extends TestCase {
   public void testTermLoanSamePayments() {
      Date start = november(20, 2003);
      Date maturity = november(20, 2006);
      Loan termLoan = Loan.newTermLoan(LOAN_AMOUNT, start, maturity, HIGH_RISK_RATING);
      termLoan.payment(1000.00, november(20, 2004));
      termLoan.payment(1000.00, november(20, 2005));
      termLoan.payment(1000.00, november(20, 2006));
      assertEquals("duration", 2.0, termLoan.duration(), TWO_DIGIT_PRECISION);
      assertEquals("capital", 210.00, termLoan.capital(), TWO_DIGIT_PRECISION);
   }
}
```

All the tests pass. I can now focus on moving more functionality related to the capital calculation from Loan to CapitalStrategy. I will spare you the details; they are similar to what I've already shown. When I'm done, CapitalStrategy now looks like this:

```
public class CapitalStrategy {
   private static final int MILLIS_PER_DAY = 86400000;
   private static final int DAYS_PER_YEAR = 365;

   public double capital(Loan loan) {
      if (loan.getExpiry() == null && loan.getMaturity() != null)
         return loan.getCommitment() * loan.duration() * riskFactorFor(loan);
      if (loan.getExpiry() != null && loan.getMaturity() == null) {
         if (loan.getUnusedPercentage() != 1.0)
            return loan.getCommitment() * loan.getUnusedPercentage()
            * loan.duration() * riskFactorFor(loan);
         else
            return
              (loan.outstandingRiskAmount() * loan.duration() * riskFactorFor(loan))
            + (loan.unusedRiskAmount() * loan.duration() * unusedRiskFactorFor(loan));
      }
      return 0.0;
   }

   private double riskFactorFor(Loan loan) {
      return RiskFactor.getFactors().forRating(loan.getRiskRating());
   }

   private double unusedRiskFactorFor(Loan loan) {
      return UnusedRiskFactors.getFactors().forRating(loan.getRiskRating());
   }
}
```

```
public double duration(Loan loan) {
    if (loan.getExpiry() == null && loan.getMaturity() != null)
        return weightedAverageDuration(loan);
    else if (loan.getExpiry() != null && loan.getMaturity() == null)
        return yearsTo(loan.getExpiry(), loan);
    return 0.0;
}

private double weightedAverageDuration(Loan loan) {
    double duration = 0.0;
    double weightedAverage = 0.0;
    double sumOfPayments = 0.0;
    Iterator loanPayments = loan.getPayments().iterator();
    while (loanPayments.hasNext()) {
        Payment payment = (Payment)loanPayments.next();
        sumOfPayments += payment.amount();
        weightedAverage += yearsTo(payment.date(), loan) * payment.amount();
    }
    if (loan.getCommitment() != 0.0)
        duration = weightedAverage / sumOfPayments;
    return duration;
}

private double yearsTo(Date endDate, Loan loan) {
    Date beginDate = (loan.getToday() == null ? loan.getStart() : loan.getToday());
    return ((endDate.getTime() - beginDate.getTime()) / MILLIS_PER_DAY) / DAYS_PER_YEAR;
}
}
```

One consequence of performing these changes is that Loan's capital and duration calculations now look like this:

```
public class Loan...
    public double capital() {
        return new CapitalStrategy().capital(this);
    }

    public double duration() {
        return new CapitalStrategy().duration(this);
    }
```

While I resist the temptation to prematurely optimize the Loan class, I don't ignore an opportunity to remove duplication. In other words, it's time to replace the two occurrences of new CapitalStrategy() with a CapitalStrategy field on Loan:

```
public class Loan...
    private CapitalStrategy capitalStrategy;
```

```
    private Loan(double commitment, double outstanding,
                Date start, Date expiry, Date maturity, int riskRating) {
        capitalStrategy = new CapitalStrategy();    ...
    }

    public double capital() {
        return capitalStrategy.capital(this);
    }

    public double duration() {
        return capitalStrategy.duration(this);
    }
```

I've now finished applying *Move Method* [F].

3. Now I'll apply *Extract Parameter (346)* to make it possible to set the value of the delegate, which is currently hard-coded. This step will be important when we get to the next step in the refactoring:

```
public class Loan...
    private Loan(...,  CapitalStrategy capitalStrategy) {
        ...
        this.capitalStrategy = capitalStrategy;
    }

    public static Loan newTermLoan(
        double commitment, Date start, Date maturity, int riskRating) {

        return new Loan(
            commitment, commitment, start, null,
            maturity, riskRating, new CapitalStrategy()
        );
    }

    public static Loan newRevolver(
        double commitment, Date start, Date expiry, int riskRating) {

        return new Loan(commitment, 0, start, expiry,
            null, riskRating, new CapitalStrategy()
        );
    }

    public static Loan newAdvisedLine(
        double commitment, Date start, Date expiry, int riskRating) {
        if (riskRating > 3) return null;
        Loan advisedLine =
            new Loan(commitment, 0, start, expiry, null, riskRating, new CapitalStrategy());
        advisedLine.setUnusedPercentage(0.1);
        return advisedLine;
    }
```

4. I can now apply *Replace Conditional with Polymorphism* [F] on Capital-
    Strategy's capital() method. My first step is to create a subclass for the capi-
    tal calculation for a term loan. This involves making some methods protected
    in CapitalStrategy (not shown below) and moving some methods to a new
    class called CapitalStrategyTermLoan (shown below):

```
public class CapitalStrategyTermLoan extends CapitalStrategy {
    public double capital(Loan loan) {
        return loan.getCommitment() * duration(loan) * riskFactorFor(loan);
    }

    public double duration(Loan loan) {
        return weightedAverageDuration(loan);
    }

    private double weightedAverageDuration(Loan loan) {
        double duration = 0.0;
        double weightedAverage = 0.0;
        double sumOfPayments = 0.0;
        Iterator loanPayments = loan.getPayments().iterator();
        while (loanPayments.hasNext()) {
            Payment payment = (Payment)loanPayments.next();
            sumOfPayments += payment.amount();
            weightedAverage += yearsTo(payment.date(), loan) * payment.amount();
        }
        if (loan.getCommitment() != 0.0)
            duration = weightedAverage / sumOfPayments;
        return duration;
    }
}
```

To test this class, I must first update Loan as follows:

```
public class Loan...
    public static Loan newTermLoan(
        double commitment, Date start, Date maturity, int riskRating) {
        return new Loan(
            commitment, commitment, start, null, maturity, riskRating,
            new CapitalStrategyTermLoan()
        );
    }
```

The tests pass. Now I continue applying *Replace Conditional with Polymorphism* [F] to produce capital strategies for the other two loan types,
revolver and advised line. Here are the changes I make to Loan:

```
public class Loan...
    public static Loan newRevolver(
        double commitment, Date start, Date expiry, int riskRating) {
        return new Loan(
            commitment, 0, start, expiry, null, riskRating,
            new CapitalStrategyRevolver()
```

**Replace
Conditional
Logic with
Strategy**

```
    );
    }

    public static Loan newAdvisedLine(
        double commitment, Date start, Date expiry, int riskRating) {
        if (riskRating > 3) return null;
        Loan advisedLine = new Loan(
            commitment, 0, start, expiry, null, riskRating,
            new CapitalStrategyAdvisedLine()
        );
        advisedLine.setUnusedPercentage(0.1);
        return advisedLine;
    }
```

Here's a look at all of the new strategy classes:

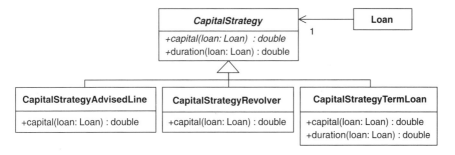

You'll notice that CapitalStrategy is now an abstract class. It now looks like this:

```
public abstract class CapitalStrategy {
    private static final int MILLIS_PER_DAY = 86400000;
    private static final int DAYS_PER_YEAR = 365;

    public abstract double capital(Loan loan);

    protected double riskFactorFor(Loan loan) {
        return RiskFactor.getFactors().forRating(loan.getRiskRating());
    }

    public double duration(Loan loan) {
        return yearsTo(loan.getExpiry(), loan);
    }

    protected double yearsTo(Date endDate, Loan loan) {
        Date beginDate = (loan.getToday() == null ? loan.getStart() : loan.getToday());
        return ((endDate.getTime() - beginDate.getTime()) / MILLIS_PER_DAY) / DAYS_PER_YEAR;
    }
}
```

And that does it for this refactoring. Capital calculations, which include duration calculations, are now performed using several concrete strategies.

Move Embellishment to Decorator

Move
Embellishment
to Decorator

Code provides an embellishment to a class's core responsibility.

Move the embellishment code to a Decorator.

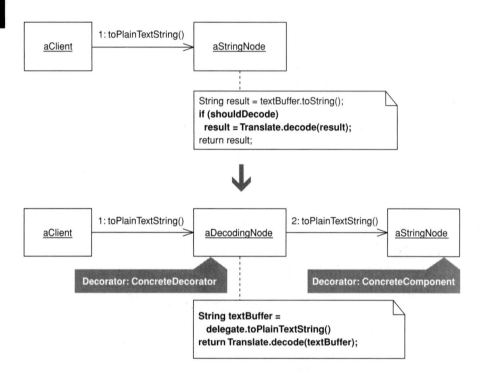

Motivation

When new features in a system are needed, it's common to add new code to old classes. Such new code often embellishes the core responsibility or primary behavior of an existing class. The trouble with some of these embellishments is that they complicate their host classes with new fields, new methods, and new logic, all of which exists for special-case behavior that needs to be executed only some of the time.

The Decorator pattern [DP] offers a good remedy: place each embellishment in its own class and let that class wrap the type of object it needs to embellish so that clients may wrap the embellishment around objects at runtime, when special-case behavior is needed.

The JUnit testing framework [Beck and Gamma] provides a good example. JUnit makes it easy to write and run tests. Each test is an object of type TestCase, and there's an easy way to tell the framework to run all of your TestCase objects. But if you want to run one test multiple times, there's no embellishment within TestCase to do so. For that extended behavior, you must decorate a TestCase object with a RepeatedTest Decorator, as the client code does in the following diagram.

Move Embellishment to Decorator

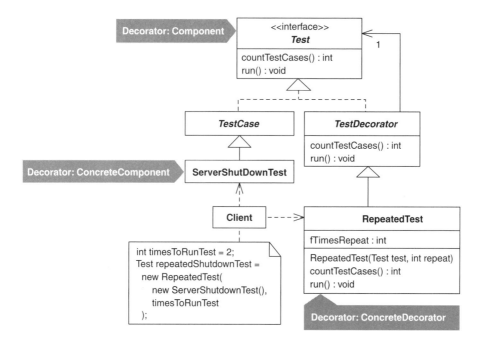

Decorator is not a pattern you'd refactor to if you wanted to move an embellishment out of a class with dozens of public methods. Why? Because a Decorator must be what *Design Patterns* [DP] calls a "transparent enclosure": it must implement *all* of the public methods of the classes it decorates (and that would require a lot of useless code for a class with dozens of public methods). Transparent enclosures wrap objects in a way that is transparent to the objects being wrapped (i.e., a decoratee doesn't know it has been decorated).

Since a Decorator and its decoratee share the same interface, Decorators are transparent to client code that uses them. Such transparency works well for client code, unless that code is deliberately checking the identity of an object. In that case, the Decorator can prevent the client code from identifying a particular object instance because the Decorator and the object it decorates are instances of different classes. For example, the following Java code

```
if (node instanceof StringNode)
```

**Move
Embellishment
to Decorator**

would not evaluate to `true` if `node` were an instance of a `StringNode` that had been decorated with a concrete Decorator. That shouldn't stop you from using this pattern, for it is often possible to rewrite client code to not rely on an object's type.

Another consideration for using this pattern involves multiple Decorators. If you've written two or more concrete Decorators for an object, clients can decorate instances of the object with more than one Decorator. In that case, the ordering of the Decorators may cause unwanted behavior. For example, a Decorator that encrypts data can interfere with a Decorator that filters out certain words if the encryption happens prior to the filtering. In the ideal case, it is best to have Decorators be so independent of each other that they can be arranged in any combination. In practice, that sometimes isn't possible; then you can consider encapsulating the Decorators and giving clients access to safe combinations of them via specific Creation Methods (see *Encapsulate Classes with Factory, 80*).

Refactoring embellishments out of a class can produce a design that is simple to those who are comfortable with object composition. To those who aren't, code that used to be in one class is now spread out across many classes. Such a separation may make code harder to understand since because it no longer resides in one place. In addition, having code reside in different objects can make it harder to debug because debugging sessions must go through one or more Decorators before getting to a decorated object. In short, if a team isn't comfortable with using object composition to "decorate" objects, the team may not be ready for this pattern.

Sometimes an embellishment provides protection logic for an object. In that case, the embellishment can be moved to a Protection Proxy [DP] (see the example from *Encapsulating Inner Classes, 86*). Structurally, a Protection Proxy is the same as a Decorator. The difference is in intent. A Protection Proxy protects an object, while a Decorator adds behavior to an object.

I like the Decorator pattern because it helps produce elegant solutions. Yet my colleagues and I don't find ourselves refactoring to it very often. We're more likely to refactor towards it and only refactor all the way to it once in a while. As usual, no matter how much you like a pattern, use it only when you really need it.

Decorator versus Strategy

Move Embellishment to Decorator (144) and *Replace Conditional Logic with Strategy (129)* are competing refactorings. Both can eliminate conditional logic associated with special-case or alternative behavior, and both do so by moving such behavior out of an existing class and into one or more new classes. Yet how these new classes are used is the difference. Decorator instances wrap themselves around an object (or each other), while one or more Strategy instances are used within an object, as shown in the following diagram.

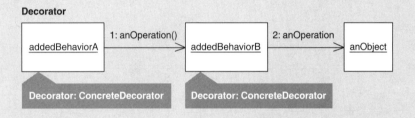

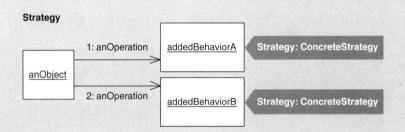

When does it make sense to refactor to Decorator versus to Strategy? There's no simple answer. You must consider numerous issues when making the decision. Here are a few.

- You can't share Decorator instances—each instance wraps one object. On the other hand, you can easily share Strategy instances by means of the Singleton or Flyweight patterns [DP].

- A Strategy can have whatever interface it wants, while a Decorator must conform to the interface of the classes it decorates.

- Decorators can transparently add behavior to many different classes, as long as the classes share the same interface as the Decorators. On the other hand, classes that want to use Strategy objects must know about their existence and how to use them.

- Using one or more Strategies within a class that holds a lot of data or implements many public methods is common practice. On the other hand, Decorator classes become too heavy and require too much memory when they're used to decorate classes with lots of data and many public methods.

To learn more about what is similar and different about Decorator and Strategy, I suggest studying these two patterns in *Design Patterns* [DP].

Benefits and Liabilities

+ Simplifies a class by removing embellishments from it.
+ Effectively distinguishes a class's core responsibility from its embellishments.
+ Helps remove duplicated embellishment logic in several related classes.
− Changes the object identity of a decorated object.
− Can make code harder to understand and debug.
− Complicates a design when combinations of Decorators can adversely affect one another.

Mechanics

Before you begin this refactoring, you must identify an *embellished class*, a class that contains an embellishment to its core responsibility. Not every class with an embellishment to its core responsibility will be a good candidate for being "decorated." First ensure that the set of public methods that your Decorator will need to implement isn't too large. Because a Decorator forms a "transparent enclosure" around the objects it decorates, a piece of client code should be able to call the same set of public methods on a decorated object as it would normally call on the object itself. If your embellished class declares and inherits lots of public methods, either reduce that number (by deleting, moving, or changing the visibility of methods) or consider applying a different refactoring, such as *Replace Conditional Logic with Strategy (129)*.

1. Identify or create an *enclosure type*, an interface or class that declares all of the public methods needed by clients of the embellished class. An enclosure type is known as Decorator: Component in *Design Patterns* [DP].

    If you already have an enclosure type, it's likely to be an interface implemented by the embellished class or a superclass of the embellished class. Classes that contain state aren't good enclosure types because Decorators will inherit their state when they don't need to. If you don't already have a proper enclosure type, create one by applying *Unify Interfaces (343)* and/or *Extract Interface* [F].

2. Find the conditional logic (a switch or if statement) that adds the embellishment to your embellished class and remove that logic by applying *Replace Conditional with Polymorphism* [F].

    Martin Fowler notes that before applying *Replace Conditional with Polymorphism*, you often need to apply *Replace Type Code with Subclasses* [F] or *Replace Type Code with State/Strategy* [F]. If you apply *Replace Type Code with Subclasses*, the first step in the mechanics requires creating a Creation Method to fully encapsulate the type code. Should you need such a Creation Method, make sure its return type is the enclosure type. In addition, when you remove the type code field from the superclass, it is not necessary to declare the accessors for the type code as abstract (even though Martin Fowler's mechanics state that you must do so).

    If you have logic that must be executed before *and/or* after your embellishment code, you'll likely need to use *Form Template Method* [F] when applying *Replace Conditional with Polymorphism*.

    ✔ Compile and test.

3. Step 2 produced one or more subclasses of the embellished class. Transform these subclasses into delegating classes by applying *Replace Inheritance with Delegation* [F]. When implementing this refactoring, be sure to do the following.

    • Make each delegating class implement the enclosure type.

    • Make the type for the delegating class's delegate field be the enclosure type.

    • Decide whether your embellishment code will execute before or after your delegating class makes its call to the delegate.

    If you applied *Form Template Method* during step 2, your delegating class may need to call non-public methods on the delegate (i.e., the embellished class) that are referenced by your Template Method. If that occurs, change the visibility of these methods to public and reapply *Unify Interfaces (343)*.

If your delegating class delegates to a method on the embellished class that can return an undecorated object instance, make sure your delegating class decorates it before handing the instance to a client.

✔ Compile and test.

Move Embellishment to Decorator

4. Each delegating class now assigns its delegate field to a new instance of the embellished class. Ensure that this assignment logic exists in a delegating class constructor. Then extract the part of the assignment statement that instantiates the embellished class into a parameter by applying *Extract Parameter (346)*. If possible, remove any unnecessary constructor parameters by repeatedly applying *Remove Parameter* [F].

✔ Compile and test.

Example

The open source HTML Parser (*http://sourceforge.net/projects/htmlparser*) allows programs to see the contents of HTML files as specific HTML objects. When the parser encounters tag data or strings sandwiched between tag data, it translates what it finds into the appropriate HTML objects, like Tag, StringNode, EndTag, ImageTag, and so forth. The parser is frequently used to:

• Translate the contents of one HTML file to another

• Report information about a piece of HTML

• Verify the contents of HTML

The *Move Embellishment to Decorator* refactoring we'll look at concerns the parser's StringNode class. Instances of this class are created at runtime when the parser finds chunks of text sandwiched between tags. For example, consider this HTML:

```
<BODY>This text will be recognized as a StringNode</BODY>
```

Given this line of HTML, the parser creates the following objects at runtime:

• Tag (for the <BODY> tag)

• StringNode (for the String, "This text will be recognized as a StringNode")

• EndTag (for the </BODY> tag)

There are a few ways to examine the contents of HTML objects: you can obtain the object's plain-text representation using toPlainTextString(), and you can obtain the object's HTML representation using toHtml(). In addition, some classes in the parser, including StringNode, implement getText() and setText() methods. Yet a call to a StringNode instance's getText() method returns the same plain-text representation that calls to toPlainTextString() and toHtml() return. So why are there three methods for obtaining the same value? It's a typical story of programmers adding new code to classes based on current needs without refactoring existing code to remove duplication. In this case, it's likely that getText() and toPlainTextString() could be consolidated into one method. In this example, I defer that refactoring work until I learn more about why this consolidation wasn't already performed.

A common embellishment to StringNode involves decoding "numeric or character entity references" found in StringNode instances. Typical character reference decodings include the following:

&amp;	decoded to	&
&divide;	decoded to	÷
&lt;	decoded to	<
&gt;	decoded to	>

The parser's Translate class has a method called decode(String dataToDecode) that can decode a comprehensive set of numeric and character entity references. Such decoding is an embellishment often applied to StringNode instances after they've been found by the parser. For example, consider the following test code, which parses a fragment of HTML and then iterates through a collection of Node instances, decoding the nodes that are instances of StringNode:

```
public void testDecodingAmpersand() throws Exception {
    String ENCODED_WORKSHOP_TITLE =
        "The Testing &amp; Refactoring Workshop";

    String DECODED_WORKSHOP_TITLE =
        "The Testing & Refactoring Workshop";

    assertEquals(
        "ampersand in string",
        DECODED_WORKSHOP_TITLE,
        parseToObtainDecodedResult(ENCODED_WORKSHOP_TITLE));
}
```

```
private String parseToObtainDecodedResult(String stringToDecode)
   throws ParserException {

   StringBuffer decodedContent = new StringBuffer();
   createParser(stringToDecode);

   NodeIterator nodes = parser.elements();
   while (nodes.hasMoreNodes()) {
      Node node = nodes.nextNode();
      if (node instanceof StringNode) {
         StringNode stringNode = (StringNode) node;
         decodedContent.append(
            Translate.decode(stringNode.toPlainTextString())); // decoding step
      }
      if (node instanceof Tag)
         decodedContent.append(node.toHtml());
   }
   return decodedContent.toString();
}
```

Decoding character and numeric references in StringNode instances is a feature that clients need only some of the time. Yet these clients always perform the decoding themselves, using the same process of iterating nodes, finding nodes that are StringNode instances, and decoding them. Instead of forcing these clients to perform the same decoding steps over and over again, the work could be consolidated in one place by building this decoding behavior into the parser.

I thought of several ways to go about this refactoring and then settled on a straightforward approach: add the decoding embellishment directly to String-Node and observe how the code looks afterward. I had some doubts about this implementation, but I wanted to see how far I could push it until a better design was needed. So, using test-driven development, I added the decoding embellishment to StringNode. This work involved updating test code, changing the Parser class, changing the StringParser class (which instantiates StringNodes) and changing StringNode.

Here's how I updated the above test to drive the creation of this decoding embellishment:

```
public void testDecodingAmpersand() throws Exception {
   String ENCODED_WORKSHOP_TITLE =
   "The Testing &amp; Refactoring Workshop";

   String DECODED_WORKSHOP_TITLE =
   "The Testing & Refactoring Workshop";

   StringBuffer decodedContent = new StringBuffer();
   Parser parser = Parser.createParser(ENCODED_WORKSHOP_TITLE);
   parser.setNodeDecoding(true);  // tell parser to decode StringNodes
   NodeIterator nodes = parser.elements();
```

Move Embellishment to Decorator

```
while (nodes.hasMoreNodes())
    decodedContent.append(nodes.nextNode().toPlainTextString());

assertEquals("decoded content",
    DECODED_WORKSHOP_TITLE,
    decodedContent.toString()
);
}
```

True to the nature of test-driven development, this updated code wouldn't even compile until I added the code necessary for parser.setNodeDecoding(true). My first step was to extend the Parser class to include a flag for toggling String-Node decoding on or off:

```
public class Parser...
    private boolean shouldDecodeNodes = false;

    public void setNodeDecoding(boolean shouldDecodeNodes) {
        this.shouldDecodeNodes = shouldDecodeNodes;
    }
```

Next, the StringParser class needed some changes. It contains a method called find(…) that locates, instantiates, and returns StringNode instances during parsing. Here's a fragment of the code:

```
public class StringParser...
    public Node find(NodeReader reader, String input, int position, boolean balance_quotes) {
        ...
        return new StringNode(textBuffer, textBegin, textEnd);
    }
```

I also changed this code to support the new decoding option:

```
public class StringParser...
    public Node find(NodeReader reader, String input, int position, boolean balance_quotes) {
        ...
        return new StringNode(
            textBuffer, textBegin, textEnd, reader.getParser().shouldDecodeNodes());
    }
```

That code wouldn't compile until I added to the Parser class the shouldDecode-Nodes() method and created a new StringNode constructor that would take the boolean value supplied by shouldDecodeNodes():

```
public class Parser...
    public boolean shouldDecodeNodes() {
        return shouldDecodeNodes;
    }
```

```
public class StringNode extends Node...
   private boolean shouldDecode = false;

   public StringNode(StringBuffer textBuffer, int textBegin, int textEnd, boolean shouldDecode) {
      this(textBuffer, textBegin, textEnd);
      this.shouldDecode = shouldDecode;
   }
```

Move Embellishment to Decorator

Finally, to complete the implementation and make the test pass, I needed to write decoding logic in StringNode:

```
public class StringNode...
   public String toPlainTextString() {
      String result = textBuffer.toString();
      if (shouldDecode)
         result = Translate.decode(result);
      return result;
   }
```

My tests were now passing. I observed that the parser's new decoding embellishment didn't unduly bloat the code. Yet once you support one embellishment, it's often easy to find others worth supporting. And sure enough, when I looked over more parser client code, I found that it was common to remove escape characters (like \n for newline, \t for tabs) from StringNode instances. So I decided to give the parser an embellishment to remove escape characters as well. Doing that meant adding another flag to the Parser class (which I called shouldRemoveEscapeCharacters), updating StringParser to call a StringNode constructor that could handle both the decoding option and the new option for removing escape characters, and adding the following new code to StringNode:

```
public class StringNode...
   private boolean shouldRemoveEscapeCharacters = false;

   public StringNode(StringBuffer textBuffer, int textBegin, int textEnd,
                      boolean shouldDecode, boolean shouldRemoveEscapeCharacters) {
      this(textBuffer, textBegin, textEnd);
      this.shouldDecode = shouldDecode;
      this.shouldRemoveEscapeCharacters = shouldRemoveEscapeCharacters;
   }

   public String toPlainTextString() {
      String result = textBuffer.toString();
      if (shouldDecode)
         result = Translate.decode(result);
      if (shouldRemoveEscapeCharacters)
         result = ParserUtils.removeEscapeCharacters(result);
      return result;
   }
```

The embellishments for decoding and escape character removal simplified client code to the parser. But I didn't like the number of changes I was forced to make across several parser classes just to support each new embellishment. Making such changes across multiple classes was an indication of the code smell *Solution Sprawl (43)*. This smell resulted from:

Move Embellishment to Decorator

- *Too much initialization logic*, that is, code to tell Parser and StringParser to toggle an embellishment on or off and to initialize StringNode instances to use one or more embellishments

- *Too much embellishment logic*, that is, special-case logic in StringNode to support each embellishment

I reasoned that the initialization problem could best be solved by handing the parser a Factory instance that instantiated the appropriately configured StringNode instances at runtime (see *Move Creation Knowledge to Factory, 68*). I further reasoned that the buildup of embellishment logic could be solved by refactoring to either a Decorator or a Strategy. I decided to revisit the initialization problem later and focus on the Decorator or Strategy refactoring now.

So which pattern would be more useful here? As I explored sibling classes of StringNode (such as RemarkNode, which represents a comment in HTML), I saw that they could also benefit from the decoding and escape character removal behavior now in StringNode. If I refactored that behavior into Strategy classes, then StringNode and its sibling classes would need to be altered to know about the Strategy classes. This would not be necessary with a Decorator implementation because the behavior in Decorators could be transparently wrapped around instances of StringNode and its siblings. That appealed to me; I did not like the idea of changing a lot of code in many classes.

What about performance? I did not give much consideration to performance because I tend to let a profiler lead me to performance problems. I further reasoned that if the Decorator refactoring led to slow performance, it wouldn't require much work to refactor it to a Strategy implementation.

Having decided that a Decorator would be better than a Strategy, I now needed to decide whether a Decorator would really be a good fit for the code in question. As I mentioned at the beginning of the Mechanics section, it's vital to learn whether a class is primitive enough to make decoration viable. Primitive, in this case, means that the class doesn't implement a large number of public methods or declare many fields. I discovered that StringNode *is* primitive, but its superclass, AbstractNode, is not. The diagram on the following page shows AbstractNode.

AbstractNode
#nodeBegin : int #nodeEnd : int
+AbstractNode(beginPosition: int, endPosition: int) +toPlainTextString() : String +toHtml() : String +toString() : String +collectInto(nodes: NodeList, filter: String) : void +collectInto(nodes: NodeList, nodeType: class) : void +elementBegin() : int +elementEnd() : int +accept(NodeVisitor) : void +setParent(tag: CompositeTag) : void +getParent() : CompositeTag

I counted ten public methods on AbstractNode. That's not exactly what I'd call a narrow interface, but it isn't broad either. I decided it's small enough to do this refactoring.

Getting ready to refactor, my goal now is to get the embellishment logic out of StringNode by putting each embellishment into its own StringNode Decorator class. If there is ever a need to support multiple embellishments, it will be possible to configure combinations of StringNode Decorators prior to executing a parse.

The following diagram illustrates where StringNode fits into the Node hierarchy and how its decoding logic looked before it was refactored to use a DecodingNode Decorator.

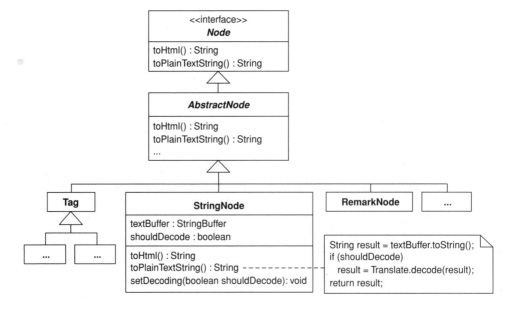

Here are the steps for refactoring StringNode's decoding logic to a Decorator.

1. My first step is to identify or create an enclosure type, a class or interface that declares all public methods of StringNode and whatever public methods it inherits. A good enclosure type won't contain fields (i.e., state). So String-Node's superclass, AbstractNode, is not a good enclosure type because it contains the two primitive int fields, nodeBegin and nodeEnd. Why does it matter whether a class contains fields? Decorators add behavior to the objects they decorate, but they don't need duplicate copies of the fields in those objects. In this case, because StringNode already inherits nodeBegin and nodeEnd from AbstractNode, Decorators of StringNode don't also need to inherit those fields.

So I rule out AbstractNode as the enclosure type. The next natural place to look is the interface that AbstractNode implements, which is called Node. The following diagram shows this interface.

```
              <<interface>>
                 Node
─────────────────────────────────────────────
+toPlainTextString() : String
+toHtml() : String
+toString() : String
+collectInto(nodes: NodeList, filter: String) : void
+collectInto(nodes: NodeList, nodeType: class) : void
+elementBegin() : int
+elementEnd() : int
+accept(NodeVisitor) : void
+setParent(tag: CompositeTag) : void
+getParent() : CompositeTag
```

This would be the perfect enclosure type, except that it doesn't include StringNode's two public methods, getText() and setText(…). I must add these methods to the Node interface in order to pave the way for creating a transparent enclosure for StringNode. I'm not happy about this step, for it means expanding the interface of Node just to accommodate this refactoring. However, I proceed anyway, knowing that a future refactoring will combine toPlainTextString() and getText(), thereby reducing the size of the Node interface.

In Java, adding the getText() and setText(…) methods to the Node interface means that all concrete classes that implement Node must implement getText() and setText(…) or inherit implementations of them. StringNode contains the implementations of getText() and setText(…), but AbstractNode and some of its subclasses (which aren't shown in this example) have no such implementation (or have only one of the two methods defined). To obtain the solution I need, I must apply the refactoring *Unify Interfaces (343)*. This refactoring adds getText() and setText(…) to Node and outfits AbstractNode with the following default (do-nothing) versions of the methods, which all subclasses either inherit and/or override:

```
public abstract class AbstractNode...
    public String getText() {
        return null;
    }

    public void setText(String text) {
    }
```

Move Embellishment to Decorator

2. I can now work towards replacing the decoding embellishment inside String-Node by applying the refactoring *Replace Conditional with Polymorphism* [F]. Applying that refactoring involves producing an inheritance structure that will look like the one shown here.

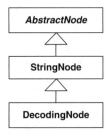

To produce this inheritance structure, I apply *Replace Type Code with Subclasses* [F]. The first step in implementing that refactoring is to apply *Self-Encapsulate Field* [F] on shouldDecode, the type code inside StringNode. The following code shows where shouldDecode is referenced or used within StringNode:

```
public class StringNode extends AbstractNode...
    private boolean shouldDecode = false;

    public StringNode(
        StringBuffer textBuffer, int textBegin, int textEnd, boolean shouldDecode) {
        this(textBuffer, textBegin, textEnd);
        this.shouldDecode = shouldDecode;
    }

    public String toPlainTextString() {
        String result = textBuffer.toString();
        if (shouldDecode)
            result = Translate.decode(result);
        return result;
    }
```

To self-encapsulate shouldDecode, I make the following changes:

```
public class StringNode extends AbstractNode...
    public StringNode(
        StringBuffer textBuffer, int textBegin, int textEnd, boolean shouldDecode) {
        this(textBuffer, textBegin, textEnd);
        setShouldDecode(shouldDecode);
    }

    public String toPlainTextString() {
        String result = textBuffer.toString();
        if (shouldDecode())
            result = Translate.decode(result);
        return result;
    }

    private void setShouldDecode(boolean shouldDecode) {
        this.shouldDecode = shouldDecode;
    }

    private boolean shouldDecode() {
        return shouldDecode;
    }
```

I've nearly self-encapsulated shouldDecode, except for the new StringNode constructor. Because it accepts the type code shouldDecode as a parameter, I need to replace this constructor with a Creation Method (as described in the mechanics to *Replace Type Code with Subclasses* [F]). The Decorator mechanics also tell me to make the return type of this Creation Method be Node, which is the enclosure type that will be vital to implementing the Decorator pattern. Here's the new Creation Method:

```
public class StringNode extends AbstractNode...
    private StringNode(
        StringBuffer textBuffer, int textBegin, int textEnd, boolean shouldDecode) {
        this(textBuffer, textBegin, textEnd);
        setShouldDecode(shouldDecode);
    }

    public static Node createStringNode(
        StringBuffer textBuffer, int textBegin, int textEnd, boolean shouldDecode) {
        return new StringNode(textBuffer, textBegin, textEnd, shouldDecode);
    }
```

And here is the updated client call to the new Creation Method:

```
public class StringParser...
    public Node find(
        NodeReader reader,String input,int position, boolean balance_quotes) {
        ...
        return StringNode.createStringNode(
            textBuffer, textBegin, textEnd, reader.getParser().shouldDecodeNodes());
```

I compile and test to see that these changes didn't break anything. Now, the second step in the mechanics for *Replace Type Code with Subclasses* [F] says:

> For each value of the type code, create a subclass. Override the getting method of the type code in the subclass to return the relevant value. [F, 224]

The type code, shouldDecode, has two values: true and false. I decide that StringNode itself will handle the false case (i.e., don't perform any decoding), while a new subclass called DecodingNode will handle the true case. I start by creating DecodingNode and overriding the shouldDecode() method (which I now make protected):

```
public class StringNode extends AbstractNode...
    protected boolean shouldDecode()...

public class DecodingNode extends StringNode {
    public DecodingNode(StringBuffer textBuffer, int textBegin, int textEnd) {
        super(textBuffer, textBegin, textEnd);
    }

    protected boolean shouldDecode() {
        return true;
    }
}
```

I now need to alter the Creation Method to create the appropriate object based on the value of shouldDecode:

```
public class StringNode extends AbstractNode...
    private boolean shouldDecode = false;

    public static Node createStringNode(
        StringBuffer textBuffer, int textBegin, int textEnd, boolean shouldDecode) {
        if (shouldDecode)
            return new DecodingNode(textBuffer, textBegin, textEnd);
        return new StringNode(textBuffer, textBegin, textEnd, shouldDecode);
    }
```

I compile and test to see that everything is still working.

At this point I can simplify StringNode by removing the shouldDecode type code, its setting method, and the constructor that accepts it. All I have to do to make this work is to return false from StringNode's shouldDecode() method:

```
public class StringNode extends AbstractNode...
    private boolean shouldDecode = false;

    public StringNode(StringBuffer textBuffer,int textBegin,int textEnd) {
        super(textBegin,textEnd);
        this.textBuffer = textBuffer;
    }
```

```
private StringNode(
    StringBuffer textBuffer, int textBegin, int textEnd, boolean shouldDecode) {
    this(textBuffer, textBegin, textEnd);
    setShouldDecode(shouldDecode);
}

public static Node createStringNode(
    StringBuffer textBuffer, int textBegin, int textEnd, boolean shouldDecode) {
    if (shouldDecode)
        return new DecodingNode(textBuffer, textBegin, textEnd);
    return new StringNode(textBuffer, textBegin, textEnd);
}

private void setShouldDecode(boolean shouldDecode) {
    this.shouldDecode = shouldDecode;
}

protected boolean shouldDecode() {
    return false;
}
```

Everything works fine after I compile and test. I've now successfully created an inheritance structure that will enable me to apply *Replace Conditional with Polymorphism* [F].

I now want to rid StringNode of the conditional logic inside toPlainTextString(). Here's how the method looks before I make changes:

```
public class StringNode extends AbstractNode...
    public String toPlainTextString() {
        String result = textBuffer.toString();
        if (shouldDecode())
            result = Translate.decode(result);
        return result;
    }
```

My first step is to give DecodingNode an overriding version of toPlainTextString():

```
public class DecodingNode extends StringNode...
    public String toPlainTextString() {
        return Translate.decode(textBuffer.toString());
    }
```

I compile and test to see that this minor change doesn't upset anything. Now I remove the logic that I had copied into DecodingNode from StringNode:

```
public class StringNode extends AbstractNode...
    public String toPlainTextString() {
        return textBuffer.toString();
        String result = textBuffer.toString();
```

```
if (shouldDecode())
    result = Translate.decode(result);
return result;
}
```

I can now safely delete the shouldDecode() method in both StringNode and DecodingNode:

```
public class StringNode extends AbstractNode...
    protected boolean shouldDecode() {
        return false;
    }
```

```
public class DecodingNode extends StringNode...
    protected boolean shouldDecode() {
        return true;
    }
```

There is also a small amount of duplication in DecodingNode's toPlainText-String(): the call to textBuffer.toString() is identical to the call in StringNode's toPlainTextString(). I can remove this duplication by having DecodingNode call its superclass, as follows:

```
public class DecodingNode extends StringNode...
    public String toPlainTextString() {
        return Translate.decode(super.toPlainTextString());
    }
```

StringNode currently has no trace of the type code shouldDecode, and the conditional decoding logic in toPlainTextString() has been replaced with polymorphism.

3. The next step is to apply the refactoring *Replace Inheritance with Delegation* [F]. That refactoring's mechanics tell me to begin by creating a field in the subclass, DecodingNode, that refers to itself:

```
public class DecodingNode extends StringNode...3.
private Node delegate = this
```

I make delegate's type be Node rather than DecodingNode because DecodingNode will soon be a Decorator and that which it decorates (and delegates to) must implement the same interface as it does (i.e., Node).

I now replace direct calls to inherited StringNode methods to make them use delegation. The only DecodingNode method that makes a call to a superclass method is toPlainTextString():

```
public class DecodingNode extends StringNode...
    public String toPlainTextString() {
        return Translate.decode(super.toPlainTextString());
    }
```

I change this call to use the new field, delegate:

```
public class DecodingNode extends StringNode...
    public String toPlainTextString() {
        return Translate.decode(delegate.toPlainTextString());
    }
```

I compile and test to see whether this still works. It doesn't! It gets the code into an infinite loop. I then notice that Martin mentions this in a note on the mechanics for *Replace Inheritance with Delegation*:

> You won't be able to replace any methods that invoke a method on super that is defined on the subclass, or they may get into an infinite recurse. These methods can be replaced only after you have broken inheritance. [F, 353]

So I undo that last step and press on with the refactoring. My next step is to break inheritance, that is, to make DecodingNode no longer a subclass of StringNode. During this step I must also make delegate point to a real instance of StringNode:

```
public class DecodingNode extends StringNode ...
    private Node delegate = this;

    public DecodingNode(StringBuffer textBuffer, int textBegin, int textEnd) {
        delegate = new StringNode(textBuffer, textBegin, textEnd);
    }
```

My compiler is happy with this code, but the following code in StringNode no longer compiles:

```
public class StringNode extends AbstractNode...
    public static Node createStringNode(
        StringBuffer textBuffer, int textBegin, int textEnd, boolean shouldDecode) {

        if (shouldDecode)
            return new DecodingNode(textBuffer, textBegin, textEnd);
        return new StringNode(textBuffer, textBegin, textEnd);
    }
```

The problem is that createStringNode wants to return objects that implement the Node interface, and DecodingNode no longer implements that interface. I solve this by making DecodingNode implement Node:

```
public class DecodingNode implements Node...
    private Node delegate;

    public DecodingNode(StringBuffer textBuffer, int textBegin, int textEnd) {
        delegate = new StringNode(textBuffer, textBegin, textEnd);
    }
```

```
public String toPlainTextString() {
    return Translate.decode(delegate.toPlainTextString());
}

public void accept(NodeVisitor visitor) {
}

public void collectInto(NodeList collectionList, Class nodeType) {
}

// etc.
```

Move
Embellishment
to Decorator

The final step of *Replace Inheritance with Delegation* involves having each of the methods I've just added to DecodingNode—methods defined by Node—call the corresponding methods on delegate:

```
public class DecodingNode implements Node...

    public void accept(NodeVisitor visitor) {
        delegate.accept(visitor);
    }

    public void collectInto(NodeList collectionList, Class nodeType) {
        delegate.collectInto(collectionList, nodeType);
    }

    // etc.
```

4. DecodingNode is now almost a Decorator. The one thing preventing it from being an actual Decorator is that the field that it delegates to, delegate, is instantiated inside DecodingNode rather then being passed in via a constructor argument. To fix that, I apply *Extract Parameter (346)* and *Remove Parameter* [F] (to remove unnecessary parameters). I make the following changes to implement those refactorings:

```
public class StringNode extends AbstractNode...
    public static Node createStringNode(
        StringBuffer textBuffer, int textBegin, int textEnd, boolean shouldDecode) {
        if (shouldDecode)
            return new DecodingNode(new StringNode(textBuffer, textBegin, textEnd));
        return new StringNode(textBuffer, textBegin, textEnd);
    }

public class DecodingNode implements Node...
    private Node delegate;

    public DecodingNode(Node newDelegate) {
        delegate = newDelegate;
    }
```

DecodingNode is now a full-fledged Decorator. The following diagram shows how it fits into the Node hierarchy.

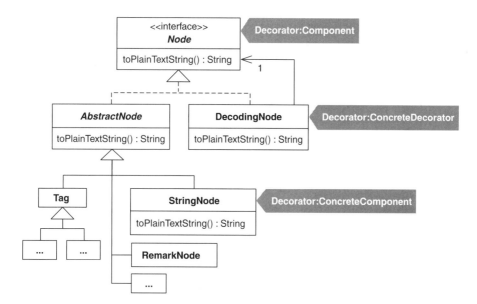

Replace State-Altering Conditionals with State

The conditional expressions that control
an object's state transitions are complex.

*Replace the conditionals with State classes that handle
specific states and transitions between them.*

**Replace
State-Altering
Conditionals
with State**

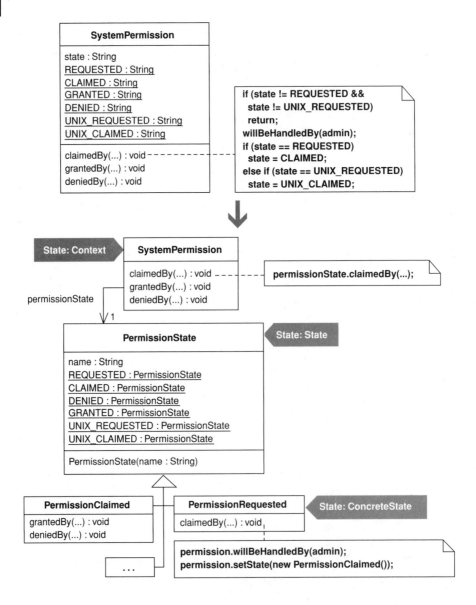

Motivation

The primary reason for refactoring to the State pattern [DP] is to tame overly complex state-altering conditional logic. Such logic, which tends to spread itself throughout a class, controls an object's state, including how states transition to other states. When you implement the State pattern, you create classes that represent specific states of an object and the transitions between those states. The object that has its state changed is known in Design Patterns [DP] as the *context*. A context delegates state-dependent behavior to a state object. State objects make state transitions at runtime by making the context point to a different state object.

Moving state-altering conditional logic out of one class and into a family of classes that represent different states can yield a simpler design that provides a better bird's-eye view of the transitions between states. On the other hand, if you can easily understand the state transition logic in a class, you likely don't need to refactor to the State pattern (unless you plan to add many more state transitions in the future). The Example section for this refactoring shows a case where state-altering conditional logic is no longer easy to follow or extend and where the State pattern can make a real difference.

Before refactoring to State, it's always a good idea to see if simpler refactorings, such as *Extract Method* [F], can help clean up the state-changing conditional logic. If they can't, refactoring to State can help remove or reduce many lines of conditional logic, yielding simpler code that's easier to understand and extend.

This *Replace State-Altering Conditionals with State* refactoring is different from Martin Fowler's *Replace Type Code with State/Strategy* [F] for the following reasons.

- *Differences between State and Strategy:* The State pattern is useful for a class that must easily transition between instances of a family of state classes, while the Strategy pattern is useful for allowing a class to delegate execution of an algorithm to an instance of a family of Strategy classes. Because of these differences, the motivation and mechanics for refactoring to these two patterns differs (see *Replace Conditional Logic with Strategy*, 129).

- *End-to-end mechanics:* Martin deliberately doesn't document a full refactoring to the State pattern because the complete implementation depends on a further refactoring he wrote, *Replace Conditional with Polymorphism* [F]. While I respect that decision, I thought it would be more helpful to readers to understand how the refactoring works from end to end, so my Mechanics and Example sections delineate all of the steps to get you from conditional state-changing logic to a State implementation.

If your state objects have no instance variables (i.e., they are *stateless*), you can optimize memory usage by having context objects share instances of the stateless state instances. The Flyweight and Singleton patterns [DP] are often used to implement sharing (e.g., see *Limit Instantiation with Singleton, 296*). However, it's always best to add state-sharing code *after* your users experience system delays and a profiler points you to the state-instantiation code as a prime bottleneck.

Replace State-Altering Conditionals with State

Benefits and Liabilities

+ Reduces or removes state-changing conditional logic.
+ Simplifies complex state-changing logic.
+ Provides a good bird's-eye view of state-changing logic.
− Complicates a design when state transition logic is already easy to follow.

Mechanics

1. The *context class* is a class that contains the *original state field*, a field that gets assigned to or compared against a family of constants during state transitions. Apply *Replace Type Code with Class (286)* on the original state field such that its type becomes a class. We'll call that new class the *state superclass*.

   The context class is known as State: Context and the state superclass as State: State in *Design Patterns* [DP].

   ✔ Compile.

2. Each constant in the state superclass now refers to an instance of the state superclass. Apply *Extract Subclass* [F] to produce one subclass (known as State: ConcreteState [DP]) per constant, then update the constants in the state superclass so that each refers to the correct subclass instance of the state superclass. Finally, declare the state superclass to be abstract.

   ✔ Compile.

3. Find a context class method that changes the value of the original state field based on state transition logic. Copy this method to the state superclass, making the simplest changes possible to make the new method work. (A common, *simple* change is to pass the context class to the method in order

to have code call methods on the context class.) Finally, replace the body of the context class method with a delegation call to the new method.

✔ Compile and test.

Repeat this step for every context class method that changes the value of the original state field based on state transition logic.

4.   Choose a state that the context class can enter, and identify which state superclass methods make this state transition to other states. Copy the identified method(s), if any, to the subclass associated with the chosen state and remove all unrelated logic.

Unrelated logic usually includes verifications of a current state or logic that transitions to unrelated states.

✔ Compile and test.

Repeat for all states the context class can enter.

5.   Delete the bodies of each of the methods copied to the state superclass during step 3 to produce an empty implementation for each method.

✔ Compile and test.

Example

To understand when it makes sense to refactor to the State pattern, it helps to study a class that manages its state without requiring the sophistication of the State pattern. SystemPermission is such a class. It uses simple conditional logic to keep track of the state of a permission request to access a software system. Over the lifetime of a SystemPermission object, an instance variable named state transitions between the states *requested*, *claimed*, *denied*, and *granted*. Here is a state diagram of the possible transitions:

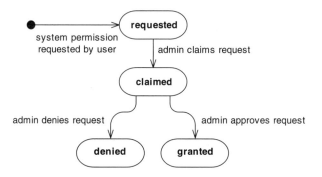

Below is the code for SystemPermission and a fragment of test code to show how the class gets used:

Replace State-Altering Conditionals with State

```
public class SystemPermission...
  private SystemProfile profile;
  private SystemUser requestor;
  private SystemAdmin admin;
  private boolean isGranted;
  private String state;

  public final static String REQUESTED = "REQUESTED";
  public final static String CLAIMED = "CLAIMED";
  public final static String GRANTED = "GRANTED";
  public final static String DENIED = "DENIED";

  public SystemPermission(SystemUser requestor, SystemProfile profile) {
    this.requestor = requestor;
    this.profile = profile;
    state = REQUESTED;
    isGranted = false;
    notifyAdminOfPermissionRequest();
  }

  public void claimedBy(SystemAdmin admin) {
    if (!state.equals(REQUESTED))
      return;
    willBeHandledBy(admin);
    state = CLAIMED;
  }

  public void deniedBy(SystemAdmin admin) {
    if (!state.equals(CLAIMED))
      return;
    if (!this.admin.equals(admin))
      return;
    isGranted = false;
    state = DENIED;
    notifyUserOfPermissionRequestResult();
  }

  public void grantedBy(SystemAdmin admin) {
    if (!state.equals(CLAIMED))
      return;
    if (!this.admin.equals(admin))
      return;
    state = GRANTED;
    isGranted = true;
    notifyUserOfPermissionRequestResult();
  }

public class TestStates extends TestCase...
  private SystemPermission permission;
```

```
public void setUp() {
  permission = new SystemPermission(user, profile);
}

public void testGrantedBy() {
  permission.grantedBy(admin);
  assertEquals("requested", permission.REQUESTED, permission.state());
  assertEquals("not granted", false, permission.isGranted());
  permission.claimedBy(admin);
  permission.grantedBy(admin);
  assertEquals("granted", permission.GRANTED, permission.state());
  assertEquals("granted", true, permission.isGranted());
}
```

Notice how the instance variable, state, gets assigned to different values as clients call specific SystemPermission methods. Now look at the overall conditional logic in SystemPermission. This logic is responsible for transitioning between states, but the logic isn't very complicated so the code doesn't require the sophistication of the State pattern.

This conditional state-changing logic can quickly become hard to follow as more real-world behavior gets added to the SystemPermission class. For example, I helped design a security system in which users needed to obtain UNIX and/or database permissions before the user could be granted general permission to access a given software system. The state transition logic that requires UNIX permission before general permission may be granted looks like this:

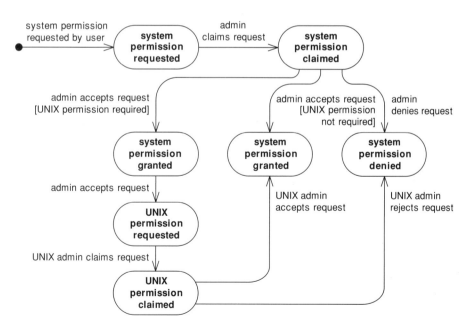

Adding support for UNIX permission makes SystemPermission's state-altering conditional logic more complicated than it used to be. Consider the following:

Replace
State-Altering
Conditionals
with State

```
public class SystemPermission...
  public void claimedBy(SystemAdmin admin) {
    if (!state.equals(REQUESTED) && !state.equals(UNIX_REQUESTED))
      return;
    willBeHandledBy(admin);
    if (state.equals(REQUESTED))
      state = CLAIMED;
    else if (state.equals(UNIX_REQUESTED))
      state = UNIX_CLAIMED;
  }

  public void deniedBy(SystemAdmin admin) {
    if (!state.equals(CLAIMED) && !state.equals(UNIX_CLAIMED))
      return;
    if (!this.admin.equals(admin))
      return;
    isGranted = false;
    isUnixPermissionGranted = false;
    state = DENIED;
    notifyUserOfPermissionRequestResult();
  }

  public void grantedBy(SystemAdmin admin) {
    if (!state.equals(CLAIMED) && !state.equals(UNIX_CLAIMED))
      return;
    if (!this.admin.equals(admin))
      return;

    if (profile.isUnixPermissionRequired() && state.equals(UNIX_CLAIMED))
      isUnixPermissionGranted = true;
    else if (profile.isUnixPermissionRequired() &&
      !isUnixPermissionGranted()) {
      state = UNIX_REQUESTED;
      notifyUnixAdminsOfPermissionRequest();
      return;
    }
    state = GRANTED;
    isGranted = true;
    notifyUserOfPermissionRequestResult();
  }
```

An attempt can be made to simplify this code by applying *Extract Method* [F]. For example, I could refactor the grantedBy() method like so:

```
public void grantedBy(SystemAdmin admin) {
  if (!isInClaimedState())
    return;
```

```
if (!this.admin.equals(admin))
  return;
if (isUnixPermissionRequestedAndClaimed())
  isUnixPermissionGranted = true;
else if (isUnixPermisionDesiredButNotRequested()) {
  state = UNIX_REQUESTED;
  notifyUnixAdminsOfPermissionRequest();
  return;
}
...
```

Replace
State-Altering
Conditionals
with State

Although that's an improvement, SystemPermission now has lots of state-specific Boolean logic (e.g., methods like isUnixPermissionRequestedAndClaimed()), and the grantedBy() method still isn't simple. It's time to see how I simplify things by refactoring to the State pattern.

1. SystemPermission has a field called state, which is of type String. The first step is to change state's type to be a class by applying the refactoring *Replace Type Code with Class (286)*. This yields the following new class:

```
public class PermissionState {
  private String name;

  private PermissionState(String name) {
    this.name = name;
  }

  public final static PermissionState REQUESTED = new PermissionState("REQUESTED");
  public final static PermissionState CLAIMED = new PermissionState("CLAIMED");
  public final static PermissionState GRANTED = new PermissionState("GRANTED");
  public final static PermissionState DENIED = new PermissionState("DENIED");
  public final static PermissionState UNIX_REQUESTED =
    new PermissionState("UNIX_REQUESTED");
  public final static PermissionState UNIX_CLAIMED = new PermissionState("UNIX_CLAIMED");

  public String toString() {
    return name;
  }
}
```

The refactoring also replaces SystemPermission's state field with one called permissionState, which is of type PermissionState:

```
public class SystemPermission...
  private PermissionState permissionState;

  public SystemPermission(SystemUser requestor, SystemProfile profile) {
    ...
```

```
    setState(PermissionState.REQUESTED);
    ...
  }

  public PermissionState getState() {
    return permissionState;
  }

  private void setState(PermissionState state) {
    permissionState = state;
  }

  public void claimedBy(SystemAdmin admin) {
    if (!getState().equals(PermissionState.REQUESTED)
    && !getState().equals(PermissionState.UNIX_REQUESTED))
      return;
    ...
  }

  etc...
```

Replace
State-Altering
Conditionals
with State

2. PermissionState now contains six constants, all of which are instances of Per-missionState. To make each of these constants an instance of a subclass of PermissionState, I apply *Extract Subclass* [F] six times to produce the result shown in the following diagram.

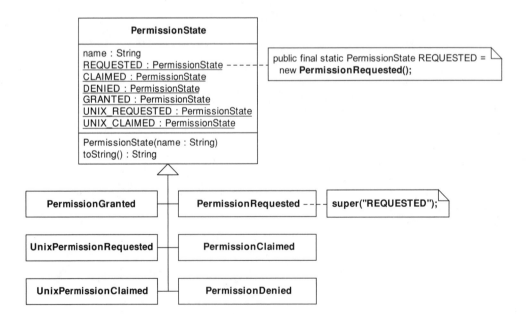

Because no client will ever need to instantiate PermissionState, I declare it to be abstract:

```
public abstract class PermissionState...
```

The compiler is happy with all of the new code, so I press on.

3. Next, I find a method on SystemPermission that changes the value of permission based on state transition logic. There are three such methods in SystemPermission: claimedBy(), deniedBy(), and grantedBy(). I start by working with claimedBy(). I must copy this method to PermissionState, making enough changes to get it to compile and then replacing the body of the original claimedBy() method with a call to the new PermissionState version:

```
public class SystemPermission...
    private void setState(PermissionState state) { // now has package-level visibility
      permissionState = state;
    }

    public void claimedBy(SystemAdmin admin) {
      permissionState.claimedBy(admin, this);
    }

    void willBeHandledBy(SystemAdmin admin) {
      this.admin = admin;
    }

abstract class PermissionState...
    public void claimedBy(SystemAdmin admin, SystemPermission permission) {
      if (!permission.getState().equals(REQUESTED) &&
          !permission.getState().equals(UNIX_REQUESTED))
        return;
      permission.willBeHandledBy(admin);
      if (permission.getState().equals(REQUESTED))
        permission.setState(CLAIMED);
      else if (permission.getState().equals(UNIX_REQUESTED)) {
        permission.setState(UNIX_CLAIMED);
      }
    }
```

After I compile and test to see that the changes worked, I repeat this step for deniedBy() and grantedBy().

4. Now I choose a state that SystemPermission can enter and identify which PermissionState methods make this state transition to other states. I'll start with the REQUESTED state. This state can only transition to the CLAIMED state, and the

transition happens in the PermissionState.claimedBy() method. I copy that
method to the PermissionRequested class:

Replace
State-Altering
Conditionals
with State

```
class PermissionRequested extends PermissionState...
  public void claimedBy(SystemAdmin admin, SystemPermission permission) {
    if (!permission.getState().equals(REQUESTED) &&
       !permission.getState().equals(UNIX_REQUESTED))
      return;
    permission.willBeHandledBy(admin);
    if (permission.getState().equals(REQUESTED))
      permission.setState(CLAIMED);
    else if (permission.getState().equals(UNIX_REQUESTED)) {
      permission.setState(UNIX_CLAIMED);
    }
  }
}
```

A lot of logic in this method is no longer needed. For example, anything
related to the UNIX_REQUESTED state isn't needed because we're only concerned
with the REQUESTED state in the PermissionRequested class. We also don't need to
check whether our current state is REQUESTED because the fact that we're in the
PermissionRequested class tells us that. So I can reduce this code to the following:

```
class PermissionRequested extends Permission...
  public void claimedBy(SystemAdmin admin, SystemPermission permission) {
    permission.willBeHandledBy(admin);
    permission.setState(CLAIMED);
  }
}
```

As always, I compile and test to make sure I didn't break anything. Now
I repeat this step for the other five states. Let's look at what is required to
produce the PermissionClaimed and PermissionGranted states.

The CLAIMED state can transition to DENIED, GRANTED, or UNIX REQUESTED. The
deniedBy() or grantedBy() methods take care of these transitions, so I copy
those methods to the PermissionClaimed class and delete unnecessary logic:

```
class PermissionClaimed extends PermissionState...
  public void deniedBy(SystemAdmin admin, SystemPermission permission) {
    if (!permission.getState().equals(CLAIMED) &&
       !permission.getState().equals(UNIX_CLAIMED))
      return;
    if (!permission.getAdmin().equals(admin))
      return;
    permission.setIsGranted(false);
    permission.setIsUnixPermissionGranted(false);
    permission.setState(DENIED);
    permission.notifyUserOfPermissionRequestResult();
  }
```

```
public void grantedBy(SystemAdmin admin, SystemPermission permission) {
  if (!permission.getState().equals(CLAIMED) &&
     !permission.getState().equals(UNIX_CLAIMED))
    return;
  if (!permission.getAdmin().equals(admin))
    return;

  if (permission.getProfile().isUnixPermissionRequired()
    && permission.getState().equals(UNIX_CLAIMED))
    permission.setIsUnixPermissionGranted(true);
  elseif (permission.getProfile().isUnixPermissionRequired()
       && !permission.isUnixPermissionGranted()) {
    permission.setState(UNIX_REQUESTED);
    permission.notifyUnixAdminsOfPermissionRequest();
    return;
  }
  permission.setState(GRANTED);
  permission.setIsGranted(true);
  permission.notifyUserOfPermissionRequestResult();
}
```

For PermissionGranted, my job is easy. Once a SystemPermission reaches the GRANTED state, it has no further states it can transition to (i.e., it's at an end state). So this class doesn't need to implement any transition methods (e.g., claimedBy()). In fact, it really needs to inherit empty implementations of the transition methods, which is exactly what will happen after the next step in the refactoring.

5. In PermissionState, I can now delete the bodies of claimedBy(), deniedBy(), and grantedBy(), leaving the following:

```
abstract class PermissionState {
  public String toString();
  public void claimedBy(SystemAdmin admin, SystemPermission permission) {}
  public void deniedBy(SystemAdmin admin, SystemPermission permission) {}
  public void grantedBy(SystemAdmin admin, SystemPermission permission) {}
}
```

I compile and test to confirm that the states continue to behave correctly. They do. The only remaining question is how best to celebrate this successful refactoring to the State pattern.

Replace Implicit Tree with Composite

You implicitly form a tree structure, using a
primitive representation, such as a String.

Replace your primitive representation with a Composite.

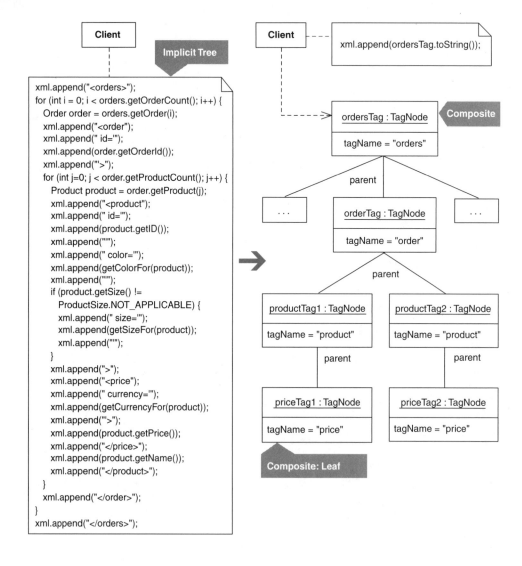

```
xml.append("<orders>");
for (int i = 0; i < orders.getOrderCount(); i++) {
  Order order = orders.getOrder(i);
  xml.append("<order");
  xml.append(" id='");
  xml.append(order.getOrderId());
  xml.append("'>");
  for (int j=0; j < order.getProductCount(); j++) {
    Product product = order.getProduct(j);
    xml.append("<product");
    xml.append(" id='");
    xml.append(product.getID());
    xml.append("'");
    xml.append(" color='");
    xml.append(getColorFor(product));
    xml.append("'");
    if (product.getSize() !=
      ProductSize.NOT_APPLICABLE) {
      xml.append(" size='");
      xml.append(getSizeFor(product));
      xml.append("'");
    }
    xml.append(">");
    xml.append("<price");
    xml.append(" currency='");
    xml.append(getCurrencyFor(product));
    xml.append("'>");
    xml.append(product.getPrice());
    xml.append("</price>");
    xml.append(product.getName());
    xml.append("</product>");
  }
  xml.append("</order>");
}
xml.append("</orders>");
```

Motivation

Data or code forms an implicit tree when it's not explicitly structured as a tree but may be represented as a tree. For example, the code that creates the XML data in the previous code sketch outputs values like this:

```
String expectedResult =
  "<orders>" +
    "<order id='321'>" +
      "<product id='f1234' color='red' size='medium'>" +
        "<price currency='USD'>" +
          "8.95" +
        "</price>" +
        "Fire Truck" +
      "</product>" +
      "<product id='p1112' color='red'>" +
        "<price currency='USD'>" +
          "230.0" +
        "</price>" +
        "Toy Porsche Convertible" +
      "</product>" +
    "</order>" +
  "</orders>";
```

The structure of this XML may be represented as the following tree.

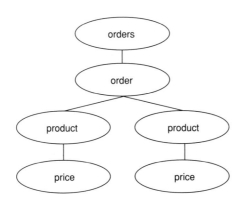

Conditional logic can also form an implicit tree. Consider the conditional logic in the following code, which queries products from a repository:

```
public class ProductFinder...
  public List belowPriceAvoidingAColor(float price, Color color) {
    List foundProducts = new ArrayList();
    Iterator products = repository.iterator();
```

```
  while (products.hasNext()) {
    Product product = (Product) products.next();
    if (product.getPrice() < price && product.getColor() != color)
      foundProducts.add(product);
  }
  return foundProducts;
}
```

**Replace Implicit
Tree with
Composite**

The structure of this conditional logic may also be represented as a tree.

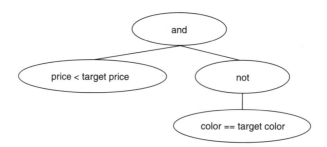

The implicit trees in these examples are different in nature, yet both may be modeled by using a Composite [DP]. What's the primary motivation for such a refactoring? To make the code simpler to work with and less bloated.

For example, producing XML as a Composite is simpler and requires less code when you don't have to repeatedly format and close tags: a Composite tag can do that work for you. Transforming the above conditional logic to a Composite has a similar motivation, with one twist: the refactoring makes sense only when there is a proliferation of similar conditional logic:

```
public class ProductFinder...
  public List byColor(Color color)...
    if (product.getColor() == color)...

  public List byColorAndBelowPrice(Color color, float price)...
    if (product.getPrice() < price && product.getColor() == color)...

  public List byColorAndAbovePrice(Color color, float price) {
    if (product.getColor() == color && product.getPrice() > price)...

  public List byColorSizeAndBelowPrice(Color color, int size, float price)...
    if (product.getColor() == color &&
        product.getSize() == size &&
        product.getPrice() < price)...
```

The above methods may be generalized to a single query method by representing each product query as a Composite. *Replace Implicit Language with*

Interpreter (269) documents this transformation, which includes the implementation of a Composite.

Data-based implicit trees, like the earlier XML example, suffer from a tight coupling between the code that builds the implicit tree and how the tree is represented. Refactoring to a Composite loosens this coupling; however, the resulting client code is then coupled to the Composite. Sometimes you need another level of indirection to loosen such coupling. For example, on one project client code sometimes needed a Composite for building XML and sometimes needed to produce XML via a DOM. This led to the refactoring *Encapsulate Composite with Builder (96)*.

Implicit tree creation may be sufficient if your system doesn't create many trees or the trees are small and manageable. You can always refactor to a Composite when it becomes hard to work with your implicit trees or your code begins to bloat because of implicit tree construction. The choice may also involve where you are in the evolution of new code. On a recent project, I was tasked with generating an HTML page from XML data using an XSLT processor. For this task, I needed to generate XML that would be used in the XSLT transformation. I knew I could use a Composite to build that XML, but I instead choose to build it by using an implicit tree. Why? Because I was more interested in going fast and facing every technical hurdle involved in doing the XSLT transformation than I was in producing good XML tree construction code. After completing the XSLT transformation, I went back to refactor the primitive tree construction code to use a Composite because that code was going to be emulated in many areas of the system.

Benefits and Liabilities

+ Encapsulates repetitive instructions like formatting, adding, or removing nodes.
+ Provides a generalized way to handle a proliferation of similar logic.
+ Simplifies construction responsibilities of a client.
− Complicates a design when it's simpler to construct implicit trees.

Mechanics

The mechanics presented in this section feature two paths for implementing this refactoring. One path, which is standard throughout the book, involves applying refactorings on an implicit tree to gradually refactor it to a Composite, while the other way involves performing test-driven development [Beck, TDD] to gradually refactor the implicit tree to a Composite. Both paths work well. I tend to use the test-driven approach when an implicit tree, like the XML in the earlier example, doesn't lend itself well to applying refactorings like *Extract Class* [F].

Replace Implicit Tree with Composite

1. Identify an *implicit leaf*, a part of the implicit tree that could be modeled with a new class. This new class will be a *leaf node* (called Composite:Leaf in *Design Patterns* [DP]). Create a leaf node class by applying refactorings like *Extract Class* [F] or by doing test-driven development—whichever is easier given your context.

    If the implicit leaf has attributes, produce equivalents for these attributes in the leaf node, such that the representation of the entire leaf node, including its attributes, matches that of the implicit leaf.

    ✔ Compile and test.

2. Replace every occurrence of the implicit leaf with an instance of the leaf node, such that the implicit tree now relies on the leaf node instead of the implicit leaf.

    ✔ Compile and test that the implicit tree still functions correctly.

3. Repeat steps 1 and 2 for any additional parts of the implicit tree that represent an implicit leaf. Make sure that all leaf nodes you create share a common interface. You can create this interface by applying *Extract Superclass* [F] or *Extract Interface* [F].

4. Identify an *implicit parent*, a part of the implicit tree that acts as a parent to implicit leaves. The implicit parent will become a parent node class (called Composite [DP]). Develop this class by applying refactorings or doing test-driven development—again, use whichever approach is easier in your context.

    Clients must be able to add leaf nodes to the parent node either through a constructor or an add(…) method. The parent node must treat all children identically (i.e., via their common interface). The parent node may or may not implement the common interface. If clients must be able to add parent nodes to parent nodes (as is mentioned in step 6) or if you don't want client code to distinguish between a leaf node and a parent node (as is the motivation for *Replace One/Many Distinctions with Composite, 224*), make the parent node implement the common interface.

5. Replace every occurrence of the implicit parent with code that uses a parent node instance, outfitted with the correct leaf node instances.

    ✔ Compile and test that the implicit tree still functions correctly.

6. Repeat steps 4 and 5 for all additional implicit parents. Make it possible to add a parent node to a parent node only if your implicit parents support similar behavior.

Example

The code that produces the implicit tree in the code sketch at the beginning of this refactoring section comes from a shopping system. In that system, there is an OrdersWriter class, which has a getContents() method. Before proceeding with the refactoring, I first break the large getContents() method into smaller methods by applying *Compose Method (123)* and *Move Accumulation to Collecting Parameter (313)*:

```
public class OrdersWriter {
  private Orders orders;

  public OrdersWriter(Orders orders) {
    this.orders = orders;
  }

  public String getContents() {
    StringBuffer xml = new StringBuffer();
    writeOrderTo(xml);
    return xml.toString();
  }

  private void writeOrderTo(StringBuffer xml) {
    xml.append("<orders>");
    for (int i = 0; i < orders.getOrderCount(); i++) {
      Order order = orders.getOrder(i);
      xml.append("<order");
      xml.append(" id='");
      xml.append(order.getOrderId());
      xml.append("'>");
      writeProductsTo(xml, order);
      xml.append("</order>");
    }
    xml.append("</orders>");
  }
```

Replace Implicit Tree with Composite

```
private void writeProductsTo(StringBuffer xml, Order order) {
  for (int j=0; j < order.getProductCount(); j++) {
    Product product = order.getProduct(j);
    xml.append("<product");
    xml.append(" id='");
    xml.append(product.getID());
    xml.append("'");
    xml.append(" color='");
    xml.append(colorFor(product));
    xml.append("'");
    if (product.getSize() != ProductSize.NOT_APPLICABLE) {
      xml.append(" size='");
      xml.append(sizeFor(product));
      xml.append("'");
    }
    xml.append(">");
    writePriceTo(xml, product);
    xml.append(product.getName());
    xml.append("</product>");
  }
}

private void writePriceTo(StringBuffer xml, Product product) {
  xml.append("<price");
  xml.append(" currency='");
  xml.append(currencyFor(product));
  xml.append("'>");
  xml.append(product.getPrice());
  xml.append("</price>");
}
```

Now that getContents() has been refactored, it's easier to see additional refactoring possibilities. One reader of this code noticed that the methods writeOrderTo(…), writeProductsTo(…), and writePriceTo(…) all loop through the domain objects Order, Product, and Price in order to extract data from them for use in producing XML. This reader wondered why the code doesn't just ask the domain objects for their XML directly, rather than having to build it externally to the domain objects. In other words, if the Order class had a toXML() method and the Product and Price classes had one as well, obtaining XML for an Order would simply involve making one call to an Order's toXML() method. That call would obtain the XML from the Order, as well as the XML from whatever Product instances were part of the Order and whatever Price was associated with each Product. This approach would take advantage of the existing structure of the domain objects, rather than recreating that structure in methods like writeOrderTo(…), writeProductsTo(…), and writePriceTo(…).

As nice as this idea sounds, it isn't a good design when a system must create many XML representations of the same domain objects. For example, the code we've been looking at comes from a shopping system that requires diverse XML representations for the domain objects:

```
<order id='987' totalPrice='14.00'>
  <product id='f1234' price='9.00' quantity='1'>
    Fire Truck
  </product>
  <product id='f4321' price='5.00' quantity='1'>
    Rubber Ball
  </product>
</order>

<orderHistory>
  <order date='20041120' totalPrice='14.00'>
    <product id='f1234'>
    <product id='f4321'>
  </order>
</orderHistory>

<order id='321'>
  <product id='f1234' color='red' size='medium'>
    <price currency='USD'>
      8.95
    </price>
    Fire Truck
  </product>
</order>
```

Replace Implicit
Tree with
Composite

Producing the above XML would be difficult and awkward using a single toXML() method on each domain object because the XML is so different in each case. Given such a situation, you can either choose to do the XML rendering external to the domain objects (as the writeOrderTo(…), writeProductsTo(…), and writePriceTo(…) methods do), or you can pursue a Visitor solution (see *Move Accumulation to Visitor, 320*).

For this shopping system, which generates a lot of diverse XML for the same domain objects, refactoring to Visitor makes a lot of sense. However, at the moment, the creation of the XML is still not simple; you have to get the formatting just right and remember to close every tag. I want to simplify this XML generation prior to refactoring to Visitor. Because the Composite pattern can help simplify the XML generation, I proceed with this refactoring.

1. To identify an implicit leaf, I study fragments of test code, such as this one:

```
String expectedResult =
"<orders>" +
  "<order id='321'>" +
    "<product id='f1234' color='red' size='medium'>" +
      "<price currency='USD'>" +
```

Replace Implicit
Tree with
Composite

```
         "8.95" +
       "</price>" +
       "Fire Truck" +
     "</product>" +
   "</order>" +
"</orders>";
```

Here, I face a decision: Which should I treat as an implicit leaf, the
<price>…</price> tag or its value, 8.95? I choose the <price>…</price> tag because
I know that the leaf node class I'll create to correspond with the implicit
leaf can easily represent the tag's value, 8.95.

Another observation I make is that every XML tag in the implicit tree
has a name, an optional number of attributes (name/value pairs), optional
children, and an optional value. I ignore the optional children part for the
moment (we'll get to that in step 4). This means that I can produce one general leaf node to represent all implicit leaves in the implicit tree. I produce
this class, which I call TagNode, using test-driven development. Here's a test I
write after already writing and passing some simpler tests:

```java
public class TagTests extends TestCase...
  private static final String SAMPLE_PRICE = "8.95";
  public void testSimpleTagWithOneAttributeAndValue() {
    TagNode priceTag = new TagNode("price");
    priceTag.addAttribute("currency", "USD");
    priceTag.addValue(SAMPLE_PRICE);
    String expected =
      "<price currency=" +
      "\"" +
      "USD" +
      "\">" +
      SAMPLE_PRICE +
      "</price>";
    assertEquals("price XML", expected, priceTag.toString());
  }
```

Here's the code to make the test pass:

```java
public class TagNode {
  private String name = "";
  private String value = "";
  private StringBuffer attributes;

  public TagNode(String name) {
    this.name = name;
    attributes = new StringBuffer("");
  }

  public void addAttribute(String attribute, String value) {
    attributes.append(" ");
```

```
      attributes.append(attribute);
      attributes.append("='");
      attributes.append(value);
      attributes.append("'");
    }

    public void addValue(String value) {
      this.value = value;
    }

    public String toString() {
      String result;
      result =
        "<" + name + attributes + ">" +
        value +
        "</" + name + ">";
      return result;
    }
```

2. I can now replace the implicit leaf in the getContents() method with a TagNode instance:

```
public class OrdersWriter...
  private void writePriceTo(StringBuffer xml, Product product) {
    TagNode priceNode = new TagNode("price");
    priceNode.addAttribute("currency", currencyFor(product));
    priceNode.addValue(priceFor(product));
    xml.append(priceNode.toString());
    xml.append("<price");
    xml.append(" currency='");
    xml.append(currencyFor(product));
    xml.append("'>");
    xml.append(product.getPrice());
    xml.append("</price>");
  }
```

I compile and run tests to ensure that the implicit tree is still rendered correctly.

3. Because TagNode models all of the implicit leaves in the XML, I do not need to repeat steps 1 and 2 to convert additional implicit leaves to leaf nodes, nor do I need to ensure that all newly created leaf nodes share a common interface—they already do.

4. Now I identify an implicit parent by studying fragments of test code. I find that a <product> tag is a parent for a <price> tag, an <order> tag is a parent for a <product> tag, and an <orders> tag is a parent for an <order> tag. Yet because each of these implicit parents is already so similar in nature to the implicit leaf identified earlier, I see that I can produce a parent node by adding

child-handling support to TagNode. I follow test-driven development to produce this new code. Here's the first test I write:

Replace Implicit
Tree with
Composite

```
public void testCompositeTagOneChild() {
  TagNode productTag = new TagNode("product");
  productTag.add(new TagNode("price"));
  String expected =
    "<product>" +
      "<price>" +
      "</price>" +
    "</product>";
  assertEquals("price XML", expected, productTag.toString());
}
```

And here's code to pass that test:

```
public class TagNode...
  private List children;

  public String toString() {
    String result;
    result = "<" + name + attributes + ">";
    Iterator it = children().iterator();
    while (it.hasNext()) {
      TagNode node = (TagNode)it.next();
      result += node.toString();
    }
    result += value;
    result += "</" + name + ">";
    return result;
  }

  private List children() {
    if (children == null)
      children = new ArrayList();
    return children;
  }

  public void add(TagNode child) {
    children().add(child);
  }
```

Here's a slightly more robust test:

```
public void testAddingChildrenAndGrandchildren() {
  String expected =
    "<orders>" +
      "<order>" +
        "<product>" +
        "</product>" +
      "</order>" +
    "</orders>";
```

```
TagNode ordersTag = new TagNode("orders");
TagNode orderTag = new TagNode("order");
TagNode productTag = new TagNode("product");
ordersTag.add(orderTag);
orderTag.add(productTag);
assertEquals("price XML", expected, ordersTag.toString());
}
```

I continue writing and running tests until I'm satisfied that TagNode can behave as a proper parent node. When I'm done, TagNode is a class that can play all three participants in the Composite pattern:

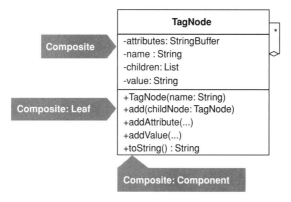

5. Now I replace every occurrence of the implicit parent with code that uses a parent node instance, outfitted with the correct leaf node instance(s). Here's an example:

```
public class OrdersWriter...
  private void writeProductsTo(StringBuffer xml, Order order) {
    for (int j=0; j < order.getProductCount(); j++) {
      Product product = order.getProduct(j);
      TagNode productTag = new TagNode("product");
      productTag.addAttribute("id", product.getID());
      productTag.addAttribute("color", colorFor(product));
      if (product.getSize() != ProductSize.NOT_APPLICABLE)
        productTag.addAttribute("size", sizeFor(product));
      writePriceTo(productTag, product);
      productTag.addValue(product.getName());
      xml.append(productTag.toString());
    }
  }

  private void writePriceTo(TagNode productTag, Product product) {
    TagNode priceTag = new TagNode("price");
    priceTag.addAttribute("currency", currencyFor(product));
    priceTag.addValue(priceFor(product));
    productTag.add(priceTag);
  }
```

I compile and run tests to ensure that the implicit tree still renders itself correctly.

6. I repeat steps 4 and 5 for all remaining implicit parents. This yields the following code, which is identical to the after code in the code sketch on the first page of this refactoring, except that the code is broken up into smaller methods:

```java
public class OrdersWriter...
  public String getContents() {
    StringBuffer xml = new StringBuffer();
    writeOrderTo(xml);
    return xml.toString();
  }

  private void writeOrderTo(StringBuffer xml) {
    TagNode ordersTag = new TagNode("orders");
    for (int i = 0; i < orders.getOrderCount(); i++) {
      Order order = orders.getOrder(i);
      TagNode orderTag = new TagNode("order");
      orderTag.addAttribute("id", order.getOrderId());
      writeProductsTo(orderTag, order);
      ordersTag.add(orderTag);
    }
    xml.append(ordersTag.toString());
  }

  private void writeProductsTo(TagNode orderTag, Order order) {
    for (int j=0; j < order.getProductCount(); j++) {
      Product product = order.getProduct(j);
      TagNode productTag = new TagNode("product");
      productTag.addAttribute("id", product.getID());
      productTag.addAttribute("color", colorFor(product));
      if (product.getSize() != ProductSize.NOT_APPLICABLE)
        productTag.addAttribute("size", sizeFor(product));
      writePriceTo(productTag, product);
      productTag.addValue(product.getName());
      orderTag.add(productTag);
    }
  }

  private void writePriceTo(TagNode productTag, Product product) {
    TagNode priceNode = new TagNode("price");
    priceNode.addAttribute("currency", currencyFor(product));
    priceNode.addValue(priceFor(product));
    productTag.add(priceNode);
  }
```

Replace Conditional Dispatcher with Command

Conditional logic is used to dispatch requests
and execute actions.

*Create a Command for each action. Store the Commands
in a collection and replace the conditional logic with
code to fetch and execute Commands.*

Replace
Conditional
Dispatcher with
Command

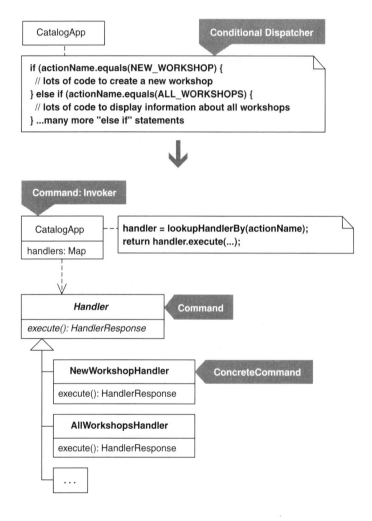

Replace
Conditional
Dispatcher with
Command

Motivation

Many systems receive, route, and handle requests. A *conditional dispatcher* is a conditional statement (such as a switch) that performs request routing and handling. Some conditional dispatchers are well suited for their jobs; others aren't.

Conditional dispatchers that are well suited for their jobs tend to route a small number of requests to small chunks of handler logic. Such dispatchers can often be viewed on a monitor without having to scroll to see all of the code. The Command pattern usually doesn't provide a useful replacement for these kinds of conditional dispatchers.

On the other hand, if your conditional dispatcher is small, it may still not be a good fit for your system. The two most common reasons to refactor from a conditional dispatcher to a Command-based solution are the following.

1. *Not enough runtime flexibility:* Clients that rely on the conditional dispatcher develop a need to dynamically configure it with new requests or handler logic. Yet the conditional dispatcher doesn't allow for such dynamic configurations because all of its routing and handling logic is hard-coded into a single conditional statement.

2. *A bloated body of code:* Some conditional dispatchers become enormous and unwieldy as they evolve to handle new requests or as their handler logic becomes ever more complex with new responsibilities. Extracting the handler logic into different methods doesn't help enough because the class that contains the dispatcher and extracted handler methods is still too large to work with.

The Command pattern provides an excellent solution to such problems. To implement it, you simply place each piece of request-handling logic in a separate "command" class that has a common method, like execute() or run(), for executing its encapsulated handler logic. Once you have a family of such commands, you can use a collection to store and retrieve instances of them; add, remove, or change instances; and execute instances by invoking their execution methods.

Routing requests and executing diverse behavior in a uniform way may be so central to a design that you may find yourself using the Command pattern early, rather than refactoring to it later. Many of the server-side, Web-based systems I've built have used the Command pattern to produce a standard way to route requests, execute actions, or forward actions to other actions. The Example section shows how to refactor to such a solution.

The authors of *Design Patterns* [DP] explain how the Command pattern is often used to support an undo/redo capability. A question that often arises in extreme programming (XP) circles is what to do when you aren't sure whether a system will need undo/redo. Do you just implement the Command pattern in case the need arises? Or is that a violation of "You aren't gonna need it," an XP principle that cautions against adding functionality to code based on speculation, not genuine need. If I'm not sure whether a system needs the Command pattern, I generally don't implement it, for I find that it isn't that hard to refactor to this pattern when the need arises. However, if your code is getting into a state in which it will be harder and harder to refactor to the Command pattern *and* there's a good chance you'll soon need an undo/redo capability, it may make sense to refactor it to use Command before doing so will be impossibly hard. It's a bit like taking out an insurance plan.

The Command pattern is easy to implement, versatile, and incredibly useful. This refactoring captures only one area in which it is useful. Because Command can solve other tricky problems, there could easily be additional refactorings to it.

Benefits and Liabilities

+ Provides a simple mechanism for executing diverse behavior in a uniform way.
+ Enables runtime changes regarding which requests are handled and how.
+ Requires trivial code to implement.
− Complicates a design when a conditional dispatcher is sufficient.

Mechanics

1. On a class containing a conditional dispatcher, find code that handles a request and apply *Extract Method* [F] on that code until you have an *execution method*, a method that invokes the code's behavior.

   ✔ Compile and test.

2. Repeat step 1 to extract all remaining chunks of request-handling code into execution methods.

3. Apply *Extract Class* [F] on each execution method to produce a *concrete command*, a class that handles a request. This step usually implies making the execution method on the concrete command public. If the execution

method in the new concrete command is too large or not quickly understandable, apply *Compose Method (123)*.

✔ Compile and test.

Replace Conditional Dispatcher with Command

After you've finished creating all of your concrete commands, look for duplicated code in them. If you find some, see if you can remove it by applying *Form Template Method (205)*.

4. Define a *command*, an interface or abstract class that declares an execution method that is the same for every concrete command. To implement this step, you'll need to analyze your concrete commands to learn what's unique or similar about them. Find answers to the following questions.

   • What parameter(s) must be passed to a common execution method?

   • What parameter(s) could be passed during a concrete command's construction?

   • What information could a concrete command obtain by calling back on a parameter, rather than having data passed direcly to the concrete command?

   • What is the simplest signature for an execution method that is the same for every concrete command?

   Consider producing an early version of your command by applying *Extract Superclass* [F] or *Extract Interface* [F] on a concrete command.

   ✔ Compile.

5. Make every concrete command implement or extend your command and update all client code to work with each concrete command via the command type.

   ✔ Compile and test.

6. On the class that contains the conditional dispatcher, define and populate a *command map*, a map that contains instances of each concrete command, keyed by a unique identifier (e.g., a command name) that may be used at runtime to fetch a command.

   If you have many concrete commands, you'll have a lot of code that adds concrete command instances to your command map. In that case, consider making your concrete commands implement the Plugin pattern, from *Patterns of Enterprise Application Architecture* [Fowler, PEAA]. This will make it possible for them to be loaded simply by supplying the appropriate configuration data (such as a list of the names of the command classes or, even better, a directory where the classes live).

✔ Compile.

7. On the class that contains the conditional dispatcher, replace the conditional code for dispatching requests with code to fetch the correct concrete command and execute it by calling its execution method. This class is now an Invoker [DP, 236].

Replace
Conditional
Dispatcher with
Command

✔ Compile and test.

Example

The example code we'll look at comes from a system I cowrote to create and organize Industrial Logic's HTML-based catalogs. Ironically, this system made heavy use of the Command pattern from its earliest evolutions. I decided to rewrite the sections of the system that used the Command pattern to *not* use the Command pattern in order to produce the kind of bloated, Command-thirsty code that I so frequently encounter in the field.

In the altered code, a class named CatalogApp is responsible for dispatching and executing actions and returning responses. It performs this work within one large conditional statement:

```
public class CatalogApp...
  private HandlerResponse executeActionAndGetResponse(String actionName, Map parameters)...
    if (actionName.equals(NEW_WORKSHOP)) {
      String nextWorkshopID = workshopManager.getNextWorkshopID();
      StringBuffer newWorkshopContents =
        workshopManager.createNewFileFromTemplate(
          nextWorkshopID,
          workshopManager.getWorkshopDir(),
          workshopManager.getWorkshopTemplate()
        );
      workshopManager.addWorkshop(newWorkshopContents);
      parameters.put("id",nextWorkshopID);
      executeActionAndGetResponse(ALL_WORKSHOPS, parameters);
    } else if (actionName.equals(ALL_WORKSHOPS)) {
      XMLBuilder allWorkshopsXml = new XMLBuilder("workshops");
      WorkshopRepository repository =
        workshopManager.getWorkshopRepository();
      Iterator ids = repository.keyIterator();
      while (ids.hasNext()) {
        String id = (String)ids.next();
        Workshop workshop = repository.getWorkshop(id);
        allWorkshopsXml.addBelowParent("workshop");
        allWorkshopsXml.addAttribute("id", workshop.getID());
```

Replace
Conditional
Dispatcher with
Command

```
      allWorkshopsXml.addAttribute("name", workshop.getName());
      allWorkshopsXml.addAttribute("status", workshop.getStatus());
      allWorkshopsXml.addAttribute("duration",
        workshop.getDurationAsString());
    }
    String formattedXml = getFormattedData(allWorkshopsXml.toString());
    return new HandlerResponse(
      new StringBuffer(formattedXml),
      ALL_WORKSHOPS_STYLESHEET
    );
  } ...many more "else if" statements
```

The complete conditional spans several pages—I'll spare you the details. The first leg of the conditional handles the creation of a new workshop. The second leg, which happens to be called by the first leg, returns XML that contains summary information for all of Industrial Logic's workshops. I'll show how to refactor this code to use the Command pattern.

1. I start by working on the first leg of the conditional. I apply *Extract Method* [F] to produce the execution method getNewWorkshopResponse():

```
public class CatalogApp...
  private HandlerResponse executeActionAndGetResponse(String actionName, Map parameters)...
    if (actionName.equals(NEW_WORKSHOP)) {
      getNewWorkshopResponse(parameters);
    } else if (actionName.equals(ALL_WORKSHOPS)) {
      ...
    } ...many more "else if" statements

  private HandlerResponse getNewWorkshopResponse(Map parameters) throws Exception {
    String nextWorkshopID = workshopManager.getNextWorkshopID();
    StringBuffer newWorkshopContents =
      workshopManager.createNewFileFromTemplate(
        nextWorkshopID,
        workshopManager.getWorkshopDir(),
        workshopManager.getWorkshopTemplate()
      );
    workshopManager.addWorkshop(newWorkshopContents);
    parameters.put("id",nextWorkshopID);
    return executeActionAndGetResponse(ALL_WORKSHOPS, parameters);
  }
```

The compiler and test code are happy with the newly extracted method.

2. I now go on to extract the next chunk of request-handling code, which deals with listing all workshops in the catalog:

```
public class CatalogApp...
  private HandlerResponse executeActionAndGetResponse(String actionName, Map parameters)...
    if (actionName.equals(NEW_WORKSHOP)) {
      getNewWorkshopResponse(parameters);
```

```
    } else if (actionName.equals(ALL_WORKSHOPS)) {
      getAllWorkshopsResponse();
    } ...many more "else if" statements

  public HandlerResponse getAllWorkshopsResponse() {
    XMLBuilder allWorkshopsXml = new XMLBuilder("workshops");
    WorkshopRepository repository =
      workshopManager.getWorkshopRepository();
    Iterator ids = repository.keyIterator();
    while (ids.hasNext()) {
      String id = (String)ids.next();
      Workshop workshop = repository.getWorkshop(id);
      allWorkshopsXml.addBelowParent("workshop");
      allWorkshopsXml.addAttribute("id", workshop.getID());
      allWorkshopsXml.addAttribute("name", workshop.getName());
      allWorkshopsXml.addAttribute("status", workshop.getStatus());
      allWorkshopsXml.addAttribute("duraction",
        workshop.getDurationAsString());
    }
    String formattedXml = getFormattedData(allWorkshopsXml.toString());
    return new HandlerResponse(
      new StringBuffer(formattedXml),
      ALL_WORKSHOPS_STYLESHEET
    );
  }
```

I compile, test, and repeat this step for all remaining chunks of request-handling code.

3. Now I begin creating concrete commands. I first produce the NewWorkshop-Handler concrete command by applying *Extract Class* [F] on the execution method getNewWorkshopResponse():

```
public class NewWorkshopHandler {
  private CatalogApp catalogApp;

  public NewWorkshopHandler(CatalogApp catalogApp) {
    this.catalogApp = catalogApp;
  }

  public HandlerResponse getNewWorkshopResponse(Map parameters) throws Exception {
    String nextWorkshopID = workshopManager().getNextWorkshopID();
    StringBuffer newWorkshopContents =
      WorkshopManager().createNewFileFromTemplate(
        nextWorkshopID,
        workshopManager().getWorkshopDir(),
        workshopManager().getWorkshopTemplate()
      );
    workshopManager().addWorkshop(newWorkshopContents);
    parameters.put("id", nextWorkshopID);
    catalogApp.executeActionAndGetResponse(ALL_WORKSHOPS, parameters);
  }
```

```
    private WorkshopManager workshopManager() {
      return catalogApp.getWorkshopManager();
    }
}
```

Replace
Conditional
Dispatcher with
Command

CatalogApp instantiates and calls an instance of NewWorkshopHandler like so:

```
public class CatalogApp...
  public HandlerResponse executeActionAndGetResponse(
    String actionName, Map parameters) throws Exception {
    if (actionName.equals(NEW_WORKSHOP)) {
      return new NewWorkshopHandler(this).getNewWorkshopResponse(parameters);
    } else if (actionName.equals(ALL_WORKSHOPS)) {
      ...
    } ...
```

The compiler and tests confirm that these changes work fine. Note that I made executeActionAndGetResponse(…) public because it's called from New-WorkshopHandler.

Before I go on, I apply *Compose Method (123)* on NewWorkshopHandler's execution method:

```
public class NewWorkshopHandler...
  public HandlerResponse getNewWorkshopResponse(Map parameters) throws Exception {
    createNewWorkshop(parameters);
    return catalogApp.executeActionAndGetResponse(
      CatalogApp.ALL_WORKSHOPS, parameters);
  }

  private void createNewWorkshop(Map parameters) throws Exception {
    String nextWorkshopID = workshopManager().getNextWorkshopID();
    workshopManager().addWorkshop(newWorkshopContents(nextWorkshopID));
    parameters.put("id",nextWorkshopID);
  }

  private StringBuffer newWorkshopContents(String nextWorkshopID) throws Exception {
    StringBuffer newWorkshopContents = workshopManager().createNewFileFromTemplate(
      nextWorkshopID,
      workshopManager().getWorkshopDir(),
      workshopManager().getWorkshopTemplate()
    );
    return newWorkshopContents;
  }
```

I repeat this step for additional execution methods that ought to be extracted into their own concrete commands and turned into Composed Methods. AllWorkshopsHandler is the next concrete command I extract. Here's how it looks:

```
public class AllWorkshopsHandler...
  private CatalogApp catalogApp;
```

```
private static String ALL_WORKSHOPS_STYLESHEET="allWorkshops.xsl";
private PrettyPrinter prettyPrinter = new PrettyPrinter();

public AllWorkshopsHandler(CatalogApp catalogApp) {
  this.catalogApp = catalogApp;
}

public HandlerResponse getAllWorkshopsResponse() throws Exception {
  return new HandlerResponse(
    new StringBuffer(prettyPrint(allWorkshopsData())),
    ALL_WORKSHOPS_STYLESHEET
  );
}

private String allWorkshopsData() ...

private String prettyPrint(String buffer) {
  return prettyPrinter.format(buffer);
}
```

Replace
Conditional
Dispatcher with
Command

After performing this step for every concrete command, I look for duplicated code across all of the concrete commands. I don't find much duplication, so there is no need to apply *Form Template Method (205)*.

4.   I must now create a command (as defined in the Mechanics section, an
interface or abstract class that declares an execution method that every
concrete command must implement). At the moment, every concrete command has an execution method with a different name, and the execution
methods take a different number of arguments (namely, one or none):

```
if (actionName.equals(NEW_WORKSHOP)) {
  return new NewWorkshopHandler(this).getNewWorkshopResponse(parameters);
} else if (actionName.equals(ALL_WORKSHOPS)) {
  return new AllWorkshopsHandler(this).getAllWorkshopsResponse();
} ...
```

Making a command will involve deciding on:

- A common execution method name

- What information to pass to and obtain from each handler

The common execution method name I choose is execute (a name that's
often used when implementing the Command pattern, but by no means the
only name to use). Now I must decide what information needs to be passed

to and/or obtained from a call to execute(). I survey the concrete commands I've created and learn that a good many of them:

- Require information contained in a Map called parameters

- Return an object of type HandlerResponse

- Throw an Exception

This means that my command must include an execution method with the following signature:

```
public HandlerResponse execute(Map parameters) throws Exception
```

I create the command by performing two refactorings on NewWorkshop-Handler. First, I rename its getNewWorkshopResponse(…) method to execute(…):

```
public class NewWorkshopHandler...
    public HandlerResponse execute(Map parameters) throws Exception
```

Next, I apply the refactoring *Extract Superclass* [F] to produce an abstract class called Handler:

```
public abstract class Handler {
  protected CatalogApp catalogApp;

  public Handler(CatalogApp catalogApp) {
    this.catalogApp = catalogApp;
  }

  public abstract HandlerResponse execute(Map parameters) throws Exception;
}
public class NewWorkshopHandler extends Handler...
    public NewWorkshopHandler(CatalogApp catalogApp) {
      super(catalogApp);
    }
```

The compiler is happy with the new class, so I move on.

5. Now that I have the command (expressed as the abstract Handler class), I'll make every handler implement it. I do this by making them all extend Handler and implement the execute() method. When I'm done, the handlers may now be invoked identically:

```
if (actionName.equals(NEW_WORKSHOP)) {
  return new NewWorkshopHandler(this).execute(parameters);
} else if (actionName.equals(ALL_WORKSHOPS)) {
  return new AllWorkshopsHandler(this).execute(parameters);
} ...
```

I compile and run the tests to find that everything is working.

Replace
Conditional
Dispatcher with
Command

6. Now comes the fun part. CatalogApp's conditional statement is merely acting like a crude Map. It would be better to turn it into a real map by storing an instance of my command in a command map. To do that, I define and populate handlers, a Map keyed by handler name:

```
public class CatalogApp...
  private Map handlers;
  public CatalogApp(...) {
    ...
    createHandlers();
    ...
  }

  public void createHandlers() {
    handlers = new HashMap();
    handlers.put(NEW_WORKSHOP, new NewWorkshopHandler(this));
    handlers.put(ALL_WORKSHOPS, new AllWorkshopsHandler(this));
    ...
  }
```

Replace
Conditional
Dispatcher with
Command

Because I don't have too many handlers, I don't resort to implementing a Plugin, as described in the Mechanics section. The compiler is happy with the new code.

7. Finally, I replace CatalogApp's large conditional statement with code that looks up a handler by name and executes it:

```
public class CatalogApp...
  public HandlerResponse executeActionAndGetResponse(
    String handlerName, Map parameters) throws Exception {
    Handler handler = lookupHandlerBy(handlerName);
    return handler.execute(parameters);
  }

  private Handler lookupHandlerBy(String handlerName) {
    return (Handler)handlers.get(handlerName);
  }
```

The compiler and test code are happy with this Command-based solution. CatalogApp now uses the Command pattern to execute an action and get back a response. This design makes it easy to declare a new handler, name it, and register it in the command map so that it may be invoked at runtime to perform an action.

Chapter 8

Generalization

Generalization is the transformation of specific code into general-purpose code. The production of generalized code frequently occurs as a result of refactoring. All seven refactorings in this chapter yield generalized code. The most common motivation for applying them is to remove duplicated code. A secondary motivation is to simplify or clarify code.

Form Template Method (205) helps remove duplication in similar methods of subclasses in a hierarchy. If the methods perform roughly the same steps, in the same order, yet the steps are slightly different, you can separate what varies from what is generic by producing a superclass method known as a Template Method [DP].

Extract Composite (214) is an application of the refactoring *Extract Superclass* [F]. It's applicable when a Composite [DP] has been implemented in multiple subclasses of a hierarchy with no good reason. By extracting a Composite to a superclass, the subclasses share one generic implementation of the Composite.

If you have some code for handling one object and separate code for handling a group of the same objects (usually in some collection), *Replace One/Many Distinctions with Composite (224)* will help you produce a generic solution that handles one or many objects without distinguishing between the two.

Replace Hard-Coded Notifications with Observer (236) is a classic example of replacing a specific solution with a general one. In this case, there is a tight coupling between objects that notify and objects that get notified. To allow instances of other classes to be notified, the code can be refactored to use an Observer [DP].

An Adapter [DP] provides another way to unify interfaces. When clients communicate with similar classes using different interfaces, there tends to be duplicated processing logic. By applying *Unify Interfaces with Adapter (247)*, clients may interact with similar classes using a generic interface. This tends to pave the way for other refactorings to remove duplicated process logic in the client code.

When a class acts as an Adapter for multiple versions of a component, library, API, or other entity, the class usually contains duplication and often lacks a simple design. Applying *Extract Adapter (258)* produces classes that implement a common interface and adapt a single version of some code.

The final refactoring in this chapter, *Replace Implicit Language with Interpreter (269)*, targets code that would be better designed were it to use an explicit language. Such code often uses numerous methods to accomplish what a language can do, only in a far more primitive and repetitive way. Refactoring such code to an Interpreter [DP] can yield a general-purpose solution that is more compact, simple, and flexible.

Form Template Method

Two methods in subclasses perform similar steps
in the same order, yet the steps are different.

*Generalize the methods by extracting their steps
into methods with identical signatures, then pull up
the generalized methods to form a Template Method.*

Form
Template
Method

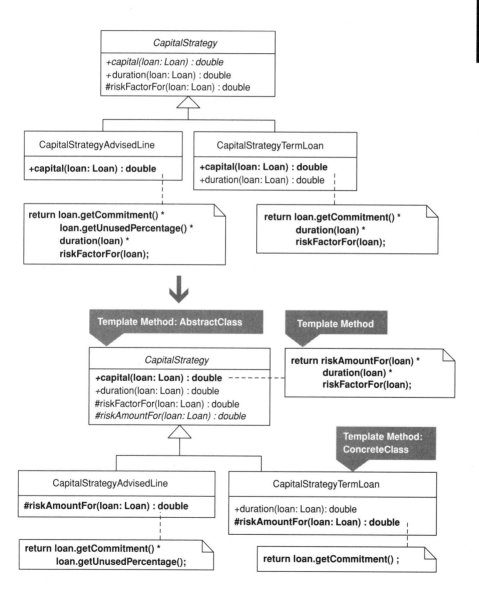

Motivation

Template Methods "implement the invariant parts of an algorithm once and leave it up to subclasses to implement the behavior that can vary" [DP, 326]. When invariant and variant behaviors are mixed together in the subclass implementations of a method, the invariant behavior is duplicated in the subclasses. Refactoring to a Template Method helps rid subclasses of their duplicated invariant behavior by moving the behavior to one place: a generalized algorithm in a superclass method.

Form Template Method

A Template Method's invariant behavior consists of the following:

- Methods called and the ordering of those methods

- Abstract methods that subclasses *must* override

- Hook methods (i.e., concrete methods) that subclasses *may* override

For example, consider the following code:

```
public abstract class Game...
    public void initialize() {
        deck = createDeck();
        shuffle(deck);
        drawGameBoard();
        dealCardsFrom(deck);
    }
    protected abstract Deck createDeck();

    protected void shuffle(Deck deck) {
        ...shuffle implementation
    }

    protected abstract void drawGameBoard();
    protected abstract void dealCardsFrom(Deck deck);
```

The list of methods called by and ordered within initialize() is invariant. The fact that subclasses must override the abstract methods is also invariant. The shuffle() implementation provided by Game is not invariant: it's a hook method that lets subclasses inherit behavior or vary it by overriding shuffle().

Because it is too tedious to implement many methods just to flesh out a Template Method in a subclass, the authors of *Design Patterns* [DP] suggest that a Template Method should minimize the number of abstract methods classes *must* override. There's also no simple way for programmers to know which methods may be overridden (i.e., hook methods) without studying the contents of a Template Method.

Template Methods often call Factory Methods [DP], like createDeck() in the above code. The refactoring *Introduce Polymorphic Creation with Factory Method (88)* provides a real-world example of this.

Languages like Java allow you to declare a Template Method final, which prevents accidental overriding of the Template Method by subclasses. In general, this is done only if client code in a system or framework totally relies on the invariant behavior in a Template Method and if allowing reinterpretation of that invariant behavior could cause client code to work incorrectly.

Martin Fowler's *Form Template Method* [F] and my version cover much of the same ground and can be thought of as the same refactoring. My mechanics use different terminology and have a different final step than Martin's. In addition, the code I've discussed in the Example section illustrates a case where the invariant behavior duplicated in subclasses is subtle, whereas Martin's example deals with a case where such duplication is explicit. If you aren't familiar with the Template Method pattern, you'd do well to study both versions of this refactoring.

Form Template Method

Benefits and Liabilities

+ Removes duplicated code in subclasses by moving invariant behavior to a superclass.
+ Simplifies and effectively communicates the steps of a general algorithm.
+ Allows subclasses to easily customize an algorithm.
− Complicates a design when subclasses must implement many methods to flesh out the algorithm.

Mechanics

1. In a hierarchy, find a *similar method* (a method in a subclass that performs similar steps in a similar order to a method in another subclass). Apply *Compose Method (123)* on the similar method (in both subclasses), extracting *identical methods* (methods that have the same signature and body in each subclass) and *unique methods* (methods that have a different signature and body in each subclass).

   When deciding whether to extract code as a unique method or an identical method, consider this: If you extract the code as a unique method, you'll eventually (during step 5) need to produce an abstract or concrete version of that unique method in the superclass. Will it make sense for sub-classes to inherit or override the unique method? If not, extract the code into an identical method.

2. Pull up the identical methods to the superclass by applying *Pull Up Method* [F].

3. To produce an identical body for each version of the similar method, apply *Rename Method* [F] on every unique method until the similar method is identical in each subclass.

    ✔ Compile and test after each application of *Rename Method* [F].

4. If the similar method doesn't already have an identical signature in each subclass, apply *Rename Method* [F] to produce an identical signature.

5. Apply *Pull Up Method* [F] on the similar method (in either subclass), defin-ing abstract methods on the superclass for each unique method. The pulled-up similar method is now a Template Method.

    ✔ Compile and test.

Example

At the end of the example used in this catalog for the refactoring *Replace Con-ditional Logic with Strategy (129)* there are three subclasses of the abstract class, CapitalStrategy:

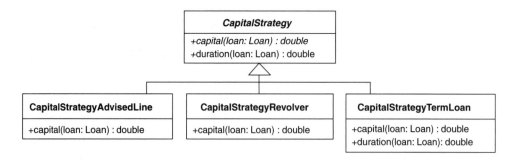

These three subclasses happen to contain a small amount of duplication, which, as we'll see in this section, can be removed by applying *Form Template Method*. It is relatively common to combine the Strategy and Template Method patterns to produce concrete Strategy classes that have little or no duplicate code in them.

The CapitalStrategy class defines an abstract method for the capital calculation:

```
public abstract class CapitalStrategy...
  public abstract double capital(Loan loan);
```

Subclasses of CapitalStrategy calculate capital similarly:

```
public class CapitalStrategyAdvisedLine...
  public double capital(Loan loan) {
    return loan.getCommitment() * loan.getUnusedPercentage() *
        duration(loan) * riskFactorFor(loan);
  }

public class CapitalStrategyRevolver...
  public double capital(Loan loan) {
    return (loan.outstandingRiskAmount() * duration(loan) * riskFactorFor(loan))
        + (loan.unusedRiskAmount() * duration(loan) * unusedRiskFactor(loan));
  }

public class CapitalStrategyTermLoan...
  public double capital(Loan loan) {
    return loan.getCommitment() * duration(loan) * riskFactorFor(loan);
  }
  protected double duration(Loan loan) {
    return weightedAverageDuration(loan);
  }
  private double weightedAverageDuration(Loan loan)...
```

I observe that CapitalStrategyAdvisedLine's calculation is identical to Capital-StrategyTermLoan's calculation, except for a step that multiplies the result by the loan's unused percentage (loan.getUnusedPercentage()). Spotting this similar sequence of steps with a slight variation means I can generalize the algorithm by refactoring to Template Method. I'll do that in the following steps and then deal with the third class, CapitalStrategyRevolver, at the end of this Example section.

1. The capital(…) method implemented by CapitalStrategyAdvisedLine and Capital-StrategyTermLoan is the similar method in this example.

   The mechanics direct me to apply *Compose Method (123)* on the capital() implementations by extracting identical methods or unique methods. Since the formulas in capital() are identical except for CapitalStrategy-AdvisedLine's step of multiplying by loan.getUnusedPercentage(), I must choose whether to extract that step into its own unique method or extract it as part of a method that includes other code. The mechanics work either way. In this case, several years of programming loan calculators for a bank aids me in making a decision. The risk amount for an advised line is calculated by multiplying the loan's commitment amount by its unused percentage (i.e., loan.getCommitment() * loan.getUnusedPercentage()). In addition, I know the standard formula for risk-adjusted capital:

$$\text{Risk Amount} \times \text{Duration} \times \text{Risk Factor}$$

That knowledge leads me to extract the CapitalStrategyAdvisedLine code, loan.getCommitment() * loan.getUnusedPercentage(), into its own method, riskAmount-For(), while performing a similar step for CapitalStrategyTermLoan:

```
public class CapitalStrategyAdvisedLine...
    public double capital(Loan loan) {
        return riskAmountFor(loan) * duration(loan) * riskFactorFor(loan);
    }
    private double riskAmountFor(Loan loan) {
        return loan.getCommitment() * loan.getUnusedPercentage();
    }

public class CapitalStrategyTermLoan...
    public double capital(Loan loan) {
        return riskAmountFor(loan) * duration(loan) * riskFactorFor(loan);
    }
    private double riskAmountFor(Loan loan) {
        return loan.getCommitment();
    }
```

Domain knowledge clearly influenced my refactoring decisions during this step. In his book *Domain-Driven Design* [Evans], Eric Evans describes how domain knowledge often directs what we choose to refactor or how we choose to refactor it.

2. This step asks me to pull up identical methods to the superclass, Capital-Strategy. In this case, the riskAmountFor(…) method is not an identical method because the code in each implementation of it varies, so I can move on to the next step.

3. Now I must ensure that any unique methods have the same signature in each subclass. The only unique method, riskAmountFor(…), already has the same signature in each subclass, so I can proceed to the next step.

4. I must now ensure that the similar method, capital(…), has the same signature in both subclasses. It does, so I proceed to the next step.

5. Because the capital(…) method in each subclass now has the same signature and body, I can pull it up to CapitalStrategy by applying *Pull Up Method*

[F]. This involves declaring an abstract method for the unique method, riskAmountFor(…):

```
public abstract class CapitalStrategy...
    public abstract double capital(Loan loan);
    public double capital(Loan loan) {
        return riskAmountFor(loan) * duration(loan) * riskFactorFor(loan);
    }
    public abstract double riskAmountFor(Loan loan);
```

The capital() method is now a Template Method. That completes the refactoring for the CapitalStrategyAdvisedLine and CapitalStrategyTermLoan subclasses.

Form
Template
Method

Before I handle the capital calculation in CapitalStrategyRevolver, I'd like to show what would have happened had I not created a riskAmountFor(…) method during step 1 of the refactoring. In that case, I would have created a unique method for CapitalStrategyAdvisedLine's step of multiplying by loan.getUnusedPercentage(). I would have called such a step unusedPercentageFor(…) and implemented it as a hook method in CapitalStrategy:

```
public abstract class CapitalStrategy...
    public double capital(Loan loan) {
        return loan.getCommitment() * unusedPercentageFor(loan) *
                duration(loan) * riskFactorFor(loan);
    }
    public abstract double riskAmountFor(Loan loan);

    protected double unusedPercentageFor(Loan loan) { // hook method
        return 1.0
    };
```

Because this hook method returns 1.0, it has no effect on calculations unless the method is overridden, as it is by CapitalStrategyAdvisedLine:

```
public class CapitalStrategyAdvisedLine...
    protected double unusedPercentageFor(Loan loan) {
        return loan.getUnusedPercentage();
    };
```

The hook method allows CapitalStrategyTermLoan to inherit its capital(…) calculation, rather than implement a riskAmount(…) method:

```
public class CapitalStrategyTermLoan...
    public double capital(Loan loan) {
        return loan.getCommitment() * duration(loan) * riskFactorFor(loan);
    }
```

```
protected double duration(Loan loan) {
   return weightedAverageDuration(loan);
}
private double weightedAverageDuration(Loan loan)...
```

So that is another way to produce a Template Method for the capital() calculation. However, it suffers from a few downsides:

Form
Template
Method

- The resulting code poorly communicates the risk-adjusted capital formula (Risk Amount × Duration × Risk Factor).

- Two of the three CapitalStrategy subclasses, CapitalStrategyTermLoan and, as we'll see, CapitalStrategyRevolver, inherit the hook method's do-nothing behavior, which, because it is a unique step in CapitalStrategyAdvisedLine, really belongs exclusively in that class.

Now let's see how CapitalStrategyRevolver would take advantage of the new capital() Template Method. Its original capital() method looks like this:

```
public class CapitalStrategyRevolver...
   public double capital(Loan loan) {
      return (loan.outstandingRiskAmount() * duration(loan) * riskFactorFor(loan))
         + (loan.unusedRiskAmount() * duration(loan) * unusedRiskFactor(loan));
   }
```

The first half of the formula resembles the general formula, Risk Amount × Duration × Risk Factor. The second half of the formula is similar, but it's dealing with the unused portion of a loan. We can refactor this code to take advantage of the Template Method as follows:

```
public class CapitalStrategyRevolver...
   public double capital(Loan loan) {
      return
         super.capital(loan)
         + (loan.unusedRiskAmount() * duration(loan) * unusedRiskFactor(loan));
   }

   protected double riskAmountFor(Loan loan) {
      return loan.outstandingRiskAmount();
   }
```

You could argue whether this new implementation is easier to understand than the previous one. Certainly some duplication in the formula has been removed. Yet is the resulting formula easier to follow? I think so, because it communicates that capital is calculated according to the general formula with

the addition of unused capital. The addition of unused capital can be made
clearer by applying *Extract Method* [F] on capital():

```
public class CapitalStrategyRevolver...
    public double capital(Loan loan) {
        return super.capital(loan) + unusedCapital(loan);
    }
    public double unusedCapital(Loan loan) {
        return loan.unusedRiskAmount() * duration(loan) * unusedRiskFactor(loan);
    }
```

Form
Template
Method

Extract Composite

Subclasses in a hierarchy implement the same Composite.

Extract a superclass that implements the Composite.

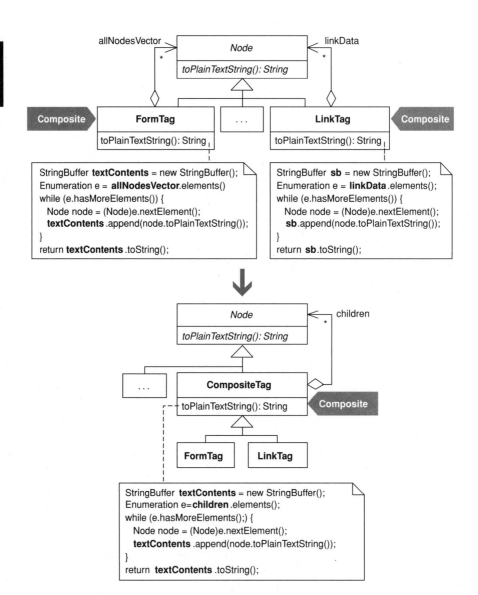

Motivation

In *Extract Superclass* [F], Martin Fowler explains that if you have two or more classes with similar features, it makes sense to move the common features to a superclass. This refactoring is similar: it addresses the case when the similar feature is a Composite [DP] that would be better off in a superclass.

Subclasses in hierarchies that store collections of children and have methods for reporting information about those children are common. When the children being collected happen to be classes in the same hierarchy, there's a good chance that much duplicate code can be removed by refactoring to Composite.

Removing such duplication can greatly simplify subclasses. On one project, I found that people were confused about how to add new behavior to the system, and much of the confusion stemmed from the complex, child-handling logic propagated in numerous subclasses. By applying *Extract Composite*, subclass code became simple, which made it easier for folks to understand how to write new subclasses. In addition, the very existence of a superclass named to express that it handled Composites communicated to developers that some rich functionality could be inherited via subclassing.

This refactoring and *Extract Superclass* [F] are essentially the same. I apply this refactoring when I'm only concerned with pulling up common child-handling logic to a superclass. Following that, if there is still more behavior that can be pulled up to a superclass but isn't related to the Composite, I apply the pull-up logic in *Extract Superclass*.

Extract Composite

Benefits and Liabilities

+ Eliminates duplicated child-storage and child-handling logic.
+ Effectively communicates that child-handling logic may be inherited.

Mechanics

These mechanics are based on the mechanics from *Extract Superclass* [F].

1. Create a *composite*, a class that will become a Composite [DP] during this refactoring. Name this class to reflect what kind of children it will contain (e.g., CompositeTag).

   ✔ Compile.

2. Make each *child container* (a class in the hierarchy that contains duplicate child-handling code) a subclass of your *composite*.

    ✔ Compile.

3. In a child container, find a child-processing method that is purely duplicated or partially duplicated across the child containers. A *purely duplicated method* has the same method body with the same or different method names across child containers. A *partially duplicated method* has a method body with common *and* uncommon code and the same or different method names across child containers.

    Whether you've found a purely duplicated or partially duplicated method, if its name isn't consistent across child containers, make it consistent by applying *Rename Method* [F].

    For a purely duplicated method, move the child collection field referenced by the method to your composite by applying *Pull Up Field* [F]. Rename this field if its name doesn't make sense for all child containers. Now move the method to the composite by applying *Pull Up Method* [F]. If the pulled-up method relies on constructor code still residing in child containers, pull up that code to the composite's constructor.

    For a partially duplicated method, see if the method body can be made consistent across all child containers by using *Substitute Algorithm* [F]. If so, refactor it as a purely duplicated method. Otherwise, extract the code that is common across all child-container implementations by using *Extract Method* [F] and pull it up to the composite by using *Pull Up Method* [F]. If the method body follows the same sequence of steps, some of which are implemented differently, see if you can apply *Form Template Method (205)*.

    ✔ Compile and test after each refactoring.

4. Repeat step 3 for child-processing methods in the child containers that contain purely duplicated or partially duplicated code.

5. Check each client of each child container to see if it can now communicate with the child container using the composite interface. If it can, make it do so.

    ✔ Compile and test after each refactoring.

Example

This refactoring occurred on the open-source HTML Parser (see *http://source-forge.net/projects/htmlparser*). When the parser parses a piece of HTML, it identifies and creates objects representing HTML tags and pieces of text. For example, here's some HTML:

```
<HTML>
   <BODY>
      Hello, and welcome to my Web page! I work for
      <A HREF="http://industriallogic.com">
         <IMG SRC="http://industriallogic.com/images/logo141x145.gif">
      </A>
   </BODY>
</HTML>
```

Extract
Composite

Given such HTML, the parser would create objects of the following types:

- Tag (for the <BODY> tag)

- StringNode (for the String, "Hello, and welcome . . .")

- LinkTag (for the <A HREF="…"> tag)

Because the link tag (<A HREF="…">) contains an image tag (<IMG SRC"…">), you might wonder what the parser does with it. The image tag, which the parser treats as an ImageTag, is treated as a child of the LinkTag. When the parser notices that the link tag contains an image tag, it constructs and gives one ImageTag object as a child to the LinkTag object.

Additional tags in the parser, such as FormTag, TitleTag, and others, are also child containers. As I studied some of these classes, it didn't take long to spot duplicate code for storing and handling child nodes. For example, consider the following:

```
public class LinkTag extends Tag...
   private Vector nodeVector;

   public String toPlainTextString() {
      StringBuffer sb = new StringBuffer();
      Node node;
      for (Enumeration e=linkData();e.hasMoreElements();) {
         node = (Node)e.nextElement();
         sb.append(node.toPlainTextString());
      }
      return sb.toString();
   }

public class FormTag extends Tag...
   protected Vector allNodesVector;

   public String toPlainTextString() {
      StringBuffer stringRepresentation = new StringBuffer();
      Node node;
```

```
    for (Enumeration e=getAllNodesVector().elements();e.hasMoreElements();) {
        node = (Node)e.nextElement();
        stringRepresentation.append(node.toPlainTextString());
    }
    return stringRepresentation.toString();
}
```

Extract
Composite

Because FormTag and LinkTag both contain children, they both have a Vector for storing children, though it goes by a different name in each class. Both classes need to support the toPlainTextString() operation, which outputs the non-HTML-formatted text of the tag's children, so both classes contain logic to iterate over their children and produce plain text. Yet the code to do this operation is nearly identical in these classes! In fact, there are several nearly identical methods in the child-container classes, all of which reek of duplication. So follow along as I apply *Extract Composite* to this code.

1. I must first create an abstract class that will become the superclass of the child-container classes. Because the child-container classes, like LinkTag and FormTag, are already subclasses of Tag, I create the following class:

```
public abstract class CompositeTag extends Tag {
    public CompositeTag(
        int tagBegin,
        int tagEnd,
        String tagContents,
        String tagLine) {
        super(tagBegin, tagEnd, tagContents, tagLine);
    }
}
```

2. Now I make the child containers subclasses of CompositeTag:

```
public class LinkTag extends CompositeTag
```

```
public class FormTag extends CompositeTag
```

```
// and so on…
```

Note that for the remainder of this refactoring, I'll show code from only two child containers, LinkTag and FormTag, even though there are others in the code base.

3. I look for a purely duplicated method across all child containers and find toPlainTextString(). Because this method has the same name in each child container, I don't have to change its name anywhere. My first step is to pull up the child Vector that stores children. I do this using the LinkTag class:

```
public abstract class CompositeTag extends Tag...
    protected Vector nodeVector;   // pulled-up field

public class LinkTag extends CompositeTag...
    private Vector nodeVector;
```

I want FormTag to use the same newly pulled-up Vector, nodeVector (yes, it's an awful name, I'll change it soon), so I rename its local child Vector to be nodeVector:

```
public class FormTag extends CompositeTag...
    protected Vector allNodesVector;
    protected Vector nodeVector;
...
```

Then I delete this local field (because FormTag inherits it):

```
public class FormTag extends CompositeTag...
    protected Vector nodeVector;
```

Now I can rename nodeVector in the composite:

```
public abstract class CompositeTag extends Tag...
    protected Vector nodeVector;
    protected Vector children;
```

I'm now ready to pull up the toPlainTextString() method to CompositeTag. My first attempt at doing this with an automated refactoring tool fails because the two methods aren't identical in LinkTag and FormTag. The trouble is that LinkTag gets an iterator on its children by means of the linkData() method, while FormTag gets an iterator on its children by means of the getAllNodesVector().elements():

```
public class LinkTag extends CompositeTag
    public Enumeration linkData() {
        return children.elements();
    }

    public String toPlainTextString()...
        for (Enumeration e=linkData();e.hasMoreElements();)
            ...

public class FormTag extends CompositeTag...
    public Vector getAllNodesVector() {
        return children;
    }
    public String toPlainTextString()...
        for (Enumeration e=getAllNodesVector().elements();e.hasMoreElements();)
            ...
```

To fix this problem, I must create a consistent method for getting access to a CompositeTag's children. I do this by making LinkTag and FormTag implement an identical method, called children(), which I pull up to CompositeTag:

```
public abstract class CompositeTag extends Tag...
    public Enumeration children() {
        return children.elements();
    }
```

Extract Composite

The automated refactoring in my IDE now lets me easily pull up toPlain-TextString() to CompositeTag. I run my tests and everything works fine.

4. In this step I repeat step 3 for additional methods that may be pulled up from the child containers to the composite. There happen to be several of these methods. I'll show you one that involves a method called toHTML(). This method outputs the HTML of a given node. Both LinkTag and FormTag have their own implementations for this method. To implement step 3, I must first decide whether toHTML() is purely duplicated or partially duplicated.

Here's a look at how LinkTag implements the method:

```
public class LinkTag extends CompositeTag
    public String toHTML() {
        StringBuffer sb = new StringBuffer();
        putLinkStartTagInto(sb);
        Node node;
        for (Enumeration e = children();e.hasMoreElements();) {
            node = (Node)e.nextElement();
            sb.append(node.toHTML());
        }
        sb.append("</A>");
        return sb.toString();
    }

    public void putLinkStartTagInto(StringBuffer sb) {
        sb.append("<A ");
        String key,value;
        int i = 0;
        for (Enumeration e = parsed.keys();e.hasMoreElements();) {
            key = (String)e.nextElement();
            i++;
            if (key!=TAGNAME) {
                value = getParameter(key);
                sb.append(key+"=\""+value+"\"");
                if (i<parsed.size()-1) sb.append(" ");
            }
        }
        sb.append(">");
    }
```

After creating a buffer, putLinkStartTagInto(…) deals with getting the contents of the start tag into the buffer, along with any attributes it may have. The start tag would be something like <A HREF="…"> or <A NAME="…">, where HREF and NAME represent attributes of the tag. The tag could have children, such as a StringNode, as in <A HREF="…">I'm a string node</A> or child ImageTag instances. Finally, there is the end tag, </A>, which must be added to the result buffer before the HTML representation of the tag is returned.

Let's now see how FormTag implements the toHTML() method:

```
public class FormTag extends CompositeTag...
   public String toHTML() {
      StringBuffer rawBuffer = new StringBuffer();
      Node node,prevNode=null;
      rawBuffer.append("<FORM METHOD=\""+formMethod+"\" ACTION=\""+formURL+"\"");
      if (formName!=null && formName.length()>0)
         rawBuffer.append(" NAME=\""+formName+"\"");
      Enumeration e = children.elements();
      node = (Node)e.nextElement();
      Tag tag = (Tag)node;
      Hashtable table = tag.getParsed();
      String key,value;
      for (Enumeration en = table.keys();en.hasMoreElements();) {
         key=(String)en.nextElement();
         if (!(key.equals("METHOD")
            || key.equals("ACTION")
            || key.equals("NAME")
            || key.equals(Tag.TAGNAME))) {
            value = (String)table.get(key);
            rawBuffer.append(" "+key+"="+"\""+value+"\"");
         }
      }
      rawBuffer.append(">");
      rawBuffer.append(lineSeparator);
      for (;e.hasMoreElements();) {
         node = (Node)e.nextElement();
         if (prevNode!=null) {
            if (prevNode.elementEnd()>node.elementBegin()) {
               // It's a new line
               rawBuffer.append(lineSeparator);
            }
         }
         rawBuffer.append(node.toHTML());
         prevNode=node;
      }
      return rawBuffer.toString();
   }
}
```

This implementation has some similarities and differences compared with the LinkTag implementation. Therefore, according to the definition presented earlier in the Mechanics section, toHTML() should be treated as a *partially duplicated* child-container method. That means that my next step is to see if I can make one implementation of this method by applying the refactoring *Substitute Algorithm* [F].

It turns out I can. It is easier than it looks because both versions of toHTML() essentially do the same three things: output the start tag along with any attributes, output any child tags, and output the close tag. Knowing that, I arrive at a common method for dealing with the start tag, which I pull up to CompositeTag:

```java
public abstract class CompositeTag extends Tag...
    public void putStartTagInto(StringBuffer sb) {
        sb.append("<" + getTagName() + " ");
        String key,value;
        int i = 0;
        for (Enumeration e = parsed.keys();e.hasMoreElements();) {
            key = (String)e.nextElement();
            i++;
            if (key!=TAGNAME) {
                value = getParameter(key);
                sb.append(key+"=\""+value+"\"");
                if (i<parsed.size()) sb.append(" ");
            }
        }
        sb.append(">");
    }

public class LinkTag extends CompositeTag...
    public String toHTML() {
        StringBuffer sb = new StringBuffer();
        putStartTagInto(sb);
        ...


public class FormTag extends CompositeTag
    public String toHTML() {
        StringBuffer rawBuffer = new StringBuffer();
        putStartTagInto(rawBuffer);
        ...
```

I perform similar operations to make a consistent way of obtaining HTML from child nodes and from an end tag. All of that work enables me to pull up one generic toHTML() method to the composite:

```java
public abstract class CompositeTag extends Tag...
    public String toHTML() {
        StringBuffer htmlContents = new StringBuffer();
        putStartTagInto(htmlContents);
```

```
    putChildrenTagsInto(htmlContents);
    putEndTagInto(htmlContents);
    return htmlContents.toString();
}
```

To complete this part of the refactoring, I'll continue to move child-related methods to CompositeTag, though I'll spare you the details.

5. The final step involves checking clients of child containers to see if they can now communicate with the child containers using the CompositeTag interface. In this case, there are no such cases in the parser itself, so I'm finished with the refactoring.

**Extract
Composite**

Replace One/Many Distinctions with Composite

A class processes single and multiple objects
using separate pieces of code.

*Use a Composite to produce one piece of code
capable of handling single or multiple objects.*

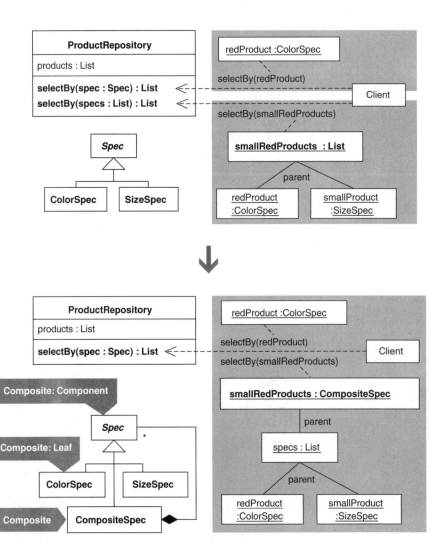

Motivation

When a class has a method for processing one object and a nearly identical method for processing a collection of the objects, a one/many distinction exists. Such a distinction can result in problems such as the following.

- *Duplicated code:* Because the method that processes one object does the same thing as the method that processes a collection of the objects, duplicated code is often spread across the two methods. It's possible to reduce this duplication without implementing a Composite [DP] (see the Example section for details), yet even if duplication is reduced, there are still two methods performing the same kind of processing.

- *Nonuniform client code:* Whether they have single objects or collections of objects, clients want their objects processed in one way. Yet the existence of two processing methods with different signatures forces clients to pass different kinds of data to the methods (i.e., one object or a collection of objects). This makes client code nonuniform, which reduces simplicity.

- *Merging of results:* The best way to explain this is with an example. Say you want to find all products that are red and priced under $5.00 *or* blue and priced above $10.00. One way to find these products is to call a ProductRepository's selectBy(List specs) method, which returns a List of results. Here's an example call to selectBy(…):

```
List redProductsUnderFiveDollars = new ArrayList();
redProductsUnderFiveDollars.add(new ColorSpec(Color.red));
redProductsUnderFiveDollars.add(new BelowPriceSpec(5.00));

List foundRedProductsUnderFiveDollars =
    productRepository.selectBy(redProductsUnderFiveDollars);
```

The main problem with selectBy(List specs) is that it can't handle an OR condition. So if you want to find all products that are red and under $5.00 *or* blue and above $10.00, you have to make separate calls to selectBy(…) and then merge the results:

```
List foundRedProductsUnderFiveDollars =
    productRepository.selectBy(redProductsUnderFiveDollars);

List foundBlueProductsAboveTenDollars =
    productRepository.selectBy(blueProductsAboveTenDollars);

List foundProducts = new ArrayList();
foundProducts.addAll(foundRedProductsUnderFiveDollars);
foundProducts.addAll(foundBlueProductsAboveTenDollars);
```

As you can see, this approach is awkward and verbose.

The Composite pattern provides a better way. It lets clients process one or many objects with a single method. This has many benefits.

- There's no duplicated code across methods because only one method handles the objects, whether one or many.

- Clients communicate with that method in a uniform way.

Replace
One/Many
Distinctions
with Composite

- Clients can make one call to obtain the results of processing a tree of objects rather than having to make several calls and merging processed results. For example, to find red products under $5.00 *or* blue products above $10.00, a client creates and passes the following Composite to the processing method:

```
                          :OrSpec
                            parent
        :AndSpec                        :AndSpec
          parent                          parent
:ColorSpec   :BelowPriceSpec   :ColorSpec   :AbovePriceSpec
color = "red"  price = $5.00   color = "blue"  price = $10.00
```

In short, replacing a one/many distinction with a Composite is a way to remove duplication, make client calls uniform, and support the processing of trees of objects. However, if these latter two particular benefits aren't all that important to your system and you can reduce most of the duplication in methods that have a one/many distinction, a Composite implementation could be overkill.

One common downside of the Composite pattern relates to type safety. To prevent clients from adding invalid objects to a Composite, the Composite code must contain runtime checks of the objects that clients attempt to add to it. This problem is also present with collections because clients can add invalid objects to collections as well.

Benefits and Liabilities

+ Removes duplicate code associated with handling one or many objects.
+ Provides a uniform way to process one or many objects.
+ Supports richer ways to process many objects (e.g., an OR expression).
− May require runtime checks for type safety during construction of the Composite.

Replace
One/Many
Distinctions
with Composite

Mechanics

In this section and the Example section, a method that works with one object is called a *one-object method* while a method that works with a collection of objects is called a *many-object method*.

1. The many-object method accepts a collection as a parameter. Create a new class that accepts the collection in a constructor and provides a getter method for it. This *composite* class will become what is known as a Composite in *Design Patterns* [DP].

   Within the many-object method, declare and instantiate an instance of your composite (i.e., the new class). In addition, find all references within the many-object method to the collection and update the code so access to the collection is obtained via the composite's getter method.

   ✔ Compile and test.

2. Apply *Extract Method* [F] on the code within the many-object method that works with the collection. Make the extracted method public. Then apply *Move Method* [F] on the extracted method to move it to your composite.

   ✔ Compile and test.

3. The many-object method will now be nearly identical to the one-object method. The main difference is that the many-object method instantiates your composite. If there are other differences, refactor to eliminate them.

   ✔ Compile and test.

4. Change the many-object method so it contains one line of code: a call to the one-object method that passes it your composite instance as an argument. You'll need to make the composite share the same interface or superclass as the type used by the one-object method.

To do this, consider making the composite a subclass of the type used by the one-object method or create a new interface (using *Extract Interface* [F]) that the composite and all objects passed to the one-object method implement.

✔ Compile and test.

5. Because the many-object method now consists of just one line of code, it can be inlined by applying *Inline Method* [F].

✔ Compile and test.

6. Apply *Encapsulate Collection* [F] on your composite. This will produce an add(…) method on the composite, which clients will call instead of passing a collection to the composite's constructor. In addition, the getter method for the collection will now return an unmodifiable collection.

✔ Compile and test.

Example

This example deals with Spec instances and how they are used to obtain a desired set of Product instances from a ProductRepository. The example also illustrates the Specification pattern [Evans] as described in *Replace Implicit Language with Interpreter (269)*.

Let's begin by studying some test code for the ProductRepository. Before any test can run, a ProductRepository (called repository) must be created. For the test code, I fill a repository with toy Product instances:

```
public class ProductRepositoryTest extends TestCase...
    private ProductRepository repository;

    private Product fireTruck =
        new Product("f1234", "Fire Truck",
            Color.red, 8.95f, ProductSize.MEDIUM);

    private Product barbieClassic =
        new Product("b7654", "Barbie Classic",
            Color.yellow, 15.95f, ProductSize.SMALL);

    private Product frisbee =
        new Product("f4321", "Frisbee",
            Color.pink, 9.99f, ProductSize.LARGE);
```

```
private Product baseball =
   new Product("b2343", "Baseball",
      Color.white, 8.95f, ProductSize.NOT_APPLICABLE);

private Product toyConvertible =
   new Product("p1112", "Toy Porsche Convertible",
      Color.red, 230.00f, ProductSize.NOT_APPLICABLE);

protected void setUp() {
   repository = new ProductRepository();
   repository.add(fireTruck);
   repository.add(barbieClassic);
   repository.add(frisbee);
   repository.add(baseball);
   repository.add(toyConvertible);
}
```

Replace
One/Many
Distinctions
with Composite

The first test we'll study looks for Product instances of a certain color by means of a call to repository.selectBy(…):

```
public class ProductRepositoryTest extends TestCase...
   public void testFindByColor() {
      List foundProducts = repository.selectBy(new ColorSpec(Color.red));
      assertEquals("found 2 red products", 2, foundProducts.size());
      assertTrue("found fireTruck", foundProducts.contains(fireTruck));
      assertTrue(
         "found Toy Porsche Convertible",
         foundProducts.contains(toyConvertible));
   }
```

The repository.selectBy(…) method looks like this:

```
public class ProductRepository...
   private List products = new ArrayList();

   public Iterator iterator() {
      return products.iterator();
   }

   public List selectBy(Spec spec) {
      List foundProducts = new ArrayList();
      Iterator products = iterator();
      while (products.hasNext()) {
         Product product = (Product)products.next();
         if (spec.isSatisfiedBy(product))
            foundProducts.add(product);
      }
      return foundProducts;
   }
```

Let's now look at another test, which calls a different repository.selectBy(…) method. This test assembles a List of Spec instances in order to select specific kinds of products from the repository:

```
public class ProductRepositoryTest extends TestCase...
    public void testFindByColorSizeAndBelowPrice() {
        List specs = new ArrayList();
        specs.add(new ColorSpec(Color.red));
        specs.add(new SizeSpec(ProductSize.SMALL));
        specs.add(new BelowPriceSpec(10.00));
        List foundProducts = repository.selectBy(specs);
        assertEquals(
            "small red products below $10.00",
            0,
            foundProducts.size());
    }
```

Replace
One/Many
Distinctions
with Composite

The List-based repository.selectBy(…) method looks like this:

```
public class ProductRepository {
    public List selectBy(List specs) {
        List foundProducts = new ArrayList();
        Iterator products = iterator();
        while (products.hasNext()) {
            Product product = (Product)products.next();
            Iterator specifications = specs.iterator();
            boolean satisfiesAllSpecs = true;
            while (specifications.hasNext()) {
                Spec productSpec = ((Spec)specifications.next());
                satisfiesAllSpecs &= productSpec.isSatisfiedBy(product);
            }
            if (satisfiesAllSpecs)
                foundProducts.add(product);
        }
        return foundProducts;
    }
```

As you can see, the List-based selectBy(…) method is more complicated than the one-Spec selectBy(…) method. If you compare the two methods, you'll notice a good deal of duplicate code. A Composite can help remove this duplication; however, there's another way to remove the duplication that doesn't involve a Composite. Consider this:

```
public class ProductRepository...
    public List selectBy(Spec spec) {
        Spec[] specs = { spec };
        return selectBy(Arrays.asList(specs));
    }

    public List selectBy(List specs)...
        // same implementation as before
```

This solution retains the more complicated List-based selectBy(…) method. However, it also completely simplifies the one-Spec selectBy(…) method, which greatly reduces the duplicated code. The only remaining duplication is the existence of the two selectBy(…) methods.

So, is it wise to use this solution instead of refactoring to Composite? Yes and no. It all depends on the needs of the code in question. For the system on which this example code was based, there is a need to support queries with OR, AND, and NOT conditions, like this one:

```
product.getColor() != targetColor ||
product.getPrice() < targetPrice
```

Replace
One/Many
Distinctions
with Composite

The List-based selectBy(…) method cannot support such queries. In addition, having just one selectBy(…) method is preferred so clients can call it in a uniform way. Therefore, I decide to refactor to the Composite pattern by implementing the following steps.

1. The List-based selectBy(…) method is the many-object method. It accepts the following parameter: List specs. My first step is to create a new class that will hold onto the value of the specs parameter and provide access to it via a getter method:

    ```
    public class CompositeSpec {
       private List specs;

       public CompositeSpec(List specs) {
          this.specs = specs;
       }

       public List getSpecs() {
          return specs;
       }
    }
    ```

    Next, I'll instantiate this class within the List-based selectBy(…) method and update code to call its getter method:

    ```
    public class ProductRepository...
       public List selectBy(List specs) {
          CompositeSpec spec = new CompositeSpec(specs);
          List foundProducts = new ArrayList();
          Iterator products = iterator();
          while (products.hasNext()) {
             Product product = (Product)products.next();
             Iterator specifications = spec.getSpecs().iterator();
             boolean satisfiesAllSpecs = true;
             while (specifications.hasNext()) {
                Spec productSpec = ((Spec)specifications.next());
                satisfiesAllSpecs &= productSpec.isSatisfiedBy(product);
    ```

```
        }
        if (satisfiesAllSpecs)
            foundProducts.add(product);
    }
    return foundProducts;
}
```

I compile and test to confirm that these changes work.

2. Now I apply *Extract Method* [F] on the selectBy(...) code that specifically deals
    with specs:

Replace
One/Many
Distinctions
with Composite

```
public class ProductRepository...
    public List selectBy(List specs) {
        CompositeSpec spec = new CompositeSpec(specs);
        List foundProducts = new ArrayList();
        Iterator products = iterator();
        while (products.hasNext()) {
            Product product = (Product)products.next();
            if (isSatisfiedBy(spec, product))
                foundProducts.add(product);
        }
        return foundProducts;
    }

    public boolean isSatisfiedBy(CompositeSpec spec, Product product) {
        Iterator specifications = spec.getSpecs().iterator();
        boolean satisfiesAllSpecs = true;
        while (specifications.hasNext()) {
            Spec productSpec = ((Spec)specifications.next());
            satisfiesAllSpecs &= productSpec.isSatisfiedBy(product);
        }
        return satisfiesAllSpecs;
    }
```

The compiler and test code are happy with this change, so I can now apply
Move Method [F] to move the isSatisfiedBy(...) method to the CompositeSpec
class:

```
public class ProductRepository...
    public List selectBy(List specs) {
        CompositeSpec spec = new CompositeSpec(specs);
        List foundProducts = new ArrayList();
        Iterator products = iterator();
        while (products.hasNext()) {
            Product product = (Product)products.next();
            if (spec.isSatisfiedBy(product))
                foundProducts.add(product);
        }
        return foundProducts;
    }
```

```
public class CompositeSpec...
    public boolean isSatisfiedBy(Product product) {
        Iterator specifications = getSpecs().iterator();
        boolean satisfiesAllSpecs = true;
        while (specifications.hasNext()) {
            Spec productSpec = ((Spec)specifications.next());
            satisfiesAllSpecs &= productSpec.isSatisfiedBy(product);
        }
        return satisfiesAllSpecs;
    }
}
```

One again, I check that the compiler and test code are happy with this change. Both are.

Replace
One/Many
Distinctions
with Composite

3. The two selectBy(...) methods are now nearly identical. The only difference is that the List-based selectBy(...) method instantiates a CompositeSpec instance:

```
public class ProductRepository...
    public List selectBy(Spec spec) {
        // same code
    }

    public List selectBy(List specs) {
        CompositeSpec spec = new CompositeSpec(specs);
        // same code
    }
```

The next step will help remove the duplicated code.

4. I now want to make the List-based selectBy(...) method call the one-Spec selectBy(...) method, like so:

```
public class ProductRepository...
    public List selectBy(Spec spec)...

    public List selectBy(List specs) {
        return selectBy(new CompositeSpec(specs));
    }
```

The compiler does not like this code because CompositeSpec does not share the same interface as Spec, the type used by the called selectBy(...) method. Spec is an abstract class that looks like this:

Spec
isSatisfiedBy(Product) : boolean

Since CompositeSpec already implements the isSatisfiedBy(…) method declared by Spec, it's trivial to make CompositeSpec a subclass of Spec:

```
public class CompositeSpec extends Spec...
```

Now the compiler is happy, as is the test code.

5. Because the List-based selectBy(…) method is now only one line of code that calls the one-Spec selectBy(…) method, I inline it by applying *Inline Method* [F]. Client code that used to call the List-based selectBy(…) now calls the one-Spec selectBy(…) method. Here's an example of such a change:

Replace
One/Many
Distinctions
with Composite

```
public class ProductRepositoryTest...
   public void testFindByColorSizeAndBelowPrice() {
      List specs = new ArrayList();
      specs.add(new ColorSpec(Color.red));
      specs.add(new SizeSpec(ProductSize.SMALL));
      specs.add(new BelowPriceSpec(10.00));
      List foundProducts = repository.selectBy(specs);
      List foundProducts = repository.selectBy(new CompositeSpec(specs));
      ...
```

There's now only one selectBy(…) method that accepts Spec objects like ColorSpec, SizeSpec, or the new CompositeSpec. This is a useful start. However, to build Composite structures that support product searches like product.get-Color() != targetColor || product.getPrice() < targetPrice, there is a need for classes like NotSpec and OrSpec. I won't show how they're created here; you can read about them in the refactoring *Replace Implicit Language with Interpreter (269)*.

6. The final step involves applying *Encapsulate Collection* [F] on the collection inside of CompositeSpec. I do this to make CompositeSpec more type-safe (i.e., to prevent clients from adding objects to it that aren't a subclass of Spec).

I begin by defining the add(Spec spec) method:

```
public class CompositeSpec extends Spec...
   private List specs;

   public void add(Spec spec) {
      specs.add(spec);
   }
```

Next, I initialize specs to an empty list:

```
public class CompositeSpec extends Spec...
   private List specs = new ArrayList();
```

Now comes the fun part. I find all callers of CompositeSpec's constructor and update them to call a new, default CompositeSpec constructor as well as the new add(…) method. Here is one such caller and the updates I make to it:

```
public class ProductRepositoryTest...
    public void testFindByColorSizeAndBelowPrice()...
        List specs = new ArrayList();
        CompositeSpec specs = new CompositeSpec();
        specs.add(new ColorSpec(Color.red));
        specs.add(new SizeSpec(ProductSize.SMALL));
        specs.add(new BelowPriceSpec(10.00));
        List foundProducts = repository.selectBy(specs);
        ...
```

Replace
One/Many
Distinctions
with Composite

I compile and test to confirm that the changes work. Once I've updated all other clients, there are no more callers to CompositeSpec's constructor that take a List. So I delete it:

```
public class CompositeSpec extends Spec...
    public CompositeSpec(List specs) {
        this.specs = specs;
    }
```

Now I update CompositeSpec's getSpecs(…) method to return an unmodifiable version of specs:

```
public class CompositeSpec extends Spec...
    private List specs = new ArrayList();

    public List getSpecs()
        return Collections.unmodifiableList(specs);
    }
```

I compile and test to confirm that my implementation of *Encapsulate Collection* works. It does. CompositeSpec is now a fine implementation of the Composite pattern:

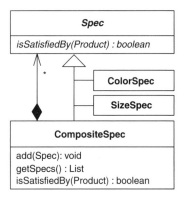

Replace Hard-Coded Notifications with Observer

Subclasses are hard-coded to notify a single
instance of another class.

*Remove the subclasses by making their superclass
capable of notifying one or more instances of any class
that implements an Observer interface.*

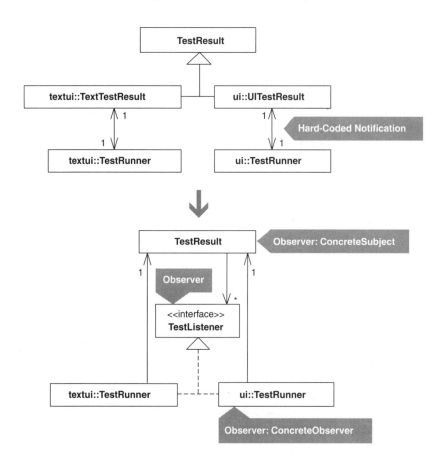

Motivation

Knowing when to refactor to an Observer [DP] first involves understanding
when you don't need an Observer. Consider the case of a single instance of a
class called Receiver that changes when an instance of a class called Notifier
changes, as shown in the following diagram.

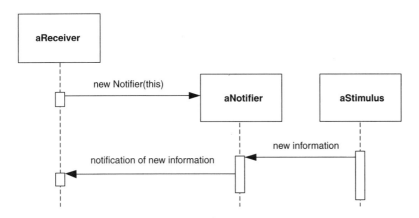

Replace
Hard-Coded
Notifications
with Observer

In this case, the Notifier instance holds onto a Receiver reference and is hard-coded to notify that reference when it receives new information. Such a tight coupling between Notifier and Receiver makes sense when one Notifier instance must notify only one Receiver instance. If that circumstance changes and a Notifier instance must notify numerous Receiver instances, or instances of other classes, the design must evolve. This is exactly what occurred on Kent Beck and Erich Gamma's JUnit framework [Beck and Gamma]. When users of the framework needed more than one party to observe changes to a TestResult instance, a hard-coded notification was refactored to use the Observer pattern (see the Example section for details).

Every implementation of the Observer pattern leads to loose coupling between a subject (a class that is the source of notifications) and its observers. The Observer interface makes this loose coupling possible. To be notified of new information, a class need only implement the Observer interface and register itself with a subject. The subject, in turn, holds onto a collection of instances that implement the Observer interface, notifying them when changes occur.

Classes that play the role of subject must contain a method for adding Observers and can optionally contain a method for removing Observers. If there is never a need to remove Observers during the life of a subject instance, there's no need to implement the remove method. Although this seems like basic common sense, many programmers fall into the trap of implementing this pattern exactly as they see its structure defined on class diagrams in books.

Two common Observer implementation problems to watch out for involve cascading notifications and memory leaks. Cascading notifications occur when a subject notifies an observer, which, by also playing the role of subject, notifies other observers, and so on. The result is an overly complicated design that's difficult to debug. A Mediator [DP] implementation may help improve such code. Memory leaks occur when an observer instance is not garbage collected because the instance is still referenced by a subject. If you remember to always remove your observers from their subjects, you'll avoid memory leaks.

The Observer pattern is used often. Because it isn't difficult to implement, you may be tempted to use this pattern before it's actually needed. Resist that temptation! If you begin with a hard-coded notification, you can always evolve a design to use an Observer when you genuinely need one.

Benefits and Liabilities

+ Loosely couples a subject with its observers.
+ Supports one or many observers.
− Complicates a design when a hard-coded notification will suffice.
− Complicates a design when you have cascading notifications.
− May cause memory leaks when observers aren't removed from their subjects.

Mechanics

A *notifier* is a class that references and sends notifications to another class. A *receiver* is a class that registers itself with a notifier and receives messages from the notifier. This refactoring details the steps for eliminating unnecessary notifiers by making their superclass a *subject* (known in *Design Patterns* as a Concrete-Subject) and transforming receivers into *observers* (known in *Design Patterns* as ConcreteObservers).

1. If a notifier performs custom behavior on behalf of its receiver, instead of performing pure notification logic, move that behavior to the notifier's receiver by applying *Move Method* [F]. When finished, the notifier contains only *notification methods* (methods that notify a receiver).
    Repeat for all notifiers.

    ✔ Compile and test.

2. Produce an observer interface by applying *Extract Interface* [F] on a receiver, selecting only those methods called by its notifier. If other notifiers call receiver methods not on the observer interface, add those methods to the observer interface so that it will work for all receivers.

    ✔ Compile.

3. Make every receiver implement the observer interface. Then make every notifier communicate with its receiver exclusively through the observer interface. Every receiver is now an observer.

✔ Compile and test.

4. Choose a notifier and apply *Pull Up Method* [F] on its notification methods. This includes pulling up the notifier's observer interface reference as well as code for setting that reference. The notifier's superclass is now the subject.

   Repeat for all *notifiers*.

✔ Compile.

5. Update each notifier's observer to register and communicate with the subject, instead of the notifier, and then delete the notifier.

✔ Compile and test.

6. Refactor the subject so it holds onto a collection of observers, rather than just one. This includes updating the way observers register themselves with their subject. It's common to create a method on the subject for adding observers (e.g., addObserver(Observer observer)). Finally, update the subject so its notification methods notify all observers in its collection of observers.

✔ Compile and test.

Example

The code sketch at the beginning of this refactoring depicts a piece of the design of Kent Beck and Erich Gamma's JUnit Testing Framework [Beck and Gamma]. In JUnit 2.x, the authors defined two TestResult subclasses called UITestResult and TextTestResult, both of which are Collecting Parameters (see *Move Accumulation to Collecting Parameter, 313*).

TestResult subclasses gather information from test case objects (e.g., whether a test passed or failed) in order to report that information to a TestRunner, a class that displays test results to the screen. The UITestResult class was hard-coded to report information for a Java Abstract Window Toolkit (AWT) TestRunner, while the TextTestResult was hard-coded to report information for a console-based

TestRunner. Here's a look at a part of the UITestResult class and the connection to its TestRunner:

```
class UITestResult extends TestResult {
    private TestRunner fRunner;
    UITestResult(TestRunner runner) {
        fRunner= runner;
    }
    public synchronized void addFailure(Test test, Throwable t) {
        super.addFailure(test, t);
        fRunner.addFailure(this, test, t);  // notification to TestRunner
    }
    ...
}

package ui;
public class TestRunner extends Frame {    // TestRunner for AWT
    private TestResult fTestResult;
    ...
    protected TestResult createTestResult() {
        return new UITestResult(this);    // hard-coded to UITestResult
    }
    synchronized public void runSuite() {
        ...
        fTestResult = createTestResult();
        testSuite.run(fTestResult);
    }
    public void addFailure(TestResult result, Test test, Throwable t) {
        ... // display the failure in a graphical AWT window
    }
}
```

Replace
Hard-Coded
Notifications
with Observer

This design was perfectly simple and good, for at this stage in JUnit's evolution, if the TestResult/TestRunner notifications had been programmed with the Observer pattern, the design would have been more sophisticated than it needed to be. That circumstance changed when users of JUnit requested the ability for multiple objects to observe a TestResult at runtime. Now the hard-coded relationship between TestRunner instances and TestResult instances wasn't sufficient. To make a TestResult instance capable of supporting many observers, an Observer implementation was necessary.

Would such a change be a refactoring or an enhancement? Making JUnit's TestRunner instances rely on an Observer implementation, rather than being hard-coded to specific TestResult subclasses, would not change their behavior; it would only make them more loosely coupled to TestResult. On the other hand, making a TestResult class hold onto a collection of observers, rather than just one solitary observer, would be new behavior. So an Observer implementation in this example is both a refactoring (i.e., a behavior-preserving transformation) and an enhancement. However, the refactoring is the essential work here, while the enhancement (supporting a collection of observers rather than just one observer) is simply a consequence of an introduction of the Observer pattern.

1. The first step involves ensuring that every notifier implements only notification methods, instead of performing custom behavior on behalf of a receiver. This is true of UITestResult and not true of TextTestResult. Rather than notifying its TestRunner of test results, TextTestResult reports test results directly to the console using Java's System.out.println() method:

```
public class TextTestResult extends TestResult...
    public synchronized void addError(Test test, Throwable t) {
        super.addError(test, t);
        System.out.println("E");
    }
    public synchronized void addFailure(Test test, Throwable t) {
        super.addFailure(test, t);
        System.out.print("F");
    }
```

By applying *Move Method* [F], I make TextTestResult contain pure notification methods, while moving its custom behavior to its associated TestRunner:

```
package textui;
public class TextTestResult extends TestResult...
    private TestRunner fRunner;
    TextTestResult(TestRunner runner) {
        fRunner= runner;
    }

    public synchronized void addError(Test test, Throwable t) {
        super.addError(test, t);
        fRunner.addError(this, test, t);
    }

    ...

package textui;
public class TestRunner...
    protected TextTestResult createTestResult() {
        return new TextTestResult(this);
    }

    // moved method
    public void addError(TestResult testResult, Test test, Throwable t) {
        System.out.println("E");
    }

    ...
```

TextTestResult now notifies its TestRunner, which reports information to the screen. I compile and test to confirm that the changes work.

2. Now I want to create an observer interface called TestListener. To create that interface, I apply *Extract Interface* [F] on the TestRunner associated with the TextTestResult. When choosing what methods to include in the new interface, I must know which methods TextTestResult calls on TestRunner. Those methods are highlighted in bold in the following listing:

```
class TextTestResult extends TestResult...
    public synchronized void addError(Test test, Throwable t) {
        super.addError(test, t);
        fRunner.addError(this, test, t);
    }

    public synchronized void addFailure(Test test, Throwable t) {
        super.addFailure(test, t);
        fRunner.addFailure(this, test, t);
    }

    public synchronized void startTest(Test test) {
        super.startTest(test);
        fRunner.startTest(this, test);
    }
```

Given this information, I extract the following interface:

```
public interface TestListener {
    public void addError(TestResult testResult, Test test, Throwable t);
    public void addFailure(TestResult testResult, Test test, Throwable t);
    public void startTest(TestResult testResult, Test test);
}

public class TestRunner implements TestListener...
```

Now I inspect the other notifier, UITestResult, to see if it calls TestRunner methods that are not on the TestListener interface. It does—it overrides a TestResult method called endTest(…):

```
package ui;
class UITestResult extends TestResult...
    public synchronized void endTest(Test test) {
        super.endTest(test);
        fRunner.endTest(this, test);
    }
```

That leads me to update TestListener with the additional method:

```
public interface TestListener...
    public void endTest(TestResult testResult, Test test);
```

I compile to confirm that everything works fine. However, it doesn't work because the TestRunner for TextTestResult implements the TestListener interface and does not declare the method endTest(...). No problem; I simply add that method to the TestRunner to make everything run:

```
public class TestRunner implements TestListener...
    public void endTest(TestResult testResult, Test test) {
    }
```

**Replace
Hard-Coded
Notifications
with Observer**

3. Now I must make UITestResult's associated TestRunner implement TestListener and also make both TextTestResult and UITestResult communicate with their TestRunner instances using the TestListener interface. Here are a few of the changes:

```
public class TestRunner extends Frame implements TestListener...

class UITestResult extends TestResult...
    protected TestListener fRunner;

    UITestResult(TestListener runner) {
        fRunner= runner;
    }

public class TextTestResult extends TestResult...
    protected TestListener fRunner;

    TextTestResult(TestListener runner) {
        fRunner= runner;
    }
```

I compile and test to confirm that these changes work.

4. Now I apply *Pull Up Method* [F] on every notification method in TextTest-Result and UITestResult. This step is tricky because the methods I'll be pulling up already exist on TestResult, the superclass of TextTestResult and UITest-Result. To do this correctly, I need to merge code from the TestResult subclasses into TestResult. This yields the following changes:

```
public class TestResult...
    protected TestListener fRunner;

    public TestResult(TestListener runner) {
        this();
        fRunner= runner;
    }
```

Replace
Hard-Coded
Notifications
with Observer

```
public TestResult() {
    fFailures= new Vector(10);
    fErrors= new Vector(10);
    fRunTests= 0;
    fStop= false;
}

public synchronized void addError(Test test, Throwable t) {
    fErrors.addElement(new TestFailure(test, t));
    fRunner.addError(this, test, t);
}

public synchronized void addFailure(Test test, Throwable t) {
    fFailures.addElement(new TestFailure(test, t));
    fRunner.addFailure(this, test, t);
}

public synchronized void endTest(Test test) {
    fRunner.endTest(this, test);
}

public synchronized void startTest(Test test) {
    fRunTests++;
    fRunner.startTest(this, test);
}
```

```
package ui;
class UITestResult extends TestResult {
}
```

```
package textui;
class TextTestResult extends TestResult {
}
```

These changes pass the compiler with no problems.

5. I can now update the TestRunner instances to work directly with TestResult. For example, here is a change I make to textui.TestRunner:

```
package textui;
public class TestRunner implements TestListener...
    protected TestResult createTestResult() {
        return new TestResult(this);
    }

    protected void doRun(Test suite, boolean wait)...
        TestResult result= createTestResult();
```

I make a similar change for ui.TestRunner. Finally, I delete both TextTest-Result and UITestResult. I compile and test. The compile is fine, yet the tests fail miserably!

I do some exploring and a little debugging. I discover that my changes to TestResult can cause a null pointer exception when the fRunner field isn't initialized. That circumstance occurs only when TestResult's original constructor is called because it doesn't initialize fRunner. I correct this problem by insulating all calls to fRunner with the following conditional logic:

```
public class TestResult...
    public synchronized void addError(Test test, Throwable t) {
        fErrors.addElement(new TestFailure(test, t));
        if (null != fRunner)
            fRunner.addError(this, test, t);
    }

    public synchronized void addFailure(Test test, Throwable t) {
        fFailures.addElement(new TestFailure(test, t));
        if (null != fRunner)
            fRunner.addFailure(this, test, t);
    }

    // etc.
```

The tests now pass and I'm happy again. The two TestRunners are now observers of the subject, TestResult. At this point I can delete both TextTestResult and UITestResult because they are no longer being used.

6. The final step involves updating TestResult so it can hold onto and notify one or many observers. I declare a List of observers like so:

```
public class TestResult...
    private List observers = new ArrayList();
```

Then I supply a method by which observers can add themselves to the observers list:

```
public class TestResult...
    public void addObserver(TestListener testListener) {
        observers.add(testListener);
    }
```

Next, I update TestResult's notification methods so they work with the list of observers. Here's one such update:

```
public class TestResult...
    public synchronized void addError(Test test, Throwable t) {
        fErrors.addElement(new TestFailure(test, t));
        for (Iterator i = observers.iterator();i.hasNext();) {
            TestListener observer = (TestListener)i.next();
            observer.addError(this, test, t);
        }
    }
```

Finally, I update the TestRunner instances so they use the new addObserver() method rather than calling a TestResult constructor. Here's the change I make to the textui.TestRunner class:

```
package textui;
public class TestRunner implements TestListener...
    protected TestResult createTestResult() {
        TestResult testResult = new TestResult();
        testResult.addObserver(this);
        return testResult;
    }
```

Replace Hard-Coded Notifications with Observer

After compiling and testing that these changes work, I can delete the now unused constructor in TestResult:

```
public class TestResult...
    public TestResult(TestListener runner) {
        this();
        fRunner= runner;
    }
```

That completes the refactoring to the Observer pattern. Now, TestResult notifications are no longer hard-coded to specific TestRunner instances, and TestResult can handle one or many observers of its results.

Unify Interfaces with Adapter

Clients interact with two classes, one of which
has a preferred interface.

Unify the interfaces with an Adapter.

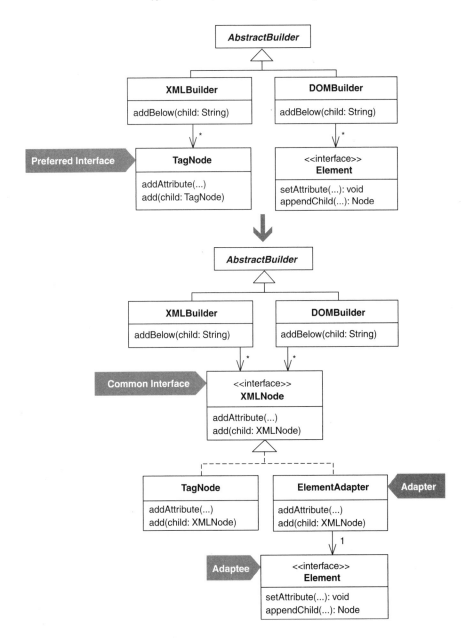

Motivation

Refactoring to an Adapter [DP] is useful when all of the following conditions are true.

- Two classes do the same thing or similar things and have different interfaces.

- Client code could be simpler, more straightforward, and more succinct if the classes shared the same interface.

- You can't simply alter the interface of one of the classes because it's part of a third-party library, or it's part of a framework that many other clients already use, or you lack source code.

The smell *Alternative Classes with Different Interfaces (43)* identifies when code could be communicating with alternative classes via a common interface but for some reason does not. A simple way to solve such a problem is to rename or move methods until the interfaces are the same. If that isn't possible, say, because you're working with code you can't change (like a third-party class or interface, such as a DOM Element), you may need to consider implementing an Adapter.

Refactoring to an Adapter tends to generalize code and pave the way for other refactorings to remove duplicate code. Typically in this situation you have separate client code for communicating with alternative classes. By introducing an Adapter to unify the interfaces of the alternative classes, you generalize how clients interact with those alternative classes. After that, other refactorings, such as *Form Template Method (205)*, can help remove duplicated processing logic in client code. This generally results in simpler, easier-to-read client code.

Benefits and Liabilities

+ Removes or reduces duplicated code by enabling clients to communicate with alternative classes via the same interface.
+ Simplifies client code by making it possible to communicate with objects via a common interace.
+ Unifies how clients interact with alternative classes.
− Complicates a design when you can change the interface of a class rather than adapting it.

Mechanics

1. A client prefers one class's interface over another, yet the client would like to communicate with both classes via a common interface. Apply *Extract Interface* [F] on the class with the client's preferred interface to produce a common interface. Update any of this class's methods that accept an argument of its own type to accept the argument as type common interface.

    The remaining mechanics will now make it possible for the client to communicate with the *adaptee* (the class with the interface the client *does not* prefer) via the common interface.

    ✔ Compile and test.

2. On the client class that uses the adaptee, apply *Extract Class* [F] to produce a primitive *adapter* (a class containing an adaptee field, a getter method for the adaptee, and a setter method or constructor parameter and code for setting the adaptee's value).

3. Update all of the client class's fields, local variables, and parameters of type adaptee to be of type adapter. This involves updating client calls on the adaptee to first obtain an adaptee reference from the adapter before invoking the adaptee method.

    ✔ Compile and test.

4. Wherever the client invokes the same adaptee method (via the adapter's getter method), apply *Extract Method* [F] to produce an adaptee invocation method. Parameterize this adaptee invocation method with an adaptee and make the method use the parameter value when it invokes the adaptee method. For example, a client makes an invocation on the adaptee, current, which is of type ElementAdapter:

```
ElementAdapter childNode = new ElementAdapter(...);
current.getElement().appendChild(childNode.getElement()); // invocation
```

    The invocation on current is extracted to the method:

```
appendChild(current, childNode);
```

    The method, appendChild(…), looks like this:

```
private void appendChild(
    ElementAdapter parent, ElementAdapter childNode) {
    parent.getElement().appendChild(childNode.getElement());
}
```

    ✔ Compile and test. Repeat this step for all client invocations of adaptee methods.

5. Apply *Move Method* [F] on an adaptee invocation method to move it from the client to the adapter. Every client call on the adaptee method should now go through the adapter.

    When moving a method to the adapter, make it resemble the corresponding method in the common interface. If the body of a moved method requires a value from the client in order to compile, avoid adding it as a parameter to the method because that will make its method signature differ from the corresponding method on the common interface. Whenever possible, find a way to pass the value without disturbing the signature (e.g., pass it via the adapter's constructor, or pass some other object reference to the adapter so it can obtain the value at runtime). If you must pass the missing value to the moved method as a parameter, you'll need to revise the corresponding method signature on the common interface to make the two equivalent.

    ✔ Compile and test.

    Repeat for all adaptee invocation methods until the adapter contains methods with the same signatures as the methods on the common interface.

6. Update the adapter to formally "implement" the common interface. This should be a trivial step given the work already accomplished. Change all adapter methods that accept an argument of type adapter to accept the argument as type common interface.

    ✔ Compile and test.

7. Update the client class so that all fields, local variables, and parameters use the common interface instead of the adapter's type.

    ✔ Compile and test.

    Client code now communicates with both classes using the common interface. To further remove duplication in this client code, you can often apply refactorings like *Form Template Method (205)* and *Introduce Polymorphic Creation with Factory Method (88)*.

Example

This example relates to code that builds XML (see *Replace Implicit Tree with Composite, 178; Encapsulate Composite with Builder, 96;* and *Introduce Polymorphic Creation with Factory Method, 88*). In this case, there are two builders: XMLBuilder and DOMBuilder. Both extend from AbstractBuilder, which implements the OutputBuilder interface:

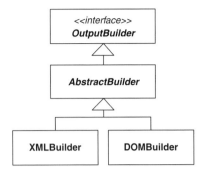

The code in XMLBuilder and DOMBuilder is largely the same, except that XMLBuilder collaborates with a class called TagNode, while DOMBuilder collaborates with objects that implement the Element interface:

```
public class DOMBuilder extends AbstractBuilder...
   private Document document;
   private Element root;
   private Element parent;
   private Element current;

   public void addAttribute(String name, String value) {
      current.setAttribute(name, value);
   }

   public void addBelow(String child) {
      Element childNode = document.createElement(child);
      current.appendChild(childNode);
      parent = current;
      current = childNode;
      history.push(current);
   }

   public void addBeside(String sibling) {
      if (current == root)
         throw new RuntimeException(CANNOT_ADD_BESIDE_ROOT);
      Element siblingNode = document.createElement(sibling);
      parent.appendChild(siblingNode);
      current = siblingNode;
      history.pop();
      history.push(current);
   }

   public void addValue(String value) {
      current.appendChild(document.createTextNode(value));
   }
```

And here's the similar code from XMLBuilder:

```
public class XMLBuilder extends AbstractBuilder...
  private TagNode rootNode;
  private TagNode currentNode;

  public void addChild(String childTagName) {
    addTo(currentNode, childTagName);
  }

  public void addSibling(String siblingTagName) {
    addTo(currentNode.getParent(), siblingTagName);
  }

  private void addTo(TagNode parentNode, String tagName) {
    currentNode = new TagNode(tagName);
    parentNode.add(currentNode);
  }

  public void addAttribute(String name, String value) {
    currentNode.addAttribute(name, value);
  }

  public void addValue(String value) {
    currentNode.addValue(value);
  }
```

Unify
Interfaces
with Adapter

These methods, and numerous others that I'm not showing in order to conserve space, are nearly the same in DOMBuilder and XMLBuilder, except for the fact that each builder works with either TagNode or Element. The goal of this refactoring is to create a common interface for TagNode and Element so that the duplication in the builder methods can be eliminated.

1. My first task is to create a common interface. I base this interface on the TagNode class because its interface is the one I prefer for client code. TagNode has about ten methods, five of which are public. The common interface needs only three of these methods. I apply *Extract Interface* [F] to obtain the desired result:

    ```
    public interface XMLNode {
      public abstract void add(XMLNode childNode);
      public abstract void addAttribute(String attribute, String value);
      public abstract void addValue(String value);
    }

    public class TagNode implements XMLNode...
      public void add(XMLNode childNode) {
        children().add(childNode);
      }
      // etc.
    ```

    I compile and test to make sure these changes worked.

2. Now I begin working on the DOMBuilder class. I want to apply *Extract Class* [F] to DOMBuilder in order to produce an adapter for Element. This results in the creation of the following class:

```
public class ElementAdapter {
    Element element;

    public ElementAdapter(Element element) {
        this.element = element;
    }

    public Element getElement() {
        return element;
    }
}
```

3. Now I update all of the Element fields in DOMBuilder to be of type ElementAdapter and update any code that needs to be updated because of this change:

```
public class DOMBuilder extends AbstractBuilder...
    private Document document;
    private ElementAdapter rootNode;
    private ElementAdapter parentNode;
    private ElementAdapter currentNode;

    public void addAttribute(String name, String value) {
        currentNode.getElement().setAttribute(name, value);
    }
    public void addChild(String childTagName) {
        ElementAdapter childNode =
            new ElementAdapter(document.createElement(childTagName));
        currentNode.getElement().appendChild(childNode.getElement());
        parentNode = currentNode;
        currentNode = childNode;
        history.push(currentNode);
    }

    public void addSibling(String siblingTagName) {
        if (currentNode == root)
            throw new RuntimeException(CANNOT_ADD_BESIDE_ROOT);
        ElementAdapter siblingNode =
            new ElementAdapter(document.createElement(siblingTagName));
        parentNode.getElement().appendChild(siblingNode.getElement());
        currentNode = siblingNode;
        history.pop();
        history.push(currentNode);
    }
```

4. Now I create an adaptee invocation method for each adaptee method called by DOMBuilder. I use *Extract Method* [F] for this purpose, making sure that each extracted method takes an adaptee as an argument and uses that adaptee in its body:

```
public class DOMBuilder extends AbstractBuilder...
    public void addAttribute(String name, String value) {
        addAttribute(currentNode, name, value);
    }

    private void addAttribute(ElementAdapter current, String name, String value) {
        currentNode.getElement().setAttribute(name, value);
    }

    public void addChild(String childTagName) {
        ElementAdapter childNode =
            new ElementAdapter(document.createElement(childTagName));
        add(currentNode, childNode);
        parentNode = currentNode;
        currentNode = childNode;
        history.push(currentNode);
    }

    private void add(ElementAdapter parent, ElementAdapter child) {
        parent.getElement().appendChild(child.getElement());
    }

    public void addSibling(String siblingTagName) {
        if (currentNode == root)
            throw new RuntimeException(CANNOT_ADD_BESIDE_ROOT);
        ElementAdapter siblingNode =
            new ElementAdapter(document.createElement(siblingTagName));
        add(parentNode, siblingNode);
        currentNode = siblingNode;
        history.pop();
        history.push(currentNode);
    }

    public void addValue(String value) {
        addValue(currentNode, value);
    }

    private void addValue(ElementAdapter current, String value) {
        currentNode.getElement().appendChild(document.createTextNode(value));
    }
```

5. I can now move each adaptee invocation method to ElementAdapter using *Move Method* [F]. I'd like the moved method to resemble the corresponding methods in the common interface, XMLNode, as much as possible. This is easy

to do for every method except addValue(…), which I'll address in a moment. Here are the results after moving the addAttribute(…) and add(…) methods:

```
public class ElementAdapter {
    Element element;

    public ElementAdapter(Element element) {
        this.element = element;
    }

    public Element getElement() {
        return element;
    }

    public void addAttribute(String name, String value) {
        getElement().setAttribute(name, value);
    }

    public void add(ElementAdapter child) {
        getElement().appendChild(child.getElement());
    }
}
```

And here are examples of changes in DOMBuilder as a result of the move:

```
public class DOMBuilder extends AbstractBuilder...
    public void addAttribute(String name, String value) {
        currentNode.addAttribute(name, value);
    }

    public void addChild(String childTagName) {
        ElementAdapter childNode =
            new ElementAdapter(document.createElement(childTagName));
        currentNode.add(childNode);
        parentNode = currentNode;
        currentNode = childNode;
        history.push(currentNode);
    }

    // etc.
```

The addValue(…) method is more tricky to move to ElementAdapter because it relies on a field within ElementAdapter called document:

```
public class DOMBuilder extends AbstractBuilder...
    private Document document;

    public void addValue(ElementAdapter current, String value) {
        current.getElement().appendChild(document.createTextNode(value));
    }
```

I don't want to pass a field of type Document to the addValue(...) method on ElementAdapter because if I do so, that method will move further away from the target, which is the addValue(...) method on XMLNode:

```
public interface XMLNode...
    public abstract void addValue(String value);
```

At this point I decide to pass an instance of Document to ElementAdapter via its constructor:

Unify
Interfaces
with Adapter

```
public class ElementAdapter...
    Element element;
    Document document;

    public ElementAdapter(Element element, Document document) {
        this.element = element;
        this.document = document;
    }
```

And I make the necessary changes in DOMBuilder to call this updated constructor. Now I can easily move addValue(...):

```
public class ElementAdapter...
    public void addValue(String value) {
        getElement().appendChild(document.createTextNode(value));
    }
```

6. Now I make ElementAdapter implement the XMLNode interface. This step is straightforward, except for a small change to the add(...) method to allow it to call the getElement() method, which is not part of the XMLNode interface:

```
public class ElementAdapter implements XMLNode...
    public void add(XMLNode child) {
        ElementAdapter childElement = (ElementAdapter)child;
        getElement().appendChild(childElement.getElement());
    }
```

7. The final step is to update DOMBuilder so that all of its ElementAdapter fields, local variables, and parameters change their type to XMLNode:

```
public class DOMBuilder extends AbstractBuilder...
    private Document document;
    private XMLNode rootNode;
    private XMLNode parentNode;
    private XMLNode currentNode;

    public void addChild(String childTagName) {
        XMLNode childNode =
            new ElementAdapter(document.createElement(childTagName), document);
        ...
    }
```

```
protected void init(String rootName) {
    document = new DocumentImpl();
    rootNode = new ElementAdapter(document.createElement(rootName), document);
    document.appendChild(((ElementAdapter)rootNode).getElement());
    ...
}
```

At this point, by adapting Element in DOMBuilder, the code in XMLBuilder is so similar to that of DOMBuilder that it makes sense to pull up the similar code to AbstractBuilder. I achieve that by applying *Form Template Method (205)* and *Introduce Polymorphic Creation with Factory Method (88)*. The following diagram shows the result.

Unify
Interfaces
with Adapter

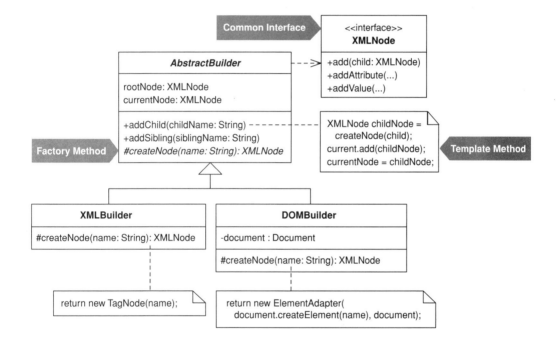

Extract Adapter

One class adapts multiple versions of a
component, library, API, or other entity.

*Extract an Adapter for a single version of the
component, library, API, or other entity.*

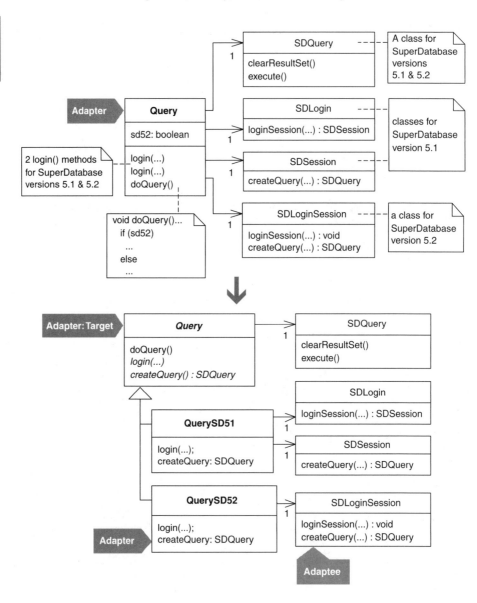

Motivation

While software must often support multiple versions of a component, library, or API, code that handles these versions doesn't have to be a confusing mess. Yet I routinely encounter code that attempts to handle multiple versions of something by overloading classes with version-specific state variables, constructors, and methods. Accompanying such code are comments like "This is for version X—please delete this code when we move to version Y!" Sure, like that's ever going to happen. Most programmers won't delete the version X code for fear that something they don't know about still relies on it. So the comments don't get deleted, and many versions supported by the code remain in the code.

Extract Adapter

Now consider an alternative: for each version of something you need to support, create a separate class. The class name could even include the version number of what it supports, to be really explicit about what it does. Such classes are called Adapters [DP]. Adapters implement a common interface and are responsible for functioning correctly with one (and usually only one) version of some code. Adapters make it easy for client code to swap in support for one library or API version or another. And programmers routinely rely on runtime information to configure their programs with the correct Adapter.

I refactor to Adapters fairly often. I like Adapters because they let me decide how I want to communicate with other people's code. In a fast-changing world, Adapters help me stay insulated from highly useful but rapidly changing APIs, such as those springing eternally from the open source world.

In some cases, Adapters may adapt too much. For example, a client needs access to behavior on an adaptee, yet it cannot access that behavior because it only has access to the adaptee via an Adapter. In that case, the Adapter must be redesigned to accommodate client needs.

Systems that depend on multiple versions of a component, library, or API tend to have a good deal of version-dependent logic scattered throughout the code (a sure sign of the *Solution Sprawl* smell, *43*). While you wouldn't want to complicate a design by refactoring to Adapter too early, it's useful to apply this refactoring as soon as you find complexity, propagating conditionality, or a maintanance issue resulting from code written to handle multiple versions.

Adapter and Facade

The Adapter pattern is often confused with the Facade pattern [DP]. Both patterns make code easier to use, yet each operates on different levels: Adapters adapt objects, while Facades adapt entire subsystems.

Facades are often used to communicate with legacy systems. For example, consider an organization with a sophisticated, two-million-line COBOL system that continually generates a good deal of the organization's income. Such a system may be hard to extend or maintain because it was never refactored. Yet because it contains important functionality, new systems must depend on it.

Facades are useful in this context. They provide new systems with simpler views of poorly designed or highly complex legacy code. These new systems can communicate with Facade objects, which in turn do all the hard work of communicating with the legacy code.

Over time, teams can rewrite entire legacy subsystems by simply writing new implementations for each Facade. The process goes like this:

- Identify a subsystem of your legacy system.

- Write Facades for that subsystem.

- Write new client programs that rely on calls to the Facades.

- Create versions of each Facade using newer technologies.

- Test that the newer and older Facades function identically.

- Update client code to use the new Facades.

- Repeat for the next subsystem.

Benefits and Liabilities

+ Isolates differences in versions of a component, library, or API.
+ Makes classes responsible for adapting only one version of something.
+ Provides insulation from frequently changing code.
− Can shield a client from important behavior that isn't available on the Adapter.

Mechanics

There are different ways to go about this refactoring, depending on how your code looks before you begin. For example, if you have a class that uses a lot of conditional logic to handle multiple versions of something, it's likely that you can create Adapters for each version by repeatedly applying *Replace Conditional with Polymorphism* [F]. If you have a case like the one shown in the code sketch—in which an existing Adapter class supports multiple versions of a library with version-specific variables and methods—you'll extract multiple Adapters using a different approach. Here I outline the mechanics for this latter scenario.

Extract Adapter

1. Identify an *overburdened adapter*, a class that adapts too many versions of something.

2. Create a *new adaper*, a class produced by applying *Extract Subclass* [F] or *Extract Class* [F] for a single version of the multiple versions supported by the overburdened adapter. Copy or move all instance variables and methods used exclusively for that version into the new adapter.

   To do this, you may need to make some private members of the overburdened adapter public or protected. It may also be necessary to initialize some instance variables via a constructor in the new adapter, which will necessitate updates to callers of the new constructor.

   ✔ Compile and test.

3. Repeat step 2 until the overburdened adapter has no more version-specific code.

4. Remove any duplication found in the new adapters by applying refactorings like *Pull Up Method* [F] and *Form Template Method (205)*.

   ✔ Compile and test.

Example

The code I'll refactor in this example, which was depicted in the code sketch at the beginning of this refactoring, is based on real-world code that handles queries to a database using a third-party library. To protect the innocent, I've renamed that library SD, which stands for SuperDatabase.

1. I begin by identifying an Adapter that is overburdened with support for multiple versions of SuperDatabase. This class, called Query, provides support for SuperDatabase versions 5.1 and 5.2.

In the following code listing, notice the version-specific instance variables, duplicate login() methods, and conditional code in doQuery():

Extract
Adapter

```
public class Query...
    private SDLogin sdLogin; // needed for SD version 5.1
    private SDSession sdSession; // needed for SD version 5.1
    private SDLoginSession sdLoginSession; // needed for SD version 5.2
    private boolean sd52; // tells if we're running under SD 5.2
    private SDQuery sdQuery; // this is needed for SD versions 5.1 & 5.2

    // this is a login for SD 5.1
    // NOTE: remove this when we convert all aplications to 5.2
    public void login(String server, String user, String password) throws QueryException {
        sd52 = false;
        try {
            sdSession = sdLogin.loginSession(server, user, password);
        } catch (SDLoginFailedException lfe) {
            throw new QueryException(QueryException.LOGIN_FAILED,
                                    "Login failure\n" + lfe, lfe);
        } catch (SDSocketInitFailedException ife) {
            throw new QueryException(QueryException.LOGIN_FAILED,
                                    "Socket fail\n" + ife, ife);
        }
    }

    // 5.2 login
    public void login(String server, String user, String password,
                    String sdConfigFileName) throws QueryException {
        sd52 = true;
        sdLoginSession = new SDLoginSession(sdConfigFileName, false);
        try {
            sdLoginSession.loginSession(server, user, password);
        } catch (SDLoginFailedException lfe) {
            throw new QueryException(QueryException.LOGIN_FAILED,
                                    "Login failure\n" + lfe, lfe);
        } catch (SDSocketInitFailedException ife) {
            throw new QueryException(QueryException.LOGIN_FAILED,
                                    "Socket fail\n" + ife, ife);
        } catch (SDNotFoundException nfe) {
            throw new QueryException(QueryException.LOGIN_FAILED,
                                    "Not found exception\n" + nfe, nfe);
        }
    }

    public void doQuery() throws QueryException {
        if (sdQuery != null)
            sdQuery.clearResultSet();
        if (sd52)
            sdQuery = sdLoginSession.createQuery(SDQuery.OPEN_FOR_QUERY);
        else
            sdQuery = sdSession.createQuery(SDQuery.OPEN_FOR_QUERY);
        executeQuery();
    }
```

2. Because Query doesn't already have subclasses, I decide to apply *Extract Subclass* [F] to isolate code that handles SuperDatabase 5.1 queries. My first step is to define the subclass and create a constructor for it:

```
class QuerySD51 extends Query {
    public QuerySD51() {
        super();
    }
}
```

Next, I find all client calls to Query's constructor and, where appropriate, change the code to call the QuerySD51 constructor. For example, I find the following client code, which holds onto a Query field called query:

```
public void loginToDatabase(String db, String user, String password)...
    query = new Query();
    try   {
        if (usingSDVersion52()) {
            query.login(db, user, password, getSD52ConfigFileName());  // Login to SD 5.2
        } else {
            query.login(db, user, password); // Login to SD 5.1
        }
        ...
    } catch(QueryException qe)...
```

I change this to:

```
public void loginToDatabase(String db, String user, String password)...
    query = new Query();
    try   {
        if (usingSDVersion52()) {
            query = new Query();
            query.login(db, user, password, getSD52ConfigFileName()); // Login to SD 5.2
        } else {
            query = new QuerySD51();
            query.login(db, user, password);  // Login to SD 5.1
        }
        ...
    } catch(QueryException qe) {
```

Next, I apply *Push Down Method* [F] and *Push Down Field* [F] to outfit QuerySD51 with the methods and instance variables it needs. During this step, I have to be careful to consider the clients that make calls to public Query methods, for if I move a public method like login() from Query to QuerySD51, the caller will not be able to call the public method unless its type is changed to QuerySD51. Because I don't want to make such changes to client code, I proceed cautiously, sometimes copying and modifying public methods instead of completely removing them from Query. While I do this, I generate duplicate code, but that doesn't bother me now—I'll get rid of the duplication in the final step of this refactoring.

```
class Query...
    private SDLogin sdLogin;
    private SDSession sdSession;
    protected SDQuery sdQuery;

    // this is a login for SD 5.1
    public void login(String server, String user, String password) throws QueryException {
        // I make this a do-nothing method
    }

    public void doQuery() throws QueryException {
        if (sdQuery != null)
            sdQuery.clearResultSet();
        if (sd52)
        sdQuery = sdLoginSession.createQuery(SDQuery.OPEN_FOR_QUERY);
        else
            sdQuery = sdSession.createQuery(SDQuery.OPEN_FOR_QUERY);
        executeQuery();
    }
```

```
class QuerySD51 {
    private SDLogin sdLogin;
    private SDSession sdSession;

    public void login(String server, String user, String password) throws QueryException {
        sd52 = false;
        try {
            sdSession = sdLogin.loginSession(server, user, password);
        } catch (SDLoginFailedException lfe) {
            throw new QueryException(QueryException.LOGIN_FAILED,
                                     "Login failure\n" + lfe, lfe);
        } catch (SDSocketInitFailedException ife) {
            throw new QueryException(QueryException.LOGIN_FAILED,
                                     "Socket fail\n" + ife, ife);
        }
    }

    public void doQuery() throws QueryException {
        if (sdQuery != null)
            sdQuery.clearResultSet();
        if (sd52)
            sdQuery = sdLoginSession.createQuery(SDQuery.OPEN_FOR_QUERY);
        else
        sdQuery = sdSession.createQuery(SDQuery.OPEN_FOR_QUERY);
        executeQuery();
    }
}
```

I compile and test that QuerySD51 works. No problems.

3. Next, I repeat step 2 to create QuerySD52. Along the way, I can make the Query class abstract, along with the doQuery() method. Here's what I have now:

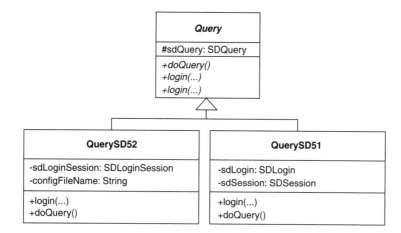

Query is now free of version-specific code, but it is not free of duplicate code.

4. Now I go on a mission to remove duplication. I quickly find some in the two implementations of doQuery():

```
abstract class Query…
    public abstract void doQuery() throws QueryException;

class QuerySD51...
    public void doQuery() throws QueryException {
        if (sdQuery != null)
            sdQuery.clearResultSet();

        sdQuery = sdSession.createQuery(SDQuery.OPEN_FOR_QUERY);
        executeQuery();
    }

class QuerySD52...
    public void doQuery() throws QueryException {
        if (sdQuery != null)
            sdQuery.clearResultSet();

        sdQuery = sdLoginSession.createQuery(SDQuery.OPEN_FOR_QUERY);
        executeQuery();
    }
```

Each of these methods simply initializes the sdQuery instance in a different way. This means that I can apply *Introduce Polymorphic Creation with Factory Method (88)* and *Form Template Method (205)* to create a single superclass version of doQuery():

```
public abstract class Query...
    protected abstract SDQuery createQuery();          // a Factory Method [DP]

    public void doQuery() throws QueryException {      // a Template Method [DP]
        if (sdQuery != null)
            sdQuery.clearResultSet();
        sdQuery = createQuery();                        // call to the Factory Method
        executeQuery();
    }

class QuerySD51...
    protected SDQuery createQuery() {
        return sdSession.createQuery(SDQuery.OPEN_FOR_QUERY);
    }

class QuerySD52...
    protected SDQuery createQuery() {
        return sdLoginSession.createQuery(SDQuery.OPEN_FOR_QUERY);
    }
```

Extract
Adapter

After compiling and testing the changes, I now face a more obvious duplication problem: Query still contains the SD 5.1 and 5.2 login() methods, even though they no longer do anything (the real login work is now handled by the subclasses). The signatures for these two login() method are identical, except for one parameter:

```
// SD 5.1 login
public void login(String server, String user, String password) throws QueryException...

// SD 5.2 login
public void login(String server, String user,
                String password, String sdConfigFileName) throws QueryException...
```

I decide to make the login() signatures the same, by simply supplying QuerySD52 with the sdConfigFileName information via its constructor:

```
class QuerySD52...
    private String sdConfigFileName;
    public QuerySD52(String sdConfigFileName) {
        super();
        this.sdConfigFileName = sdConfigFileName;
    }
```

Now Query has only one abstract login() method:

```
abstract class Query...
    public abstract void login(String server, String user,
                            String password) throws QueryException...
```

Client code is updated as follows:

```
public void loginToDatabase(String db, String user, String password)...
    if (usingSDVersion52())
        query = new QuerySD52(getSD52ConfigFileName());
    else
        query = new QuerySD51();

    try {
        query.login(db, user, password);
        ...
    } catch(QueryException qe)...
```

I'm nearly done. Because Query is an abstract class, I decide to rename it AbstractQuery, which communicates more about its nature. But making that name change necessitates changing client code to declare variables of type AbstractQuery instead of Query. I don't want to do that, so I apply *Extract Interface* [F] on AbstractQuery to obtain a Query interface that AbstractQuery can implement:

```
interface Query {
    public void login(String server, String user, String password) throws QueryException;
    public void doQuery() throws QueryException;
}

abstract class AbstractQuery implements Query...
    public abstract void login(String server, String user,
                            String password) throws QueryException...
```

Now, subclasses of AbstractQuery implement login(), while AbstractQuery doesn't even need to declare the login() method because it is an abstract class.

I compile and test to see that everything works as planned. Each version of SuperDatabase is now fully adapted. The code is smaller and treats each version in a more uniform way, all of which makes it easier to:

- See similarities and differences between the versions

- Remove support for older, unused versions

- Add support for newer versions

Variations

Adapting with Anonymous Inner Classes

The first version of Java (JDK 1.0) included an interface called Enumeration, which was used to iterate over collections like Vector and Hashtable collections. Over time, better collections classes were added to the JDK, along with a new interface called Iterator. To make it possible to interoperate with code written using the Enumeration interface, the JDK provided the following Creation Method, which used Java's anonymous inner class capability to adapt an Iterator with an Enumeration:

Extract Adapter

```
public class Collections...
    public static Enumeration enumeration(final Collection c) {
        return new Enumeration() {
            Iterator i = c.iterator();

            public boolean hasMoreElements() {
                return i.hasNext();
            }
            public Object nextElement() {
                return i.next();
            }
        };
    }
```

Replace Implicit Language with Interpreter

Numerous methods on a class combine elements
of an implicit language.

*Define classes for elements of the implicit language so that
instances may be combined to form interpretable expressions.*

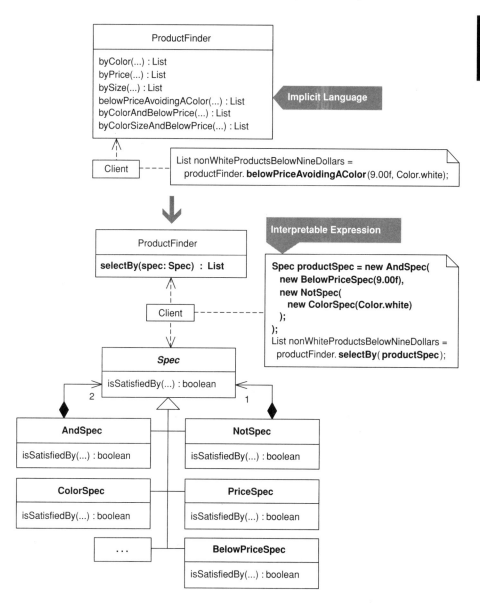

Motivation

An Interpreter [DP] is useful for interpreting simple languages. A simple language is one that has a grammar that may be modeled using a small number of classes. Sentences and expressions in simple languages are formed by combining instances of the grammar's classes, typically using a Composite [DP] structure.

Programmers divide into two camps with respect to the Interpreter pattern: those who are comfortable implementing it and those who aren't. However, whether or not you're comfortable with terms like parse trees and abstract syntax trees, terminal and nonterminal expressions, implementing an Interpreter is only slightly more complicated than implementing a Composite. The trick is knowing when you need an Interpreter.

You don't need an Interpreter for complex languages or for really simple ones. For complex languages, it's usually best to use a tool (such as JavaCC) that supports parsing, grammar definition, and interpretation. For example, on one project, my colleagues and I used a parser generator to produce a grammar that had more than 20 classes—too many to comfortably program by hand using the Interpreter pattern. On another project, our language's grammar was so simple and uniform that we didn't use any classes to interpret each expression in the language.

If a language's grammar requires fewer than a dozen classes to implement, it may be useful to model using the Interpreter pattern. Search expressions for objects or database values often have such grammars. Typical searches require the use of words like "and," "not," and "or" (called *nonterminal expressions*), as well as values like "$10.00," "small," and "blue" (called *terminal expressions*). For example:

- Find products below $10.00.

- Find products below $10.00 and not white.

- Find products that are blue, small, and below $20.00.

Such search expressions are often programmed into systems without using an explicit language. Consider this class:

```
ProductFinder…
    public List byColor(Color colorOfProductToFind)...
    public List byPrice(float priceLimit)...
    public List bySize(int sizeToFind)...
    public List belowPrice(float price) ...
    public List belowPriceAvoidingAColor(float price, Color color)...
    public List byColorAndBelowPrice(Color color, float price)...
    public List byColorSizeAndBelowPrice(Color color, int size, float price)...
```

Programmed in this way, a product-finding language is *implicit:* present, but unexpressed. Two problems result from this approach. First, you must create a new method for each new combination of product criteria. Second, the product-finding methods tend to duplicate a lot of product-finding code. An Interpreter solution (shown in the Example section) is better because it can support a large variety of product queries with a little over a half-dozen small classes and no duplication of code.

Refactoring to an Interpreter involves the start-up cost of defining classes for a grammar and altering client code to compose instances of the classes to represent language expressions. Is that price worth it? It is if the alternative is lots of duplicated code to handle a combinatorial explosion of implicit language expressions, such as the many finder methods in the ProductFinder class just shown.

Replace Implicit Language with Interpreter

Two patterns that make heavy use of Interpreter are Specification [Evans] and Query Object [Fowler, PEAA]. Both model search expressions using simple grammars and compositions of objects. These patterns provide a useful way to separate a search expression from its representation. For example, a Query Object models a query in a generic way, which allows you to convert it into a SQL representation (or some other representation) when you want to perform an actual database query.

Interpreters are often used within systems to allow for the runtime configuration of behavior. For example, a system may accept a user's query preferences through a user interface and then dynamically produce an interpretable object structure that represents the query. In this way, Interpreters can provide a level of power and flexibility that isn't possible when all behavior in a system is static and can't be configured dynamically.

Benefits and Liabilities

+ Supports combinations of language elements better than an implicit language does.
+ Requires no new code to support new combinations of language elements.
+ Allows for runtime configuration of behavior.
− Has a start-up cost for defining a grammar and changing client code to use it.
− Requires too much programming when your language is complex.
− Complicates a design when a language is simple.

Mechanics

These mechanics are heavily weighted towards the use of Interpreter in the context of the Specification and Query Object patterns because most of the Interpreter implementations I've written or encountered have been implementations of those two patterns. In this context, an implicit language is modeled using numerous object selection methods, each of which iterates across a collection to select a specific set of objects.

Replace Implicit Language with Interpreter

1. Find an object selection method that relies on a single criterion argument (e.g., `double targetPrice`) to find a set of objects. Create a concrete specification class for the criterion argument, which accepts the argument's value in a constructor and provides a getter method for it. Within the object selection method, declare and instantiate a variable of type concrete specification and update the code so access to the criterion is obtained via the concrete specification's getter method.

    Name your concrete specification by what it does (e.g., `ColorSpec` helps find products by a given color).

    If your object selection method relies on multiple criteria for its object selection, apply this step and step 2 for each piece of the criterion. In step 4, you'll deal with composing concrete specifications into composite specifications.

    ✔ Compile and test that object selection still works correctly.

2. Apply *Extract Method* [F] on the conditional statement in the object selection method to produce a method called `isSatisfiedBy()`, which should have a Boolean result. Now apply *Move Method* [F] to move this method to the concrete specification.

    Create a specification superclass (if you haven't already created one) by applying *Extract Superclass* [F] on the concrete specification. Make this superclass abstract and have it declare a single abstract method for `isSatisfiedBy(…)`.

    ✔ Compile and test that object selection still works correctly.

3. Repeat steps 1 and 2 for similar object selection methods, including methods that rely on the criteria for object selection.

4. If you have an object selection method that relies on multiple concrete specifications (i.e., the method now instantiates more than one concrete specification for use in its object selection logic), apply a modified version of step 1 by creating a *composite specification* (a class composed of the concrete

specifications instantiated inside the object selection method). You may pass the concrete specifications to the composite specification via its constructor or, if there are many concrete specifications, supply an add(…) method on the composite specification.

Then apply step 2 on the object selection method's conditional statement to move the logic to the composite specification's isSatisfiedBy(…) method. Make the composite specification extend from the specification superclass.

5. Each object selection method now works with one specification object (i.e., one concrete specification or one composite specification). In addition, the object selection methods are identical except for specification creation code. Remove duplicated code in the object selection methods by applying *Extract Method* [F] on the identical code from any object selection method. Name the extracted method something like selectBy(…) and have it accept one argument of type specification interface and return a collection of objects (e.g., public List selectBy(Spec spec)).

Replace Implicit Language with Interpreter

✔ Compile and test.

Adjust all object selection methods to call the selectBy(…) method.

✔ Compile and test.

6. Apply *Inline Method* [F] on every object selection method.

✔ Compile and test.

Example

The code sketch and the Motivation section already gave you an introduction to this example, which is inspired from an inventory management system. That system's Finder classes (AccountFinder, InvoiceFinder, ProductFinder, and so forth) eventually came to suffer from a Combinatorial Explosion smell (45), which necessitated the refactoring to Specification. It's worth noting that this does not reveal a problem with Finder classes: the point is that a time may come when a refactoring to Specification is justified.

I begin by studying the tests and code for a ProductFinder that is in need of this refactoring. I'll start with the test code. Before any test can run, I need a ProductRepository object that's filled with various Product objects and a ProductFinder object that knows about the ProductRepository:

```
public class ProductFinderTests extends TestCase...
    private ProductFinder finder;
```

```
private Product fireTruck =
   new Product("f1234", "Fire Truck",
      Color.red, 8.95f, ProductSize.MEDIUM);

private Product barbieClassic =
   new Product("b7654", "Barbie Classic",
      Color.yellow, 15.95f, ProductSize.SMALL);

private Product frisbee =
   new Product("f4321", "Frisbee",
      Color.pink, 9.99f, ProductSize.LARGE);

private Product baseball =
   new Product("b2343", "Baseball",
      Color.white, 8.95f, ProductSize.NOT_APPLICABLE);

private Product toyConvertible =
   new Product("p1112", "Toy Porsche Convertible",
      Color.red, 230.00f, ProductSize.NOT_APPLICABLE);

protected void setUp() {
   finder = new ProductFinder(createProductRepository());
}

private ProductRepository createProductRepository() {
   ProductRepository repository = new ProductRepository();
   repository.add(fireTruck);
   repository.add(barbieClassic);
   repository.add(frisbee);
   repository.add(baseball);
   repository.add(toyConvertible);
   return repository;
}
```

The "toy" products above work fine for test code. Of course, the production code uses real product objects, which are obtained using object-relational mapping logic.

Now I look at a few simple tests and the implementation code that satisfies them. The testFindByColor() method checks whether the ProductFinder.byColor(…) method correctly finds red toys, while testFindByPrice() checks whether Product-Finder.byPrice(…) correctly finds toys at a given price:

```
public class ProductFinderTests extends TestCase...
   public void testFindByColor() {
      List foundProducts = finder.byColor(Color.red);
      assertEquals("found 2 red products", 2, foundProducts.size());
      assertTrue("found fireTruck", foundProducts.contains(fireTruck));
      assertTrue(
         "found Toy Porsche Convertible",
         foundProducts.contains(toyConvertible));
   }
```

Replace Implicit Language with Interpreter

```
public void testFindByPrice() {
   List foundProducts = finder.byPrice(8.95f);
   assertEquals("found products that cost $8.95", 2, foundProducts.size());
   for (Iterator i = foundProducts.iterator(); i.hasNext();) {
      Product p = (Product) i.next();
      assertTrue(p.getPrice() == 8.95f);
   }
}
```

Here's the implementation code that satisfies these tests:

```
public class ProductFinder...
   private ProductRepository repository;

   public ProductFinder(ProductRepository repository) {
      this.repository = repository;
   }

   public List byColor(Color colorOfProductToFind) {
      List foundProducts = new ArrayList();
      Iterator products = repository.iterator();
      while (products.hasNext()) {
         Product product = (Product) products.next();
         if (product.getColor().equals(colorOfProductToFind))
            foundProducts.add(product);
      }
      return foundProducts;
   }
   public List byPrice(float priceLimit) {
      List foundProducts = new ArrayList();
      Iterator products = repository.iterator();
      while (products.hasNext()) {
         Product product = (Product) products.next();
         if (product.getPrice() == priceLimit)
            foundProducts.add(product);
      }
      return foundProducts;
   }
```

There's plenty of duplicate code in these two methods. I'll be getting rid of that duplication during this refactoring. Meanwhile, I explore some more tests and code that are involved in the Combinatorial Explosion problem. Below, one test is concerned with finding Product instances by color, size, and below a certain price, while the other test is concerned with finding Product instances by color and above a certain price:

```
public class ProductFinderTests extends TestCase...
   public void testFindByColorSizeAndBelowPrice() {
      List foundProducts =
         finder.byColorSizeAndBelowPrice(Color.red, ProductSize.SMALL, 10.00f);
```

```
        assertEquals(
          "found no small red products below $10.00",
          0,
          foundProducts.size());


        foundProducts =
          finder.byColorSizeAndBelowPrice(Color.red, ProductSize.MEDIUM, 10.00f);
        assertEquals(
          "found firetruck when looking for cheap medium red toys",
          fireTruck,
          foundProducts.get(0));
    }

    public void testFindBelowPriceAvoidingAColor() {
      List foundProducts =
        finder.belowPriceAvoidingAColor(9.00f, Color.white);
      assertEquals(
        "found 1 non-white product < $9.00",
        1,
        foundProducts.size());
      assertTrue("found fireTruck", foundProducts.contains(fireTruck));


      foundProducts = finder.belowPriceAvoidingAColor(9.00f, Color.red);
      assertEquals(
        "found 1 non-red product < $9.00",
        1,
        foundProducts.size());
      assertTrue("found baseball", foundProducts.contains(baseball));
    }
```

Here's how the implementation code looks for these tests:

```
public class ProductFinder...
    public List byColorSizeAndBelowPrice(Color color, int size, float price) {
      List foundProducts = new ArrayList();
      Iterator products = repository.iterator();
      while (products.hasNext()) {
        Product product = (Product) products.next();
        if (product.getColor() == color
            && product.getSize() == size
            && product.getPrice() < price)
          foundProducts.add(product);
      }
      return foundProducts;
    }
    public List belowPriceAvoidingAColor(float price, Color color) {
      List foundProducts = new ArrayList();
      Iterator products = repository.iterator();
      while (products.hasNext()) {
        Product product = (Product) products.next();
```

Replace Implicit Language with Interpreter

```
        if (product.getPrice() < price && product.getColor() != color)
            foundProducts.add(product);
    }
    return foundProducts;
}
```

Again, I see plenty of duplicate code because each of the specific finder methods iterates over the same repository and selects just those Product instances that match the specified criteria. I'm now ready to begin the refactoring.

1. The first step is to find an object selection method that relies on a criterion argument for its selection logic. The ProductFinder method byColor(Color color-OfProductToFind) meets this requirement:

Replace Implicit
Language with
Interpreter

```
public class ProductFinder...
    public List byColor(Color colorOfProductToFind) {
        List foundProducts = new ArrayList();
        Iterator products = repository.iterator();
        while (products.hasNext()) {
            Product product = (Product) products.next();
            if (product.getColor().equals(colorOfProductToFind))
                foundProducts.add(product);
        }
        return foundProducts;
    }
```

I create a concrete specification class for the criterion argument, Color colorOfProductToFind. I call this class ColorSpec. It needs to hold onto a Color field and provide a getter method for it:

```
public class ColorSpec {
    private Color colorOfProductToFind;

    public ColorSpec(Color colorOfProductToFind) {
        this.colorOfProductToFind = colorOfProductToFind;
    }

    public Color getColorOfProductToFind() {
        return colorOfProductToFind;
    }
}
```

Now I can add a variable of type ColorSpec to the byColor(…) method and replace the reference to the parameter, colorOfProductToFind, with a reference to the specification's getter method:

```
public List byColor(Color colorOfProductToFind) {
    ColorSpec spec = new ColorSpec(colorOfProductToFind);
    List foundProducts = new ArrayList();
```

```
Iterator products = repository.iterator();
while (products.hasNext()) {
    Product product = (Product) products.next();
    if (product.getColor().equals(spec.getColorOfProductToFind()))
        foundProducts.add(product);
}
return foundProducts;
}
```

After these changes, I compile and run my tests. Here's one such test:

```
public void testFindByColor() {
    List foundProducts = finder.byColor(Color.red);
    assertEquals("found 2 red products", 2, foundProducts.size());
    assertTrue("found fireTruck", foundProducts.contains(fireTruck));
    assertTrue("found Toy Porsche Convertible", foundProducts.contains(toyConvertible));

}
```

2. Now I'll apply *Extract Method* [F] to extract the conditional statement in the while loop to an isSatisfiedBy(…) method:

```
public List byColor(Color colorOfProductToFind) {
    ColorSpec spec = new ColorSpec(colorOfProductToFind);
    List foundProducts = new ArrayList();
    Iterator products = repository.iterator();
    while (products.hasNext()) {
        Product product = (Product) products.next();
        if (isSatisfiedBy(spec, product))
            foundProducts.add(product);
    }
    return foundProducts;
}

private boolean isSatisfiedBy(ColorSpec spec, Product product) {
    return product.getColor().equals(spec.getColorOfProductToFind());
}
```

The isSatisfiedBy(…) method can now be moved to ColorSpec by applying *Move Method* [F]:

```
public class ProductFinder...
    public List byColor(Color colorOfProductToFind) {
        ColorSpec spec = new ColorSpec(colorOfProductToFind);
        List foundProducts = new ArrayList();
        Iterator products = repository.iterator();
        while (products.hasNext()) {
            Product product = (Product) products.next();
            if (spec.isSatisfiedBy(product))
                foundProducts.add(product);
        }
        return foundProducts;
    }
```

```
public class ColorSpec...
    public boolean isSatisfiedBy(Product product) {
        return product.getColor().equals(getColorOfProductToFind());
    }
```

Finally, I create a specification superclass by applying *Extract Superclass* [F] on ColorSpec:

```
public abstract class Spec {
    public boolean isSatisfiedBy(Product product);
}
```

Replace Implicit
Language with
Interpreter

I make ColorSpec extend this class:

```
public class ColorSpec extends Spec...
```

I compile and test to see that Product instances can still be selected by a given color correctly. Everything works fine.

3. Now I repeat steps 1 and 2 for similar object selection methods. This includes methods that work with criteria (i.e., multiple pieces of criterion). For example, the byColorAndBelowPrice(...) method accepts two arguments that act as criteria for selecting Product instances out of the repository:

```
public List byColorAndBelowPrice(Color color, float price) {
    List foundProducts = new ArrayList();
    Iterator products = repository.iterator();
    while (products.hasNext()) {
        Product product = (Product)products.next();
        if (product.getPrice() < price && product.getColor() == color)
            foundProducts.add(product);
    }
    return foundProducts;
}
```

By implementing steps 1 and 2, I end up with the BelowPriceSpec class:

```
public class BelowPriceSpec extends Spec {
    private float priceThreshold;

    public BelowPriceSpec(float priceThreshold) {
        this.priceThreshold = priceThreshold;
    }
    public boolean isSatisfiedBy(Product product) {
        return product.getPrice() < getPriceThreshold();
    }
    public float getPriceThreshold() {
        return priceThreshold;
    }
}
```

Now I can create a new version of byColorAndBelowPrice(…) that works with the two concrete specifications:

```
public List byColorAndBelowPrice(Color color, float price) {
   ColorSpec colorSpec = new ColorSpec(color);
   BelowPriceSpec priceSpec = new BelowPriceSpec(price);
   List foundProducts = new ArrayList();
   Iterator products = repository.iterator();
   while (products.hasNext()) {
      Product product = (Product)products.next();
      if (colorSpec.isSatisfiedBy(product) &&
         priceSpec.isSatisfiedBy(product))
         foundProducts.add(product);
   }
   return foundProducts;
}
```

Replace Implicit
Language with
Interpreter

4. The byColorAndBelowPrice(…) method uses criteria (color and price) in its object selection logic. I'd like to make this method, and others like it, work with a composite specification rather than with individual specifications. To do that, I'll implement a modified version of step 1 and an unmodified version of step 2. Here's how byColorAndBelowPrice(…) looks after step 1:

```
public List byColorAndBelowPrice(Color color, float price) {
   ColorSpec colorSpec = new ColorSpec(color);
   BelowPriceSpec priceSpec = new BelowPriceSpec(price);
   AndSpec spec = new AndSpec(colorSpec, priceSpec);

   List foundProducts = new ArrayList();
   Iterator products = repository.iterator();
   while (products.hasNext()) {
      Product product = (Product)products.next();
      if (spec.getAugend().isSatisfiedBy(product) &&
         spec.getAddend().isSatisfiedBy(product))
         foundProducts.add(product);
   }
   return foundProducts;
}
```

The AndSpec class looks like this:

```
public class AndSpec {
   private Spec augend, addend;

   public AndSpec(Spec augend, Spec addend) {
      this.augend = augend;
      this.addend = addend;
   }
```

```
    public Spec getAddend() {
        return addend;
    }
    public Spec getAugend() {
        return augend;
    }
}
```

After implementing step 2, the code now looks like this:

```
public List byColorAndBelowPrice(Color color, float price) {
    ...
    AndSpec spec = new AndSpec(colorSpec, priceSpec);

    while (products.hasNext()) {
        Product product = (Product)products.next();
        if (spec.isSatisfiedBy(product))
            foundProducts.add(product);
    }
    return foundProducts;
}

public class AndSpec extends Spec...
    public boolean isSatisfiedBy(Product product) {
        return getAugend().isSatisfiedBy(product) &&
            getAddend().isSatisfiedBy(product);
    }
```

I now have a composite specification that handles an AND operation to join two concrete specifications. In another object selection method called belowPriceAvoidingAColor(…), I have more complicated conditional logic:

```
public class ProductFinder...
    public List belowPriceAvoidingAColor(float price, Color color) {
        List foundProducts = new ArrayList();
        Iterator products = repository.iterator();
        while (products.hasNext()) {
            Product product = (Product) products.next();
            if (product.getPrice() < price && product.getColor() != color)
                foundProducts.add(product);
        }
        return foundProducts;
    }
```

This code requires two composite specifications (AndProductSpecification and NotProductSpecification) and two concrete specifications. The conditional logic in the method can be portrayed as shown in the diagram on the following page.

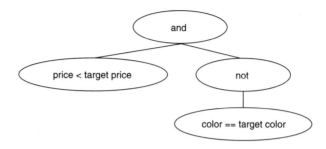

My first task is to produce a NotSpec:

```
public class NotSpec extends Spec {
   private Spec specToNegate;

   public NotSpec(Spec specToNegate) {
      this.specToNegate = specToNegate;
   }
   public boolean isSatisfiedBy(Product product) {
      return !specToNegate.isSatisfiedBy(product);
   }
}
```

Then I modify the conditional logic to use AndSpec and NotSpec:

```
public List belowPriceAvoidingAColor(float price, Color color) {
   AndSpec spec =
      new AndSpec(
         new BelowPriceSpec(price),
         new NotSpec(
            new ColorSpec(color)
         )
      );

   List foundProducts = new ArrayList();
   Iterator products = repository.iterator();
   while (products.hasNext()) {
      Product product = (Product) products.next();
      if (spec.isSatisfiedBy(product))
         foundProducts.add(product);
   }
   return foundProducts;
}
```

That takes care of the belowPriceAvoidingAColor(…) method. I continue replacing logic in the object selection methods until all of them use either one concrete specification or one composite specification.

5. The bodies of all object selection methods are now identical, except for the specification creation logic:

```
Spec spec = ...create some spec
List foundProducts = new ArrayList();
Iterator products = repository.iterator();
while (products.hasNext()) {
    Product product = (Product) products.next();
    if (spec.isSatisfiedBy(product))
        foundProducts.add(product);
}
return foundProducts;
```

> **Replace Implicit Language with Interpreter**

This means I can apply *Extract Method* [F] on everything except the specification creation logic in any object selection method to produce a selectBy(…) method. I decide to perform this step on the belowPrice(…) method:

```
public List belowPrice(float price) {
    BelowPriceSpec spec = new BelowPriceSpec(price);
    return selectBy(spec);
}

private List selectBy(ProductSpecification spec) {
    List foundProducts = new ArrayList();
    Iterator products = repository.iterator();
    while (products.hasNext()) {
        Product product = (Product)products.next();
        if (spec.isSatisfiedBy(product))
            foundProducts.add(product);
    }
    return foundProducts;
}
```

I compile and test to make sure this works. Now I make remaining Product-Finder object selection methods call the same selectBy(…) method. For example, here's the call to belowPriceAvoidingAColor(…):

```
public List belowPriceAvoidingAColor(float price, Color color) {
    ProductSpec spec =
        new AndProduct(
            new BelowPriceSpec(price),
            new NotSpec(
                new ColorSpec(color)
            )
        );
    return selectBy(spec);
}
```

6. Now every object selection method can be inlined using *Inline Method* [F]:

```
public class ProductFinder...
    public List byColor(Color colorOfProductToFind) {
        ColorSpec spec = new ColorSpec(colorOfProductToFind));
        return selectBy(spec);
    }
```

```
public class ProductFinderTests extends TestCase...
    public void testFindByColor()...
        List foundProducts = finder.byColor(Color.red);
        ColorSpec spec = new ColorSpec(Color.red));
        List foundProducts = finder.selectBy(spec);
```

Replace Implicit
Language with
Interpreter

I compile and test to make sure that everything's working. Then I conclude this refactoring by repeating step 6 for every object selection method.

Chapter 9

Protection

A refactoring that improves the protection of existing code must do so in a way that doesn't alter the behavior of the existing code. All three refactorings in this section do just that. Your motivation for applying them may be to improve protection or it may be a standard refactoring motivation, such as to reduce duplication or to simplify or clarify code.

Replace Type Code with Class (286) helps protect a field from assignments to incorrect or unsafe values. This is particularly important when a field controls what behavior gets executed at runtime because an incorrect assignment could put an object into an invalid state. *Replace Type Code with Class (286)* uses a class rather than an enum to constrain what values may be assigned to a field. Does an enum provide a better way to implement this refactoring or even render this refactoring out of date? It does not. The main difference between a class and an enum is that you can add behavior to a class. This is important because the class produced during *Replace Type Code with Class (286)* may need to be extended with behavior as you apply a sequence of refactorings. This is exactly what occurs during the refactoring *Replace State-Altering Conditionals with State (166)*.

Limit Instantiation with Singleton (296) is useful when you want to control how many instances of a class can be instantiated. Typical motivations for applying this refactoring are to reduce memory usage or improve performance. A poor motivation for refactoring to a Singleton [DP] is to give a piece of code access to hard-to-reach information (see *Inline Singleton, 114,* for a discussion of this). In general, it's best to apply *Limit Instantiation with Singleton (296)* only when a profiler informs you that doing so is worthwhile.

Introduce Null Object (301) is a refactoring that helps transform how code is protected from null values. If you have a lot of the same conditional logic that checks for the same null value, you can likely simplify and condense the code by refactoring it to use a Null Object [Woolf].

Replace Type Code with Class

A field's type (e.g., a String or int) fails to protect it
from unsafe assignments and invalid equality comparisons.

*Constrain the assignments and equality comparisons
by making the type of the field a class.*

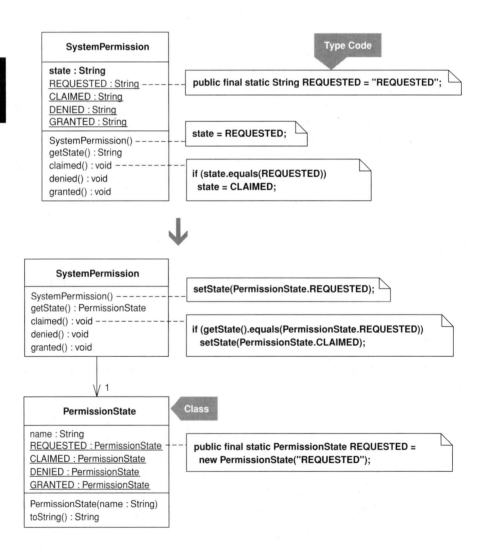

Motivation

A primary motivation for refactoring from a type code to a class is to make code type-safe. One way to do that is to constrain the possible values that may be assigned to or equated with a field or variable. Consider the following type-unsafe code:

```
public void testDefaultsToPermissionRequested() {
   SystemPermission permission = new SystemPermission();
   assertEquals(permission.REQUESTED, permission.state());
   assertEquals("REQUESTED", permission.state());
}
```

This code creates a SystemPermission object. The constructor for this object sets its state field equal to the SystemPermission.REQUESTED state:

Replace Type
Code with
Class

```
public SystemPermission() {
   state = REQUESTED;
}
```

Other methods within SystemPermission assign state to system permission states such as GRANTED and DENIED. Given that each of these state types was defined using String constants (like public final static String REQUESTED = "REQUESTED") and state was defined as type String, the two assert statements above both pass because the state field, which is accessed via the call to permission.state(), is considered equal to both SystemPermission.REQUESTED and the String, "REQUESTED."

What's the problem with this? The problem is that using a String value in this context is error prone. For example, what if an assert statement were accidently written like this:

```
assertEquals("REQEUSTED", permission.state());
```

Would that assert pass? No, for the String, "REQEUSTED", has been accidently misspelled! Using a String as the type for SystemPermission's state field also leaves it exposed to errors like this one:

```
public class SystemPermission...
   public void setState(String newState){
      state = newState;
   }
```

```
permission.setState("REQESTED"); // another misspelling of "REQUESTED"
```

Here, the misspelling of "REQESTED" will not cause a compiler error but *will* allow a SystemPermission instance to enter an invalid state. Once it enters that invalid state, SystemPermission's state transition logic won't allow it to ever leave that invalid state.

Using a class instead of a String to represent SystemPermission's state field will reduce such errors because it ensures that all assignments and comparisons are performed using a family of type-safe constants. These constants are considered to be type-safe because their type, which is a class, protects them from being impersonated by other constants. For example, in the following code, the type-safe constant, REQUESTED, lives in one class and can't be mistaken for any other value:

```
public class PermissionState {
    public final static PermissionState REQUESTED = new PermissionState();
```

Clients that want to perform assignment or equality statements using REQUESTED can only obtain a reference to it by calling PermissionState.REQUESTED.

Using a class to obtain type safety for a family of constants was described by Joshua Bloch as the Type-Safe Enum pattern [Bloch]. Joshua does an excellent job of explaining this pattern and how to deal with the serialization/deserialization issues associated with it. Languages that provide native support for what are commonly called "enums" might seem to render this refactoring useless. That isn't the case, for after you perform this refactoring, you'll often extend your code to support more behavior, which isn't possible with enums. For example, the first step in the mechanics for *Replace State-Altering Conditionals with State (166)* builds upon this refactoring but could not build upon a language-based enum.

Replace Type Code with Class

Benefits and Liabilities

+ Provides better protection from invalid assignments and comparisons.
− Requires more code than using unsafe type does.

Mechanics

In the steps below a *type-unsafe constant* is a constant defined using a primitive or non-class-based type, such as a String or int.

1. Identify a *type-unsafe field*, a field declared as a primitive or non-class-based type that is assigned to or compared against a family of type-unsafe constants. Self-encapsulate the type-unsafe field by applying *Self Encapsulate Field* [F].

   ✔ Compile and test.

2. Create a *new class*, a concrete class that will soon replace the type used for the type-unsafe field. Name this class after the kinds of types it will store. For the moment, don't provide any constructor for the new class.

3. Choose a constant value that the type-unsafe field is assigned to and/or compared against and define a new version of this constant in your new class by creating a constant that is an instance of the new class. In Java, it's common to declare this constant to be `public final static`.

   Repeat this step for all constant values assigned to or compared against the type-unsafe field.

   ✔ Compile.

   You've now defined a family of constants in the new class. If it is important to prevent clients from adding members to that family of constants, declare a single private constructor for the new class or, if your language allows it, mark the new class as `final`.

4. In the class that declared the type-unsafe field, create a *type-safe field*, a field whose type is the new class. Create a setting method for it.

5. Wherever an assignment is made to the type-unsafe field, add a similar assignment statement to the type-safe field, using the appropriate constant in the new class.

   ✔ Compile.

6. Change the getter method for the type-unsafe field so that its return value is obtained from the type-safe field. This requires making the constants in the new class capable of returning the correct value.

   ✔ Compile and test.

7. In the class that declared the type-unsafe field, delete the type-unsafe field, the setter method for it, and all calls to the setting method.

   ✔ Compile and test.

8. Find all references to the type-unsafe constants and replace them with calls to the corresponding constant in the new class. As part of this step, change the getter method for the type-unsafe field so its return type is the new class and make all changes necessary to callers of the revised getter method.

   Equality logic that once relied on primitives will now rely on comparing instances of the new class. Your language may provide a default way to do such equality logic. If not, write code to ensure that the equality logic works correctly with new class instances.

✔ Compile and test.

Delete the now unused type-unsafe constants.

Example

This example, which was shown in the code sketch at the beginning of this refactoring and mentioned in the Motivation section, deals with handling permission requests to access software systems. We'll begin by looking at relevant parts of the class, SystemPermission:

Replace Type
Code with
Class

```java
public class SystemPermission {
   private String state;
   private boolean granted;

   public final static String REQUESTED = "REQUESTED";
   public final static String CLAIMED = "CLAIMED";
   public final static String DENIED = "DENIED";
   public final static String GRANTED = "GRANTED";

   public SystemPermission() {
      state = REQUESTED;
      granted = false;
   }

   public void claimed() {
      if (state.equals(REQUESTED))
         state = CLAIMED;
   }

   public void denied() {
      if (state.equals(CLAIMED))
         state = DENIED;
   }

   public void granted() {
      if (!state.equals(CLAIMED)) return;
      state = GRANTED;
      granted = true;
   }

   public boolean isGranted() {
      return granted;
   }

   public String getState() {
      return state;
   }
}
```

1. The type-unsafe field in SystemPermission is called state. It is assigned to and compared against a family of String constants also defined within System-Permission. The goal is to make state type-safe by making its type be a class rather than a String.

    I begin by self-encapsulating state:

```
public class SystemPermission...
    public SystemPermission() {
        setState(REQUESTED);
        granted = false;
    }

    public void claimed() {
        if (getState().equals(REQUESTED))
            setState(CLAIMED);
    }

    private void setState(String state) {
        this.state = state;
    }

    public String getState() {  // note: this method already existed
        return state;
    }

    // etc.
```

Replace Type Code with Class

This is a trivial change, and my compiler and tests are happy with it.

2. I create a new class and call it PermissionState because it will soon represent the state of a SystemPermission instance.

```
public class PermissionState {
}
```

3. I choose one constant value that the type-unsafe field is assigned to or compared against and I create a constant representation for it in PermissionState. I do this by declaring a public final static in PermissionState that is an instance of PermissionState:

```
public final class PermissionState {
    public final static PermissionState REQUESTED = new PermissionState();
}
```

    I repeat this step for each constant in SystemPermission, yielding the following code:

```
public class PermissionState {
    public final static PermissionState REQUESTED = new PermissionState();
    public final static PermissionState CLAIMED = new PermissionState();
```

```
    public final static PermissionState GRANTED = new PermissionState();
    public final static PermissionState DENIED = new PermissionState();
}
```

The compiler accepts this new code.

Now I must decide whether I want to prevent clients from extending or instantiating PermissionState in order to ensure that the only instances of it are its own four constants. In this case, I don't need such a rigorous level of type safety, so I don't define a private constructor or use the final keyword for the new class.

4. Next, I create a type-safe field inside SystemPermission, using the Permission-State type. I also create a setter method for it:

Replace Type Code with Class

```
public class SystemPermission...
    private String state;
    private PermissionState permission;

    private void setState(PermissionState permission) {
        this.permission = permission;
    }
```

5. Now I must find all assignment statements to the type-unsafe field, state, and make similar assignment statements to the type-safe field, permission:

```
public class SystemPermission...
    public SystemPermission() {
        setState(REQUESTED);
        setState(PermissionState.REQUESTED);
        granted = false;
    }

    public void claimed() {
        if (getState().equals(REQUESTED)) {
            setState(CLAIMED);
            setState(PermissionState.CLAIMED);
        }
    }

    public void denied() {
        if (getState().equals(CLAIMED)) {
            setState(DENIED);
            setState(PermissionState.DENIED);
        }
    }

    public void granted() {
        if (!getState().equals(CLAIMED))
            return;
```

```
      setState(GRANTED);
      setState(PermissionState.GRANTED);
      granted = true;
   }
```

I confirm that the compiler is OK with these changes.

6. Next, I want to change the getter method for state to return a value obtained from the *type-safe field*, permission. Because the getter method for state returns a String, I'll have to make permission capable of returning a String as well. My first step is to modify PermissionState to support a toString() method that returns the name of each constant:

```
public class PermissionState {
   private final String name;

   private PermissionState(String name) {
      this.name = name;
   }

   public String toString() {
      return name;
   }

   public final static PermissionState REQUESTED = new PermissionState("REQUESTED");
   public final static PermissionState CLAIMED = new PermissionState("CLAIMED");
   public final static PermissionState GRANTED = new PermissionState("GRANTED");
   public final static PermissionState DENIED = new PermissionState("DENIED");
}
```

Replace Type Code with Class

I can now update the getter method for state:

```
public class SystemPermission...
   public String getState() {
      return state;
      return permission.toString();
   }
```

The compiler and tests confirm that everything is still working.

7. I can now delete the type-unsafe field, state, SystemPermission calls to its private setter method, and the setter method itself:

```
public class SystemPermission...
   private String state;
   private PermissionState permission;
   private boolean granted;

   public SystemPermission() {
      setState(REQUESTED);
```

```
        setState(PermissionState.REQUESTED);
        granted = false;
    }

    public void claimed() {
        if (getState().equals(REQUESTED)) {
            setState(CLAIMED);
            setState(PermissionState.CLAIMED);
        }
    }

    public void denied() {
        if (getState().equals(CLAIMED)) {
            setState(DENIED);
            setState(PermissionState.DENIED);
        }
    }

    public void granted() {
        if (!getState().equals(CLAIMED))
            return;
        setState(GRANTED);
        setState(PermissionState.GRANTED);
        granted = true;
    }

    private void setState(String state) {
        this.state = state;
    }
```

I test that SystemPermission still works as usual. It does.

8. Now I replace all code that references SystemPermission's type-unsafe constants with code that references PermissionState's contant values. For example, SystemPermission's claimed() method still references the "REQUESTED" type-unsafe constant:

```
public class SystemPermission...
    public void claimed() {
        if (getState().equals(REQUESTED))  // equality logic with type-unsafe constant
            setState(PermissionState.CLAIMED);
    }
```

I update this code as follows:

```
public class SystemPermission...
    public PermissionState getState() {
        return permission.toString();
    }
```

(margin) **Replace Type Code with Class**

```
   public void claimed() {
      if (getState().equals(PermissionState.REQUESTED)) {
         setState(PermissionState.CLAIMED);
   }
```

I make similar changes throughout SystemPermission. In addition, I update all callers on getState() so that they now work exclusively with Permission-State constants. For example, here's a test method that requires updating:

```
public class TestStates...
   public void testClaimedBy() {
      SystemPermission permission = new SystemPermission();
      permission.claimed();
      assertEquals(SystemPermission.CLAIMED, permission.getState());
   }
```

I change this code as follows:

```
public class TestStates...
   public void testClaimedBy() {
      SystemPermission permission = new SystemPermission();
      permission.claimed();
      assertEquals(PermissionState.CLAIMED, permission.getState());
   }
```

After making similar changes throughout the code, I compile and test to confirm that the new type-safe equality logic works correctly.

Finally, I can safely delete SystemPermission's type-unsafe constants because they are no longer being used:

```
public class SystemPermission...
   public final static String REQUESTED = "REQUESTED";
   public final static String CLAIMED = "CLAIMED";
   public final static String DENIED = "DENIED";
   public final static String GRANTED = "GRANTED";
```

Now SystemPermission's assignments to its permission field and all equality comparions with its permission field are type-safe.

Limit Instantiation with Singleton

Your code creates multiple instances of an object, and
that uses too much memory or slows system performance.

Replace the multiple instances with a Singleton.

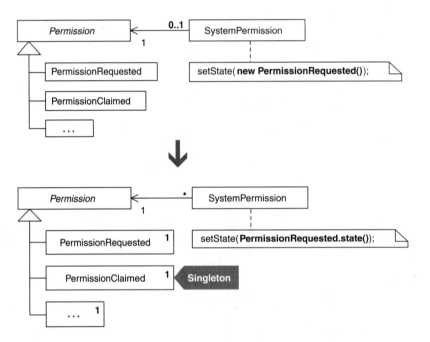

Motivation

If you want to be a good software designer, don't optimize code prematurely.
Prematurely optimized code is harder to refactor than code that hasn't been
optimized. In general, you'll discover more alternatives for improving your
code before it has been optimized than after.

If you use the Singleton [DP] pattern out of habit, because it "makes your
code more efficient," you're prematurely optimizing. You suffer from *Singletonitis*

and had better follow the advice in *Inline Singleton (114)*. On the other hand, sometimes it's a good decision to refactor to a Singleton, as in the following scenario.

- Users of your system are complaining about system performance.

- Your profiler tells you that you can improve performance by not instantiating certain objects over and over again.

- The objects you want to share have no state or contain state that is sharable.

A colleague and I profiled a system that handles security permissions. The system uses the State [DP] pattern (see *Replace State-Altering Conditionals with State, 166*). Every state transition leads to the instantiation of a new State object. We profiled the system to check memory usage and performance. While the instantiation of State objects wasn't the biggest bottleneck in the system, it did contribute to slow performance under a heavy load.

Limit
Instantiation
with
Singleton

Based on this research, we determined that it made sense to refactor to a Singleton in order to limit the instantiation of stateless State objects. And that's the general idea behind this refactoring: wait for a good reason to limit instantiation and when you find one, then refactor to a Singleton. Of course, we profiled after implementing the Singleton, and memory usage was much improved.

For other reasons to refactor to a Singleton that don't involve improving performance, see the wise words provided by Kent Beck, Ward Cunningham, and Martin Fowler earlier in this catalog at *Inline Singleton (114)*.

Benefits and Liabilities

+ Improves performance.
- Is easily accessible from anywhere. In many cases, this may indicate a design flaw (see *Inline Singleton, 114*).
- Is not useful when an object has state that can't be shared.

Mechanics

Before you perform this refactoring, make sure the object you want to turn into a Singleton has no state or has state that is sharable. Because most classes that end up becoming Singletons have one constructor, these mechanics assume you have one constructor on your class.

1. Identify a *multiple instance class*, a class that gets instantiated more than once by one or more clients. Apply the mechanics from *Replace Constructors with Creation Methods (57)* even though your class has only one constructor. The return type for your new Creation Method should be the multiple instance class.

   ✔ Compile and test.

2. Declare a *singleton field*, a private static field of type multiple instance class in the multiple instance class and, if possible, initialize it to an instance of the multiple instance class.

   It may not be possible to initialize this field because to do so, you need arguments passed by a client at runtime. In that case, simply define the field and don't initialize it.

   ✔ Compile.

3. Make your Creation Method return the value in the singleton field. If it must be lazily instantiated, do that lazy instantiation in the Creation Method, based on whatever parameters are passed in.

   ✔ Compile and test.

Example

This example is based on the security code example found in the refactoring *Replace State-Altering Conditionals with State (166)*. If you study the code produced after applying that refactoring, you'll find that each State instance is a Singleton. However, these Singleton State instances weren't created for performance reasons; they resulted from performing the refactoring *Replace Type Code with Class (286)*.

When I initially refactored to the State pattern on the security code project, I did not apply *Replace Type Code with Class (286)*. I wasn't yet aware of how much that refactoring simplifies the later steps in refactoring to the State pattern. My earlier approach to the State refactoring involved instantiating Permission subclasses each time they were needed, paying no regard to the Singleton pattern.

On that project, my colleague and I profiled our code and found several places where it could be optimized. One of those places involved the frequent instantiation of the state classes. So, as part of an overall effort to improve performance, the code to repeatedly instantiate the Permission subclasses was refactored to use the Singleton pattern. I describe the steps here.

1. There are six State classes, each of which is a multiple instance class because clients instantiate them multiple times. In this example, I'll work with the PermissionRequested class, which looks like this:

```
public class PermissionRequested extends Permission {
   public static final String NAME= "REQUESTED";

   public String name() {
      return NAME;
   }

   public void claimedBy(SystemAdmin admin, SystemPermission permission) {
      permission.willBeHandledBy(admin);
      permission.setState(new PermissionClaimed());
   }
}
```

Limit
Instantiation
with
Singleton

PermissionRequested doesn't define a constructor because it uses Java's default constructor. Because the first step in the mechanics is to convert its constructor(s) to Creation Methods, I define a Creation Method like so:

```
public class PermissionRequested extends Permission...
   public static Permission state() {
      return new PermissionRequested();
   }
```

You'll notice that I use Permission as the return type for this Creation Method. I do that because I want all client code to interact with State subclasses via the interface of their superclass. I also update all callers of the constructor to now call the Creation Method:

```
public class SystemPermission...
   private Permission state;
   public SystemPermission(SystemUser requestor, SystemProfile profile) {
      this.requestor = requestor;
      this.profile = profile;
      state = new PermissionRequested();
      state = PermissionRequested.state();
      ...
   }
```

I compile and test to make sure that this trivial change didn't break anything.

2. Now I create the singleton field, a private static field of type Permission in PermisionRequested, and initialize it to an instance of PermissionRequested:

```
public class PermissionRequested extends Permission...
   private static Permission state = new PermissionRequested();
```

I compile to confirm that my syntax is correct.

3. Finally, I change the Creation Method, state(), to return the value in the state field:

```
public class PermissionRequested extends Permission...
   public static Permission state() {
      return state;
}
```

Limit Instantiation with Singleton

I compile and test once again and everything works. I now repeat these steps for the remaining State classes until all of them are Singletons. At that point, I run the profiler to check how memory usage and performance have been affected. Hopefully, things have improved. If not, I may decide to undo these steps, as I'd always rather work with regular objects than Singletons.

Introduce Null Object

Logic for dealing with a null field or variable
is duplicated throughout your code.

*Replace the null logic with a Null Object, an object
that provides the appropriate null behavior.*

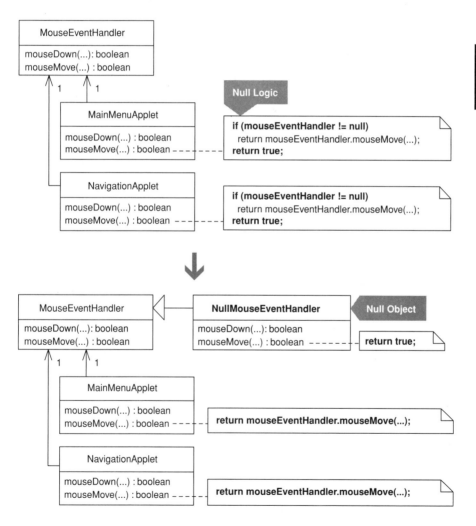

Motivation

If a client calls a method on a field or variable that is null, an exception may be raised, a system may crash, or similar problems may occur. To protect our systems from such unwanted behavior, we write checks to prevent null fields or variables from being called and, if necessary, specify alternative behavior to execute when nulls are encountered:

```
if (someObject != null)
    someObject.doSomething();
else
    performAlternativeBehavior();
```

**Introduce
Null Object**

Repeating such null logic in one or two places in a system isn't a problem, but repeating it in multiple places bloats a system with unnecessary code. Compared with code that is free of null logic, code that is full of it generally takes longer to comprehend and requires more thinking about how to extend. Null logic also fails to provide null protection for new code. So if new code is written and programmers forget to include null logic for it, null errors can begin to occur.

The *Null Object* pattern[1] provides a solution to such problems. It removes the need to check whether a field or variable is null by making it possible to *always* call the field or variable safely. The trick is to assign the field or variable to the right object at the right time. When a field or variable can be null, you can make it refer to an instance of a Null Object, which provides do-nothing, default, or harmless behavior. Later, the field or variable can be assigned to something other than a Null Object. Until that happens, all invocations safely route through the Null Object.

The introduction of a Null Object into a system ought to shrink code size or at least keep it even. If its implementation significantly increases the number of lines of code compared with just using null logic, that's a good sign that you don't need a Null Object. Kent Beck tells a story about this in his book *Test-Driven Development* [Beck, TDD]. He once suggested refactoring to a Null Object to his programming partner, Erich Gamma, who quickly calculated the difference in lines of code and explained how refactoring to a Null Object

---

1. Bruce Anderson aptly named this pattern *active nothing* [Anderson] because a Null Object actively performs behavior that does nothing. Martin Fowler described how a Null Object is an example of a broader pattern called Special Case [Fowler, PEAA]. Ralph Johnson and Bobby Woolf described how null versions of patterns like Strategy [DP], Proxy [DP], Iterator [DP], and others are often used to eliminate null checks [Woolf].

would actually add many more lines of code than they already had with their null logic.

Java's Abstract Window Toolkit (AWT) could have benefited from using a Null Object. Some of its components, like panels or dialog boxes, can contain widgets that get laid out using a layout manager (like FlowLayout, GridLayout, and so forth). Code that dispatched layout requests to a layout manager was filled with checks for a null layout manager (if (layoutManager != null)). A better design would have been to use a NullLayout as the default layout manager for all components that used layout managers. If the default layout manager for these components was a NullLayout, the code that dispatched requests to the layout manager could have done so without caring whether it was talking to a NullLayout manager or a real layout manager.

The existence of a Null Object doesn't guarantee that null logic won't be written. For example, if a programmer isn't aware that a Null Object is already protecting the code from nulls, he or she may write null logic for code that won't ever be null. Finally, if a programmer expects a null to be returned under certain conditions and writes important code to handle that situation, a Null Object implementation could cause unexpected behavior.

My version of this refactoring extends Martin Fowler's *Introduce Null Object* [F] by supplying mechanics to deal with a common situation: a class is sprinkled with null logic for a field because an instance of the class may attempt to use the field before the field has been assigned to a non-null value. Given such code, the mechanics to refactor to a Null Object are different from those defined in Martin's mechanics for this refactoring.

Null Objects are often (though not always) implemented by subclassing or by implementing an interface, as shown in the following diagram.

Introduce Null Object

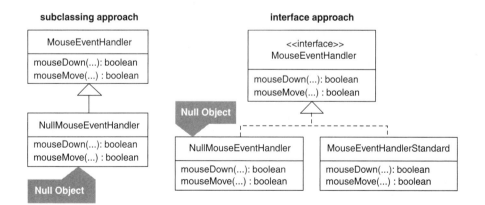

Creating a Null Object by subclassing involves overriding all inherited public methods to provide the appropriate null behavior. A risk associated with this approach is that if a new method gets added to the superclass, programmers must remember to override the method with null behavior in the Null Object. If they forget to do this, the Null Object will inherit implementation logic that could cause unwanted behavior at runtime. Making a Null Object implement an interface rather than being a subclass removes this risk.

Introduce Null Object

Benefits and Liabilities

+ Prevents null errors without duplicating null logic.
+ Simplifies code by minimizing null tests.
− Complicates a design when a system needs few null tests.
− Can yield redundant null tests if programmers are unaware of a Null Object implementation.
− Complicates maintenance. Null Objects that have a superclass must override all newly inherited public methods.

Mechanics

These mechanics assume you have the same null logic scattered throughout your code because a field or local variable may be referenced when it is still null. If your null logic exists for any other reason, consider applying Martin Fowler's mechanics for *Introduce Null Object* [F]. The term *source class* in the following steps refers to the class that you'd like to protect from nulls.

1. Create a *null object* by applying *Extract Subclass* [F] on the source class or by making your new class implement the interface implemented by the source class. If you decide to make your null object implement an interface, but that interface doesn't yet exist, create it by applying *Extract Interface* [F] on the source class.

   ✔ Compile.

2. Look for a *null check* (client code that invokes a method on an instance of the source class if it is not null, or performs alternative behavior if it is null). Overide the invoked method in the null object so it implements the alternative behavior.

   ✔ Compile.

3. Repeat step 2 for other null checks associated with the source class.

4. Find a class that contains one or more occurrences of the null check and initialize the field or local variable that is referenced in the null check to an instance of the null object. Perform this initialization at the earliest possible time during the lifetime of an instance of the class (e.g., upon instantiation).

   This code should not affect pre-existing code that assigns the field or local variable to an instance of the source class. The new code simply performs an assignment to a null object prior to any other assignments.

   ✔ Compile.

5. In the class you selected in step 4, remove every occurrence of the null check.

   ✔ Compile and test.

**Introduce
Null Object**

6. Repeat steps 4 and 5 for every class with one or more occurrences of the null check.

If your system creates many instances of the null object, you may want to use a profiler to determine whether it would make sense to apply *Limit Instantiation with Singleton (296)*.

Example

At a time when most of the world used either Netscape 2 or 3 or Internet Explorer 3 (all of which contained Java version 1.0), my company won a bid to create the Java version of a well-known music and television Web site. The site featured applets with many clickable menus and submenus, animated promotions, music news, and lots of cool graphics. The main Web page featured a frame that was divided into three sections, two of which contained applets.

Main Menu Applet	
HTML Content	Navigation Applet

The company's staff needed to easily control how the applets behaved when users interacted with them. Staff members wanted to control applet behavior without having to call programmers every time they needed to change a piece of functionality. We were able to accommodate their needs by using the Command pattern [DP] and by creating and using a custom mouse event handler class called MouseEventHandler. Instances of MouseEventHandler could be configured (via a script) to execute Commands whenever users moved their mouse over or clicked on regions within image maps.

Introduce
Null Object

Background for the Example: Mouse Events in Java 1.0

In Java 1.0, the mouse event model for Java applets relied on inheritance. If you wanted an applet to receive and handle mouse events, you would subclass java.applet.Applet and override the mouse event methods you needed, as shown in the following diagram.

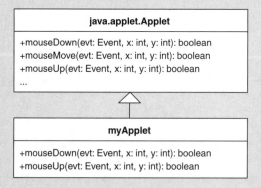

Once your applet was instantiated and running on a Web page, its mouse event methods would be called in response to mouse movements or clicks by a user.

The code worked perfectly except for one problem. During start-up, our applets would load into a browser window and initialize themselves. Part of the initialization process included getting MouseEventHandler objects instantiated and configured. To inform each MouseEventHandler instance about which areas of an applet were clickable and what Commands to run when those areas were clicked, we needed to read data and pass it to each instance. While loading that data didn't take a lot of time, it did leave a window of time in which our Mouse-

EventHandler instances weren't ready to receive mouse events. If a user happened to move or click the mouse on an applet before our custom mouse event handlers were fully instantiated and configured, the browser would bark errors onto the console and the applets would become unstable.

There was an easy fix: find every place where MouseEventHandler instances could be called when they were still null (i.e., not yet instantiated) and write code to insulate them from such calls. This solved the start-up problem, yet we were unhappy with the new design. Now, numerous classes in our system featured an abundance of null checks:

```
public class NavigationApplet extends Applet...
  public boolean mouseMove(Event event, int x, int y) {
    if (mouseEventHandler != null)
      return mouseEventHandler.mouseMove(graphicsContext, event, x, y );
    return true;
  }

  public boolean mouseDown(Event event, int x, int y) {
    if (mouseEventHandler != null)
      return mouseEventHandler.mouseDown(graphicsContext, event, x, y );
    return true;
  }

  public boolean mouseUp(Event event, int x, int y) {
    if (mouseEventHandler != null)
      return mouseEventHandler.mouseUp(graphicsContext, event, x, y );
    return true;
  }

  public boolean mouseExit(Event event, int x, int y) {
    if (mouseEventHandler != null)
      return mouseEventHandler.mouseExit(graphicsContext, event, x, y );
    return true;
  }
```

Introduce
Null Object

To remove the null checks, we refactored the applets so they used a NullMouseEventHandler at start-up and then switched to using a MouseEventHandler instance when one was ready. Here are the steps we followed to make this change.

1. We applied *Extract Subclass* [F] to define NullMouseEventHandler, a subclass of our own mouse event handler:

```
public class NullMouseEventHandler extends MouseEventHandler {
  public NullMouseEventHandler(Context context) {
    super(context);
  }
}
```

That code compiled just fine, so we moved on.

2. Next, we found a null check, like this one:

```
public class NavigationApplet extends Applet...
  public boolean mouseMove(Event event, int x, int y) {
    if (mouseEventHandler != null)  // null check
      return mouseEventHandler.mouseMove(graphicsContext, event, x, y);
    return true;
  }
```

The method invoked in the above null check is mouseEventHandler.mouse-Move(...). The code invoked if mouseEventHandler equals null is the code that the mechanics direct us to implement in an overridden mouseMove(...) method on NullMouseEventHandler. That was easily implemented:

**Introduce
Null Object**

```
public class NullMouseEventHandler...
  public boolean mouseMove(MetaGraphicsContext mgc, Event event, int x, int y) {
    return true;
  }
```

The new method compiled with no problems.

3. We repeated step 2 for all other occurrences of the null check in our code. We found the null check in numerous methods on three different classes. When we completed this step, NullMouseEventHandler had many new methods. Here are a few of them:

```
public class NullMouseEventHandler...
  public boolean mouseDown(MetaGraphicsContext mgc, Event event, int x, int y) {
    return true;
  }

  public boolean mouseUp(MetaGraphicsContext mgc, Event event, int x, int y) {
    return true;
  }

  public boolean mouseEnter(MetaGraphicsContext mgc, Event event, int x, int y) {
    return true;
  }

  public void doMouseClick(String imageMapName, String APID) {
  }
```

The above code compiled with no difficulties.

4. Then we initialized mouseEventHandler, the field referenced in the null check within the NavigationApplet class, to an instance of the NullMouseEventHandler:

```
public class NavigationApplet extends Applet...
  private MouseEventHandler mouseEventHandler = new NullMouseEventHandler(null);
```

The null that was passed to the NullMouseEventHandler's constructor forwarded to the constructor of its superclass, MouseEventHandler. Because we didn't like passing such nulls around, we altered NullMouseEventHandler's constructor to do this work:

```
public class NullMouseEventHandler extends MouseEventHandler {
  public NullMouseEventHandler(Context context) {
    super(null);
  }
}

public class NavigationApplet extends Applet...
  private MouseEventHandler mouseEventHandler = new NullMouseEventHandler();
```

5. Next came the fun part. We deleted all occurrences of the null check in such classes as NavigationApplet:

Introduce
Null Object

```
public class NavigationApplet extends Applet...
  public boolean mouseMove(Event event, int x, int y) {
    if (mouseEventHandler != null)
      return mouseEventHandler.mouseMove(graphicsContext, event, x, y );
    return true;
  }

  public boolean mouseDown(Event event, int x, int y) {
    if (mouseEventHandler != null)
      return mouseEventHandler.mouseDown(graphicsContext, event, x, y);
    return true;
  }

  public boolean mouseUp(Event event, int x, int y) {
    if (mouseEventHandler != null)
      return mouseEventHandler.mouseUp(graphicsContext, event, x, y);
    return true;
  }

  // etc.
```

After doing that, we compiled and tested whether the changes worked. In this case, we had no automated tests, so we had to run the Web site in a browser and try repeatedly to cause problems with our mouse as the NavigationApplet applet started up and began running. Everything worked well.

6. We repeated steps 4 and 5 for other classes that featured the same null check until it had been completely eliminated from all classes that originally contained it.

Because our system used only two instances of the NullMouseEventHandler, we did not make it a Singleton [DP].

Chapter 10

Accumulation

A good deal of code in software systems accumulates information. The refactorings in this section target the improvement of code that accumulates information within an object or across several objects.

A Collecting Parameter [Beck, SBPP] is an object that visits methods in order to accumulate information from them. The visited methods may reside within one object or many objects. Each visited method provides the Collecting Parameter with information. When all relevant methods have been visited, the accumulated information can be obtained from the Collecting Parameter.

Move Accumulation to Collecting Parameter (313) is often used in conjunction with the refactoring *Compose Method (123)*. The combination of these refactorings applies best when you have a long method that has many lines of code for accumulating information. To break the method into smaller parts, each of which handles a piece of the accumulation, you extract methods that accept and write to a Collecting Parameter.

The Collecting Parameter pattern resembles a Visitor [DP] in its ability to accumulate information from several objects. It differs from a Visitor in how it does the accumulation. Whereas visited objects pass themselves to a Visitor instance, objects that are visited by a Collecting Parameter simply call methods on the Collecting Parameter to provide it with information. If you have a lot of diverse information to accumulate from heterogeneous objects (i.e., objects with different interfaces), a Visitor will likely provide a cleaner design than a Collecting Parameter. That said, I frequently encounter code that could benefit from *Move Accumulation to Collecting Parameter (313)*, while I infrequently encounter code that needs *Move Accumulation to Visitor (320)*.

Unlike a Collecting Parameter, a Visitor is only useful for accumulating information from many objects, not one. It is also more applicable when you're accumulating information from heterogeneous objects, not homogeneous ones (i.e., objects that share the same interface). Because a Visitor is harder to implement than a Collecting Parameter, it's better to consider a Collecting Parameter solution before considering a Visitor one.

Accumulation

While the Visitor pattern is useful for certain types of accumulation, it is by no means limited to accumulation in what it can do. For example, a Visitor can visit an object structure and add objects to that structure during its journey. I use Visitors infrequently even for information accumulation, so I did not write about other refactorings to Visitor; they too are rare.

Accumulation

Move Accumulation to Collecting Parameter

You have a single bulky method
that accumulates information to a local variable.

*Accumulate results to a Collecting Parameter
that gets passed to extracted methods.*

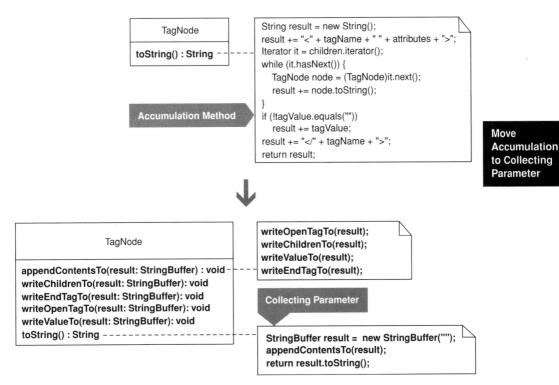

Motivation

Kent Beck defined the Collecting Parameter pattern in his classic book, *Small-talk Best Practice Patterns*. A Collecting Parameter is an object that you pass to methods in order to collect information from those methods. This pattern is often coupled with Composed Method [Beck, SBPP] (see the refactoring *Compose Method, 123*).

To decompose a bulky method into a Composed Method, you often need to decide how to accumulate information from the methods called by the Composed Method. Instead of having each of the methods return a result, which you later combine into a final result, you can incrementally accumulate a result by passing a Collecting Parameter to each of the methods. The methods write their information to the Collecting Parameter, which accumulates all of the results.

A Collecting Parameter may also be passed to methods on multiple objects. When it visits multiple objects, a Collecting Parameter accumulates information in one of two ways. Either each object calls back on a method or methods on the Collecting Parameter to pass data to it, or the objects pass themselves to the Collecting Parameter, which then calls back on the objects to obtain their data.

Collecting Parameters are programmed to accumulate data from specific classes with specific interfaces. They don't work so well when they must accumulate data from classes that hold diverse data and have diverse interfaces for accessing that data. For that case, a Visitor may be a better approach (see *Move Accumulation to Visitor, 320*).

(see *Move Accumulation to Visitor, 320*).

Collecting Parameter works nicely with the Composite [DP] pattern because you can use a Collecting Parameter to recursively accumulate information from a Composite structure. The JUnit framework by Kent Beck and Erich Gamma uses a Collecting Parameter named TestResult to accumulate test result information from every test in a Composite of test cases.

I combined Collecting Parameter with Composite when I refactored a class's toString() method. A profiler had shown that the string concatenation in toString() was slow. (This happened before compiler makers had made string concatenation just as fast as using a StringBuffer.) So my initial goal was to replace a lot of slow string concatenation code with faster StringBuffer code, but when I realized that a simple replacement would generate lots of StringBuffer instances (because the code is recursive), I retreated from this approach. Then my programming partner at the time, Don Roberts, seized the keyboard, saying "I've got it, I've got it!" He quickly refactored the code to use a single StringBuffer as a Collecting Parameter. The resulting code had a simpler design that communicated better with the reader.

Move Accumulation to Collecting Parameter

Benefits and Liabilities

+ Helps transform bulky methods into smaller, simpler, easier-to-read methods.
+ Can make resulting code run faster.

Mechanics

1. Identify an *accumulation method*, a method that accumulates information into a result. The *result*, a local variable, will become a Collecting Parameter. If the result's type won't let you iteratively gather data across methods, change its type. For example, Java's String won't let you accumulate results across methods, so use a StringBuffer (see the Example section for more on this).

    ✔ Compile.

2. In the accumulation method, find an information accumulation step and apply *Extract Method* [F] to extract it into a private method. Make sure the method's return type is void, and pass the result to it as a parameter. Inside the extracted method, write information to the result.

    ✔ Compile and test.

3. Repeat step 2 for every accumulation step, until the original code has been replaced with calls to extracted methods that accept and write to the result. The accumulation method should now contain three lines of code that

    - Instantiate a result.

    - Pass a result to the first of many methods.

    - Obtain a result's collected information.

    ✔ Compile and test.

By applying steps 2 and 3, you will be applying *Compose Method (123)* on the accumulation method and the various extracted methods you produce.

Example

In this example, I'll show you how to refactor Composite-based code to use a Collecting Parameter. I'll start with a Composite that can model an XML tree (see *Replace Implicit Tree with Composite, 178* for a complete example).

The Composite is modeled with a single class, called TagNode, which has a toString() method. The toString() method recursively walks the nodes in an XML tree and produces a final String representation of what it finds. It does a fair amount of work in 11 lines of code. In the steps presented here, I refactor toString() to make it simpler and easier to understand.

Move
Accumulation
to Collecting
Parameter

1. The following toString() method recursively accumulates information from every tag in a Composite structure and stores results in a variable called result:

```
class TagNode...
    public String toString() {
        String result = new String();
        result += "<" + tagName + " " + attributes + ">";
        Iterator it = children.iterator();
        while (it.hasNext()) {
            TagNode node = (TagNode)it.next();
            result += node.toString();
        }
        if (!value.equals(""))
            result += value;
        result += "</" + tagName + ">";
        return result;
    }
```

Move Accumulation to Collecting Parameter

I change result's type to be a StringBuffer:

```
StringBuffer result = new StringBuffer("");
```

After changing the + calls to append, the compiler is happy with this change.

2. I identify the first information accumulation step: code that concatenates an XML open tag along with any attributes to the result variable. I apply *Extract Method* [F] on this code as follows, so that this line:

```
result += "<" + tagName + " " + attributes + ">";
```

is extracted to:

```
private void writeOpenTagTo(StringBuffer result) {
    result.append("<");
    result.append(name);
    result.append(" ");
    result.append(attributes.toString());
    result.append(">");
}
```

The original code now looks like this:

```
StringBuffer result = new StringBuffer("");
writeOpenTagTo(result);
...
```

I compile and test to confirm that everything is OK.

3. Next, I want to continue applying *Extract Method* [F] on parts of the
   toString() method. I focus on the code that adds child XML nodes to result.
   This code contains a recursive step (highlighted in bold):

```
class TagNode...
   public String toString()...
      Iterator it = children.iterator();
      while (it.hasNext()) {
         TagNode node = (TagNode)it.next();
         result += node.toString();
      }
      if (!value.equals(""))
         result += value;
      ...
   }
```

   The recursive step means that the Collecting Parameter needs to be
   passed to the toString() method. But that's a problem, as the following code
   shows:

Move
Accumulation
to Collecting
Parameter

```
private void writeChildrenTo(StringBuffer result) {
   Iterator it = children.iterator();
   while (it.hasNext()) {
      TagNode node = (TagNode)it.next();
      node.toString(result); // can't do this because toString() doesn't take arguments.
   }
   ...
}
```

   Because toString() doesn't take a StringBuffer as an argument, I can't simply extract the method. I have to find another solution. I decide to solve the
   problem using a helper method, which will do the work that toString() used
   to do but will take a StringBuffer as a Collecting Parameter:

```
public String toString() {
   StringBuffer result = new StringBuffer("");
   appendContentsTo(result);
   return result.toString();
}

private void appendContentsTo(StringBuffer result) {
   writeOpenTagTo(result);
   ...
}
```

Now the recursion that's needed can be handled by the appendContentsTo() method:

```
private void appendContentsTo(StringBuffer result) {
   writeOpenTagTo(result);
   writeChildrenTo(result);
   ...
}

private void writeChildrenTo(StringBuffer result) {
   Iterator it = children.iterator();
   while (it.hasNext()) {
      TagNode node = (TagNode)it.next();
      node.appendContentsTo(result);  // now recursive call will work
   }
   if (!value.equals(""))
      result.append(value);
}
```

As I stare at the writeChildrenTo() method, I realize that it is handling two steps: adding children recursively and adding a value to a tag, when one exists. To make these two separate steps stand out, I extract the code for handling a value into its own method:

Move Accumulation to Collecting Parameter

```
private void writeValueTo(StringBuffer result) {
   if (!value.equals(""))
      result.append(value);
}
```

To finish the refactoring, I extract one more method that writes an XML close tag. Here's how the final code looks:

```
public class TagNode...
   public String toString() {
      StringBuffer result = new StringBuffer("");
      appendContentsTo(result);
      return result.toString();
   }

   private void appendContentsTo(StringBuffer result) {
      writeOpenTagTo(result);
      writeChildrenTo(result);
      writeValueTo(result);
      writeEndTagTo(result);
   }
```

```
private void writeOpenTagTo(StringBuffer result) {
    result.append("<");
    result.append(name);
    result.append(attributes.toString());
    result.append(">");
}

private void writeChildrenTo(StringBuffer result) {
    Iterator it = children.iterator();
    while (it.hasNext()) {
        TagNode node = (TagNode)it.next();
        node.appendContentsTo(result);
    }
}

private void writeValueTo(StringBuffer result) {
    if (!value.equals(""))
        result.append(value);
}

private void writeEndTagTo(StringBuffer result) {
    result.append("</");
    result.append(name);
    result.append(">");
}
}
```

Move
Accumulation
to Collecting
Parameter

I compile, run my tests, and everything is good. The toString() method is now very simple, while the appendContentsTo() method is a fine example of a Composed Method (see *Compose Method, 123*).

Move Accumulation to Visitor

A method accumulates information from
heterogeneous classes.

*Move the accumulation task to a Visitor that can
visit each class to accumulate the information.*

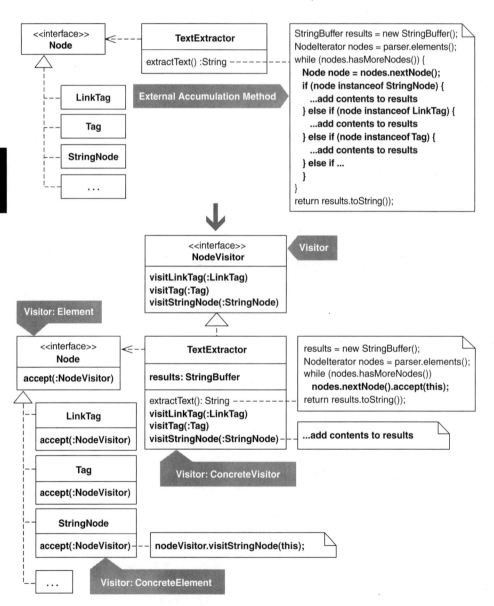

Motivation

Ralph Johnson, one of the four authors of *Design Patterns* [DP], once observed, "Most of the time you don't need Visitor, but when you do need Visitor, you *really* need Visitor!" So when do you *really* need Visitor? Let's review what Visitors are before answering that question.

A Visitor is a class that performs an operation on an object structure. The classes that a Visitor visits are heterogeneous, which means they hold unique information and provide a specific interface to that information. Visitors can easily interact with heterogeneous classes by means of *double-dispatch*. This means that each of a set of classes accepts a Visitor instance as a parameter (via an "accept" method: accept(Visitor visitor)) and then calls back on the Visitor, passing itself to its corresponding visit method, as shown in the following diagram.

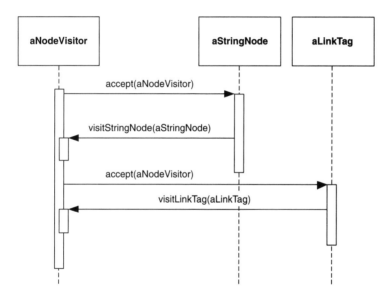

Because the first argument passed to a Visitor's visit(…) method is an instance of a specific type, the Visitor can call type-specific methods on the instance without performing type-casting. This makes it possible for Visitors to visit classes in the same hierarchy or different hierarchies.

The job of many real-world Visitors is to accumulate information. The Collecting Parameter pattern is also useful in this role (see *Move Accumulation to Collecting Parameter, 313*). Like a Visitor, a Collecting Parameter may be passed to multiple objects to accumulate information from them. The key difference lies in the ability to easily accumulate information from heterogeneous classes. While Visitors have no trouble with this task due to double-dispatch,

Collecting Parameters don't rely on double-dispatch, which limits their ability to gather diverse information from classes with diverse interfaces.

Now let's get back to the question: When do you *really* need a Visitor? In general, you need a Visitor when you have numerous algorithms to run on the same heterogeneous object structure and no other solution is as simple or succinct as a Visitor. For example, say you have three domain classes, none of which share a common superclass and all of which feature code for producing different XML representations.

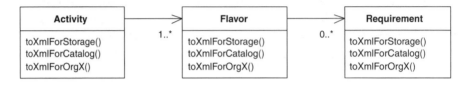

**Move
Accumulation
to Visitor**

What's wrong with this design? The main problem is that you have to add a new toXml method to each of these domain classes every time you have a new XML representation. In addition, the toXml methods bloat the domain classes with representation code, which is better kept separate from the domain logic, particularly when you have a lot of it. In the Mechanics section, I refer to the toXml methods as *internal accumulation methods* because they are internal to the classes used in the accumulation. Refactoring to a Visitor changes the design as shown in the following diagram.

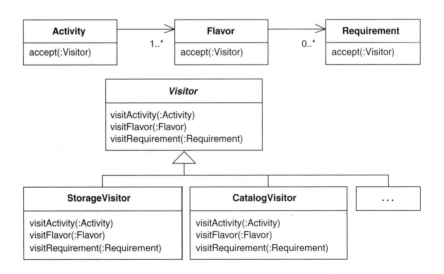

With this new design, the domain classes may be represented using whatever Visitor is appropriate. Furthermore, the copious representation logic that once crowded the domain classes is now encapsulated in the appropriate Visitor.

Another case when a Visitor is needed is when you have numerous *external accumulation methods*. Such methods typically use an Iterator [DP] and resort to type-casting heterogeneous objects to access specific information:

```
public String extractText()...
   while (nodes.hasMoreNodes()) {
      Node node = nodes.nextNode();
      if (node instanceof StringNode) {
         StringNode stringNode = (StringNode)node;
         results.append(stringNode.getText());
      } else if (node instanceof LinkTag) {
         LinkTag linkTag = (LinkTag)node;
         if (isPreTag)
            results.append(link.getLinkText());
         else
            results.append(link.getLink());
      } else if ...
   }
```

Move
Accumulation
to Visitor

Type-casting objects to access their specific interfaces is acceptable if it's not done frequently. However, if this activity becomes frequent, it's worth considering a better design. Would a Visitor provide a better solution? Perhaps—unless your heterogeneous classes suffer from the smell Alternative Classes with Different Interfaces [F]. In that case, you could likely refactor the classes to have a common interface, thereby making it possible to accumulate information without type-casting or implementing a Visitor. On the other hand, if you can't make heterogeneous classes look homogeneous by means of a common interface *and* you have numerous external accumulation methods, you can likely arrive at a better solution by refactoring to a Visitor. The opening code sketch and the Example section show such a case.

Finally, there are times when you have neither an external nor an internal accumulation method, yet your design could be improved by replacing your existing code with a Visitor. On the HTML Parser project, we once accomplished an information accumulation step by writing two new subclasses as shown in the figure on the following page.

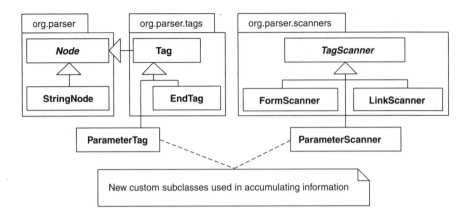

After we studied the new subclasses we'd written, we realized that one Visitor could take the place of the subclasses and the code would be simpler and more succinct. Yet we didn't jump to implementing a Visitor at that point; we felt that we needed further justification before taking on the nontrivial task of a Visitor refactoring. We found that justification when we discovered several external accumulation methods in client code to the HTML Parser. This illustrates the kind of thinking that ought to go into a decision to refactor to Visitor because such a refactoring is by no means a simple transformation.

If the set of classes your would-be Visitor must visit is growing frequently, it's generally advisable to avoid a Visitor solution because it involves writing an accept method on each new visitable class along with a corresponding visit method on the Visitor. On the other hand, it's best to not follow this rule religiously. When I considered refactoring to Visitor on the HTML Parser project, I found that the initial set of classes the Visitor would need to visit was too large and changed too frequently. After further inquiry, I determined that only a subset of the classes actually needed to be visited; the rest of the classes could be visited by using the visit method for their superclass.

Some programmers object to the Visitor pattern for one reason or another before they get to know it. For example, one programmer told me that he didn't like Visitor because it "breaks encapsulation." In other words, if a Visitor can't perform its work on a visitee because one or more of the visitee methods aren't public, the method(s) must be made public (thereby breaking encapsulation) to let the Visitor do its work. True. Yet many Visitor implementations require *no* visibility changes on visitees (see the upcoming Example section) and, even if a few visibility changes *are* required, the price you pay for compromising a visitee's encapsulation may be far lower than the price you pay to live with a non-Visitor solution.

Another objection raised against the Visitor pattern is that it adds too much complexity or obscurity to code. One programmer said, "Looking at the visit loop tells you nothing about what is being performed." The "visit loop" is code that iterates over visitees in an object structure and passes the Visitor to each one of them. While it's true that a visit loop reveals little about what concrete Visitors actually do, it's clear what the visit loop does if you understand the Visitor pattern. So the complexity or obscurity of a Visitor implementation depends a lot on an individual's or team's comfort level with the pattern. In addition, if a Visitor is really needed in a system, it will make overly complex or obscure code simpler.

The double-edged sword of the Visitor pattern is its power and sophistication. When you need a Visitor, you *really* need one, as Ralph says. Unfortunately, too many programmers feel the need to use Visitor for the wrong reasons, like showing off or because they're still "patterns happy." Always consider simpler solutions before refactoring to Visitor, and use this pattern most judiciously.

Move
Accumulation
to Visitor

Benefits and Liabilities

+ Accommodates numerous algorithms for the same heterogeneous object structure.
+ Visits classes in the same or different hierarchies.
+ Calls type-specific methods on heterogeneous classes without type-casting.
- Complicates a design when a common interface can make heterogeneous classes homogeneous.
- A new visitable class requires a new accept method along with a new visit method on each Visitor.
- May break encapsulation of visited classes.

Mechanics

An *accumulation method* gathers information from heterogeneous classes. An *external accumulation method* exists on a class that isn't one of the heterogeneous classes, while an *internal accumulation method* exists on the heterogeneous classes themselves. In this section you will find mechanics for both internal and external accumulation methods. In addition, I've provided a third set of mechanics for *Visitor replacement*, which you can use if you have neither an internal nor an external accumulation method yet can achieve a better design by rewriting your accumulation code as a Visitor.

External Accumulation Method

The class that contains your accumulation method is known in this refactoring as the *host*. Does it make sense for your host to play the role of Visitor? If your host is already playing too many roles, extract the accumulation method into a new host by performing *Replace Method with Method Object* [F] prior to this refactoring.

1. In the accumulation method, find any local variables that are referenced in multiple places by the accumulation logic. Convert these local variables to fields of the host class.

   ✔ Compile and test.

2. Apply *Extract Method* [F] on the accumulation logic for a given *accumulation source*, a class from which information is accumulated. Adjust the extracted method so it accepts an argument of the accumulation source's type. Name the extracted method accept(…).

   Repeat this step on accumulation logic for the remaining accumulation sources.

   ✔ Compile and test.

3. Apply *Extract Method* [F] on the body of an accept(…) method to produce a method called visitClassName(), where ClassName is the name of the accumulation source associated with the accept(…) method. The new method will accept one argument of the accumulation source's type (e.g., visitEndTag(End-Tag endTag)).

   Repeat this step for every accept(…) method.

4. Apply *Move Method* [F] to move every accept(…) method to its corresponding accumulation source. Each accept(…) method will now accept an argument of the host's type.

   ✔ Compile and test.

5. In the accumulation method, apply *Inline Method* [F] on every call to an accept(…) method.

   ✔ Compile and test.

6. Apply *Unify Interfaces (343)* on the superclasses and/or interfaces of the accumulation sources so the accept(…) method may be called polymorphically.

(margin tab: Move Accumulation to Visitor)

7. Generalize the accumulation method to call the accept(…) method polymorphically for every accumulation source.

    ✔ Compile and test.

8. Apply *Extract Interface* [F] on the host to produce a *visitor interface*, an interface that declares the visit methods implemented by the host.

9. Change the signature on every occurrence of the accept(…) method so it uses the visitor interface.

    ✔ Compile and test.

The host is now a Visitor.

Internal Accumulation Method

Use these mechanics when your accumulation method is implemented by the heterogeneous classes from which information is gathered. These mechanics assume that the heterogeneous classes are part of a hierarchy because that is a common case. The steps for these mechanics are largely based on mechanics defined in the paper "A Refactoring Tool for Smalltalk" [Roberts, Brant, and Johnson].

Move Accumulation to Visitor

1. Create a visitor by creating a new class. Consider using visitor in the class name.

    ✔ Compile.

2. Identify a *visitee*, a class from which the visitor will accumulate data. Add a method to the visitor called visitClassName(…), where ClassName is the name of the visitee (e.g., visitor.visitEndTag(…)). Make the visit method's return type void, and make it take a visitee argument (e.g., public void visitStringNode(StringNode stringNode)).

    Repeat this step for every class in the hierarchy from which the visitor must accumulate information.

    ✔ Compile.

3. On every visitee, apply *Extract Method* [F] on the body of the accumulation method so it calls a new method, which will be called the *accept method*. Make the signature of the accept method identical in all classes, so every accumulation method contains the same code for calling its accept method.

    ✔ Compile and test.

4. The accumulation method is now identical in every class. Apply *Pull Up Method* [F] to move it to the hierarchy's superclass.

   ✔ Compile and test.

5. Apply *Add Parameter* [F] to add an argument of type visitor to every implementation of the accept method. Make the accumulation method pass in a new instance of the visitor when it calls the accept method.

   ✔ Compile.

6. Produce a visit method on the visitor by applying *Move Method* [F] on a visitee's accept method. The accept method now calls a visit method that accepts an argument of type visitee.

   For example, given a visitee called StringNode and a visitor called Visitor, we'd have the following code:

```
class StringNode...
   void accept(Visitor visitor) {
      visitor.visitStringNode(this);
   }

class Visitor {
   void visitStringNode(StringNode stringNode)…
}
```

   Repeat this step for every visitee.

   ✔ Compile and test.

Visitor Replacement

This refactoring assumes you have neither an internal nor an external accumulation method, yet your code would be better if it were replaced with a Visitor.

1. Create a concrete visitor by creating a new class. Consider using visitor in the class name.

   If you're creating your second concrete visitor, apply *Extract Superclass* [F] on your first concrete visitor to create your abstract visitor, and change message signatures on all visitees (defined in step 2) so they accept an abstract visitor instead of your first concrete visitor. When applying *Extract Superclass* [F], don't pull up any data or methods that are specific to a concrete visitor and not generic to all concrete visitors.

2. Identify a visitee, a class from which the concrete visitor must accumulate data. Add a method to the concrete visitor called visitClassName, where ClassName is the name of the visitee (e.g., concreteVisitor.visitEndTag(…)). Make the

Move Accumulation to Visitor

visit method's return type void and make it take a visitee argument (e.g., `public void visitStringNode(StringNode stringNode)`).

3. Add to the same visitee (from step 2) a public accept method that takes as a parameter the concrete visitor or, if you have one, the abstract visitor. Make the body of this method call back on the concrete visitor's visit method, passing a reference to the visitee.

    For example:

```
class Tag...
    public void accept(NodeVisitor nodeVisitor){
    nodeVisitor.visitTag(this)
    }
```

4. Repeat steps 2 and 3 for every visitee. You now have the skeleton of your concrete visitor.

5. Implement a public method on your concrete visitor to obtain its accumulated result. Make the accumulated result be empty or null.

    ✔ Compile.

Move
Accumulation
to Visitor

6. In the accumulation method, define a local field for the concrete visitor and instantiate it. Next, find accumulation method code where information is accumulated from each visitee, and add code to call each visitee's accept method, passing in the concrete visitor instance. When you're done, update the accumulation method so it uses the concrete visitor's accumulated result instead of its normal result. This last part will cause your tests to break.

7. Implement the method bodies for each visit method on the concrete visitor. This step is big, and there's no single set of mechanics that will work for it because all cases vary. As you copy code from the accumulation method into each visit method, make it fit into its new home by

    *   Ensuring each visit method can access essential data/logic from its visitee

    *   Declaring and initializing concrete visitor fields that are accessed by two or more of the visit methods

    *   Passing essential data (used in accumulation) from the accumulation method to the concrete visitor's constructor (e.g., a `TagAccumulatingVisitor` accumulates all Tag instances that match the string, `tagNameToFind`, which is a value supplied via a constructor argument)

    ✔ Compile and test that the accumulated results returned by the accumulation method are all correct.

8. Remove as much old code from the accumulation method as possible.

   ✔ Compile and test.

9. You should now be left with code that iterates over a collection of objects, passing the concrete visitor to the accept method for each visitee. If some of the objects being iterated over don't have an accept method (i.e., aren't visitees), define a do-nothing accept method on those classes (or on their base class), so your iteration code doesn't have to distinguish between objects when it calls the accept method.

   ✔ Compile and test.

10. Create a local accept method by applying *Extract Method* [F] on the accumulation method's iteration code. This new method should take the concrete visitor as its sole argument and should iterate over a collection of objects, passing the concrete visitor to each object's accept method.

11. Move the local accept method to a place where it will more naturally fit, such as a class that other clients can easily access.

    ✔ Compile and test.

Example

It takes a good deal of patience to find a real-world case in which refactoring to a Visitor actually makes sense. I found numerous such cases while refactoring code in an open source, streaming HTML parser (see *http://sourceforge.net/projects/htmlparser*). The refactoring I'll discuss here occurred on an external accumulation method. To help you understand this refactoring, I need to give a brief overview of how the parser works.

As the parser parses HTML or XML, it recognizes tags and strings. For example, consider this HTML:

```
<HTML>
   <BODY>
      Hello, and welcome to my Web page! I work for
      <A HREF="http://industriallogic.com">
         <IMG SRC="http://industriallogic.com/images/logo141x145.gif">
      </A>
   </BODY>
</HTML>
```

The parser recognizes the following objects when parsing this HTML:

- Tag (for the <BODY> tag)
- StringNode (for the String, "Hello, and welcome . . .")

- LinkTag (for the <A HREF="…">…</A> tags)

- ImageTag (for the <IMG SRC="…"> tag)

- EndTag (for the </BODY> tag)

Users of the parser commonly accumulate information from HTML or XML documents. The TextExtractor class provides an easy way to accumulate textual data from documents. The heart of this class is a method called extractText():

```
public class TextExtractor...
   public String extractText() throws ParserException {
      Node node;
      boolean isPreTag = false;
      boolean isScriptTag = false;
      StringBuffer results = new StringBuffer();

      parser.flushScanners();
      parser.registerScanners();

      for (NodeIterator e = parser.elements(); e.hasMoreNodes();) {
         node = e.nextNode();
         if (node instanceof StringNode) {
            if (!isScriptTag) {
               StringNode stringNode = (StringNode) node;
               if (isPreTag)
                  results.append(stringNode.getText());
               else {
                  String text = Translate.decode(stringNode.getText());
                  if (getReplaceNonBreakingSpace())
                     text = text.replace('\u00a0', ' ');
                  if (getCollapse())
                     collapse(results, text);
                  else
                     results.append(text);
               }
            }
         } else if (node instanceof LinkTag) {
            LinkTag link = (LinkTag) node;
            if (isPreTag)
               results.append(link.getLinkText());
            else
               collapse(results, Translate.decode(link.getLinkText()));
            if (getLinks()) {
               results.append("<");
               results.append(link.getLink());
               results.append(">");
            }
         } else if (node instanceof EndTag) {
            EndTag endTag = (EndTag) node;
            String tagName = endTag.getTagName();
```

```
        if (tagName.equalsIgnoreCase("PRE"))
            isPreTag = false;
        else if (tagName.equalsIgnoreCase("SCRIPT"))
            isScriptTag = false;
    } else if (node instanceof Tag) {
        Tag tag = (Tag) node;
        String tagName = tag.getTagName();
        if (tagName.equalsIgnoreCase("PRE"))
            isPreTag = true;
        else if (tagName.equalsIgnoreCase("SCRIPT"))
            isScriptTag = true;
    }
  }
  return (results.toString());
}
```

This code iterates all nodes returned by the parser, figures out each node's type (using Java's instanceof operator), and then type-casts and accumulates data from each node with some help from local variables and user-configurable Boolean flags.

In deciding whether or how to refactor this code, I consider the following questions:

- Would a Visitor implementation provide a simpler, more succinct solution?

- Would a Visitor implementation enable similar refactorings in other areas of the parser or in client code to the parser?

- Is there a simpler solution than a Visitor? For example, can I accumulate data from each node by using one common method?

- Is the existing code sufficient?

I quickly determine that I cannot accumulate data from the nodes by using one common accumulation method. For instance, the code gathers either all of a LinkTag's text or just its link (i.e., URL) by calling two different methods. I also determine that there is no easy way to avoid all of the instanceof calls and type-casts without moving to a Visitor implementation. Is it worth it? I determine that it is because other areas in the parser and client code could also be improved by using a Visitor.

Before beginning the refactoring, I must decide whether it makes sense for the TextExtractor class to play the role of Visitor or whether to extract a class from it that will play the Visitor role. In this case, because TextExtractor performs only the single responsibility of text extraction, I decide that it will make a perfectly good Visitor. Having made my choice, I proceed with the refactoring.

Move Accumulation to Visitor

1. The accumulation method, extractText(), contains three local variables referenced across multiple legs of a conditional statement. I convert these local variables into TextExtractor fields:

```
public class TextExtractor...
    private boolean isPreTag;
    private boolean isScriptTag;
    private StringBuffer results;

    public String extractText()...
        boolean isPreTag = false;
        boolean isScriptTag = false;
        StringBuffer results = new StringBuffer();
        ...
```

I compile and test to confirm that the changes work.

2. Now I apply *Extract Method* [F] on the first chunk of accumulation code for the StringNode type:

Move
Accumulation
to Visitor

```
public class TextExtractor...
    public String extractText()...
        ...
        for (NodeIterator e = parser.elements(); e.hasMoreNodes();) {
            node = e.nextNode();
            if (node instanceof StringNode) {
                accept(node);
            } else if (...

    private void accept(Node node) {
        if (!isScriptTag) {
            StringNode stringNode = (StringNode) node;
            if (isPreTag)
                results.append(stringNode.getText());
            else {
                String text = Translate.decode(stringNode.getText());
                if (getReplaceNonBreakingSpace())
                    text = text.replace('\u00a0', ' ');
                if (getCollapse())
                    collapse(results, text);
                else
                    results.append(text);
            }
        }
    }
```

The accept() method currently type-casts its node argument to a StringNode. I will be creating accept() methods for each of the accumulation sources, so I must customize this one to accept an argument of type StringNode:

```
public class TextExtractor...
    public String extractText()...
        ...
        for (NodeIterator e = parser.elements(); e.hasMoreNodes();) {
            node = e.nextNode();
            if (node instanceof StringNode) {
                accept((StringNode)node);
            } else if (...

    private void accept(StringNode stringNode)...
        if (!isScriptTag) {
            StringNode stringNode = (StringNode) node;
            ...
```

After compiling and testing, I repeat this step for all other accumulation sources. This yields the following code:

Move
Accumulation
to Visitor

```
public class TextExtractor...
    public String extractText()...

        for (NodeIterator e = parser.elements(); e.hasMoreNodes();) {
            node = e.nextNode();
            if (node instanceof StringNode) {
                accept((StringNode)node);
            } else if (node instanceof LinkTag) {
                accept((LinkTag)node);
            } else if (node instanceof EndTag) {
                accept((EndTag)node);
            } else if (node instanceof Tag) {
                accept((Tag)node);
            }
        }
        return (results.toString());
    }
```

3. Now I apply *Extract Method* [F] on the body of the accept(StringNode string-Node) method to produce a visitStringNode() method:

```
public class TextExtractor...
    private void accept(StringNode stringNode) {
        visitStringNode(stringNode);
    }

    private void visitStringNode(StringNode stringNode) {
        if (!isScriptTag) {
            if (isPreTag)
                results.append(stringNode.getText());
```

```
      else {
         String text = Translate.decode(stringNode.getText());
         if (getReplaceNonBreakingSpace())
            text = text.replace('\u00a0', ' ');
         if (getCollapse())
            collapse(results, text);
         else
            results.append(text);
      }
   }
}
```

After compiling and testing, I repeat this step for all of the accept() methods, yielding the following:

```
public class TextExtractor...
   private void accept(Tag tag) {
      visitTag(tag);
   }
   private void visitTag(Tag tag)...

   private void accept(EndTag endTag) {
      visitEndTag(endTag);
   }
   private void visitEndTag(EndTag endTag)...

   private void accept(LinkTag link) {
      visitLinkTag(link);
   }
   private void visitLinkTag(LinkTag link)...

   private void accept(StringNode stringNode) {
      visitStringNode(stringNode);
   }
   private void visitStringNode(StringNode stringNode)...
```

Move Accumulation to Visitor

4. Next, I apply *Move Method* [F] to move every accept() method to the accumulation source with which it is associated. For example, the following method:

```
public class TextExtractor...
   private void accept(StringNode stringNode) {
      visitStringNode(stringNode);
   }
```

is moved to StringNode:

```
public class StringNode...
   public void accept(TextExtractor textExtractor) {
      textExtractor.visitStringNode(this);
   }
```

and adjusted to call StringNode like so:

```
public class TextExtractor...
    private void accept(StringNode stringNode) {
        stringNode.accept(this);
    }
```

This transformation requires modifying TextExtractor so its visitString-Node(…) method is public. Once I compile and test that the new code works, I repeat this step to move the accept() methods for Tag, EndTag, and LinkTag to those classes.

5. Now I can apply *Inline Method* [F] on every call to accept() within extract-Text():

Move Accumulation to Visitor

```
public class TextExtractor...
    public String extractText()...
        for (NodeIterator e = parser.elements(); e.hasMoreNodes();) {
            node = e.nextNode();
            if (node instanceof StringNode) {
                ((StringNode)node).accept(this);
            } else if (node instanceof LinkTag) {
                ((LinkTag)node).accept(this);
            } else if (node instanceof EndTag) {
                ((EndTag)node).accept(this);
            } else if (node instanceof Tag) {
                ((Tag)node).accept(this);
            }
        }
        return (results.toString());
    }

    private void accept(Tag tag) {
        tag.accept(this);
    }
    private void accept(EndTag endTag) {
        endTag.accept(this);
    }

    private void accept(LinkTag link) {
        link.accept(this);
    }

    private void accept(StringNode stringNode) {
        stringNode.accept(this);
    }
```

I compile and test to confirm that all is well.

6. At this point, I want extractText() to call accept() polymorphically, rather than having to type-cast node to call the appropriate accept() method for each

accumulation source. To make that possible, I apply *Unify Interfaces (343)* on the superclass and associated interface for StringNode, LinkTag, Tag, and EndTag:

```
public interface Node...
    public void accept(TextExtractor textExtractor);

public abstract class AbstractNode implements Node...
    public void accept(TextExtractor textExtractor) {
    }
```

7. Now I can change extractText() to call the accept() method polymorphically:

```
public class TextExtractor...
    public String extractText()
        ...
        for (NodeIterator e = parser.elements(); e.hasMoreNodes();) {
            node = e.nextNode();
            node.accept(this);
        }
```

Compiling and testing confirms that everything is working.

8. At this point, I extract a visitor interface from TextExtractor like so:

```
public interface NodeVisitor {
    public void visitTag(Tag tag);
    public void visitEndTag(EndTag endTag);
    public void visitLinkTag(LinkTag link);
    public void visitStringNode(StringNode stringNode);
}

public class TextExtractor implements NodeVisitor...
```

9. The final step is to change every accept() method so it takes a NodeVisitor argument rather than a TextExtractor:

```
public interface Node...
    public void accept(NodeVisitor nodeVisitor);

public abstract class AbstractNode implements Node...
    public void accept(NodeVisitor nodeVisitor) {
    }

public class StringNode extends AbstractNode...
    public void accept(NodeVisitor nodeVisitor) {
        nodeVisitor.visitStringNode(this);
    }

// etc.
```

Move
Accumulation
to Visitor

I compile and test to confirm that TextExtractor now works beautifully as a Visitor. This refactoring has paved the way for additional refactorings to Visitor in the parser, none of which I will do without first taking a nice, long break.

Move
Accumulation
to Visitor

Chapter 11

Utilities

The refactorings in this section are low-level transformations used by the higher-level refactorings in the catalog. These refactorings fit well with the refactorings in *Refactoring* [F].

Chain Constructors (340) is about removing duplication in constructors by having them call each other. This refactoring is used by the refactoring *Replace Constructors with Creation Methods (57)*.

Unify Interfaces (343) is useful when you need a superclass and/or interface to share the same interface as a subclass. The usual motivation for applying this refactoring is to make it possible to treat objects polymorphically. The refactorings *Move Embellishment to Decorator (144)* and *Move Accumulation to Visitor (320)* both make use of this refactoring.

Extract Parameter (346) is useful when a field is assigned to a locally instantiated value and you'd rather have that value supplied by a parameter. While this can be useful in many situations, the refactoring *Move Embellishment to Decorator (144)* uses this refactoring just after the application of *Replace Inheritance with Delegation* [F].

Chain Constructors

You have multiple constructors that contain duplicate code.

Chain the constructors together to obtain the least amount of duplicate code.

```
public class Loan {
  ...
  public Loan(float notional, float outstanding, int rating, Date expiry) {
    this.strategy = new TermROC();
    this.notional = notional;
    this.outstanding = outstanding;
    this.rating =rating;
    this.expiry = expiry;
  }
  public Loan(float notional, float outstanding, int rating, Date expiry, Date maturity) {
    this.strategy = new RevolvingTermROC();
    this.notional = notional;
    this.outstanding = outstanding;
    this.rating = rating;
    this.expiry = expiry;
    this.maturity = maturity;
  }
  public Loan(CapitalStrategy strategy, float notional, float outstanding,
              int rating, Date expiry, Date maturity) {
    this.strategy = strategy;
    this.notional = notional;
    this.outstanding = outstanding;
    this.rating = rating;
    this.expiry = expiry;
    this.maturity = maturity;
  }
}
```

$\downarrow$

```
public class Loan {
  ...
  public Loan(float notional, float outstanding, int rating, Date expiry) {
    this(new TermROC(), notional, outstanding, rating, expiry, null);
  }
  public Loan(float notional, float outstanding, int rating, Date expiry, Date maturity) {
    this(new RevolvingTermROC(), notional, outstanding, rating, expiry, maturity);
  }
  public Loan(CapitalStrategy strategy, float notional, float outstanding,
              int rating, Date expiry, Date maturity) {
    this.strategy = strategy;
    this.notional = notional;
    this.outstanding = outstanding;
    this.rating = rating;
    this.expiry = expiry;
    this.maturity = maturity;
  }
}
```

Motivation

Code that's duplicated across two or more of a class's constructors is an invitation for trouble. If someone adds a new variable to a class and updates a constructor to initialize the variable, but then neglects to update the other constructors—*bang*, say hello to your next defect. The more constructors you have in a class, the more duplication will hurt you. It is therefore a good idea to reduce or remove duplication in your constructors.

We often accomplish this refactoring with *constructor chaining*: specific constructors call more general-purpose constructors until a final constructor is reached. If you have one constructor at the end of every chain, it is a *catch-all constructor* because it handles every constructor call. A catch-all constructor often accepts more parameters than other constructors.

If you find that having many constructors on your class detracts from its usability, consider applying *Replace Constructors with Creation Methods (57)*.

Mechanics

1. Find two constructors that contain duplicate code. Determine whether one can call the other such that duplicate code can be safely (and, hopefully, easily) deleted from one of these constructors. Then make the one constructor call the other constructor such that duplicate code is reduced or eliminated.

   ✔ Compile and test.

2. Repeat step 1 for all constructors in the class, including ones you've already touched, in order to obtain as little duplication across all constructors as possible.

3. Change the visibility of any constructors that may not need to be public.

   ✔ Compile and test.

Chain Constructors

Example

For this example I'll use the scenario shown in the code sketch at the beginning of this refactoring. A single Loan class has three constructors to represent different types of loans, as well as tons of bloated and ugly duplication:

```
public Loan(float notional, float outstanding, int rating, Date expiry) {
    this.strategy = new TermROC();
    this.notional = notional;
    this.outstanding = outstanding;
```

```
        this.rating = rating;
        this.expiry = expiry;
    }

    public Loan(float notional, float outstanding, int rating, Date expiry, Date maturity) {
        this.strategy = new RevolvingTermROC();
        this.notional = notional;
        this.outstanding = outstanding;
        this.rating = rating;
        this.expiry = expiry;
        this.maturity = maturity;
    }

    public Loan(CapitalStrategy strategy, float notional, float outstanding, int rating,
            Date expiry, Date maturity) {
        this.strategy = strategy;
        this.notional = notional;
        this.outstanding = outstanding;
        this.rating = rating;
        this.expiry = expiry;
        this.maturity = maturity;
    }
```

Let's see what happens when I refactor this code.

<table>
<tr>
<td>

**Chain
Constructors**

</td>
<td>

1. I study the first two constructors. They do contain duplicate code, but so
does that third constructor. I consider which constructor it would be easier
for the first constructor to call. I see that it could call the third constructor
with a minimum amount of work. So I change the first constructor to be:

</td>
</tr>
</table>

```
    public Loan(float notional, float outstanding, int rating, Date expiry) {
        this(new TermROC(), notional, outstanding, rating, expiry, null);
    }
```

✔ I compile and test to see that the change works.

2. I repeat step 1 to remove as much duplication as possible. This leads me to
the second constructor. It appears that it too can call the third constructor,
as follows:

```
    public Loan(float notional, float outstanding, int rating, Date expiry, Date maturity) {
        this(new RevolvingTermROC(), notional, outstanding, rating, expiry, maturity);
    }
```

I'm now aware that the third constructor is my class's catch-all constructor because it handles all of the construction details.

3. I check all callers of the three constructors to determine whether I can
change the public visibility of any of them. In this case, I can't. (Take my
word for it—you can't see the code that calls these methods.)

✔ I compile and test to complete the refactoring.

Unify Interfaces

You need a superclass and/or interface to have
the same interface as a subclass.

*Find all public methods on the subclass that are missing on the
superclass/interface. Add copies of these missing methods to
the superclass, altering each one to perform null behavior.*

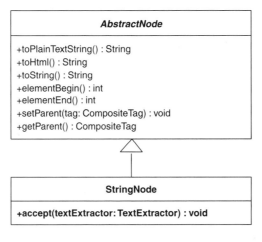

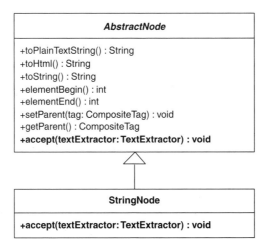

Motivation

To process objects polymorphically, the classes of the objects need to share a common interface, whether a superclass or an actual interface. This refactoring addresses the case when a superclass or interface needs to have the same interface as a subclass.

I came across the need for this refactoring on two separate occasions. Once when I was applying *Move Embellishment to Decorator (144)*, an emerging Decorator [DP] needed the same interface as a subclass. The easiest way to make that happen was to apply *Unify Interfaces*. Similarly, during an application of the refactoring *Move Accumulation to Visitor (320)*, duplicate code could be removed if certain objects shared the same interface, which *Unify Interfaces* made possible.

After applying this refactoring on a superclass and subclass, I sometimes apply *Extract Interface* [F] on the superclass to produce a stand-alone interface. I usually do this when an abstract base class contains state fields and I don't want implementors of the common base class, such as a Decorator, to inherit those fields. See *Move Embellishment to Decorator (144)* for an example.

Unify Interfaces is often a temporary step on the way to somewhere else. For example, after you perform this refactoring, you may perform a sequence of refactorings that allows you to remove methods you added while unifying your interfaces. Other times, a default implementation of a method on an abstract base class may no longer be needed after applying *Extract Interface* [F].

Mechanics

Find a *missing method*, a public method on the subclass that isn't declared on the superclass and/or interface.

1. Add a copy of the missing method to the superclass/interface. If you're adding the missing method to a superclass, modify its body to perform null behavior.

   ✔ Compile.

   Repeat until the superclass/interface and subclass share the same interface.

   ✔ Test that all code related to the superclass works as expected.

Example

I need to unify the interfaces of a subclass called StringNode and its superclass, AbstractNode. StringNode inherits most of its public methods from AbstractNode, with the exception of one method:

```
public class StringNode extends AbstractNode...
    public void accept(textExtractor: TextExtractor) {
        // implementation details…
    }
}
```

1. I add a copy of the accept(…) method to AbstractNode, modifying its body to provide null behavior:

   ```
   public abstract class AbstractNode...
       public void accept(textExtractor: TextExtractor) {
       }
   ```

   At this point, the interfaces of AbstractNode and StringNode have been unified. I compile and test to ensure that everything works fine. It does.

Extract Parameter

*A method or constructor assigns a field
to a locally instantiated value.*

*Assign the field to a parameter supplied by a client by
extracting one-half of the assignment statement to a parameter.*

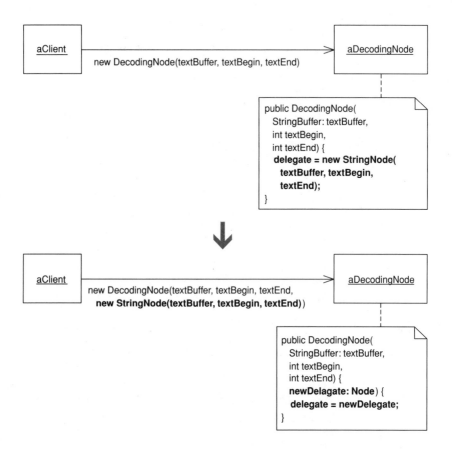

**Extract
Parameter**

Motivation

Sometimes you want to assign a field inside an object to a value provided by another object. If the field is already assigned to a local value, you can extract one-half of the assignment statement to a parameter so that a client can supply the field's value rather than the host object.

I needed this refactoring after performing *Replace Inheritance with Delegation* [F]. At the end of that refactoring, a delegating class contains a field for an object it delegates to (the delegatee). The delegating class assigns this delegate field to a new instance of the delegate. Yet I needed a client object to supply the delegate's value. *Extract Parameter* allowed me to simply extract the delegate instantiation code to a parameter value supplied by a client.

Mechanics

1. The assignment statement for the field must be in a constructor or method before you can do this refactoring. If it isn't already in a constructor or method, move it to one.

2. Apply *Add Parameter* [F] to pass in the value for the field, using the field's type as the type for the parameter. Make the parameter's value be the value the field is assigned to within its host object. Alter the assignment statement so the field is assigned to the new parameter.

   ✔ Compile and test.

When you have finished this refactoring, you may wish to remove unused parameters by applying *Remove Parameter* [F].

**Extract
Parameter**

Example

This example comes from a step I perform during the refactoring *Move Embellishment to Decorator (144)*. The HTML Parser's `DecodingNode` class contains a field called `delegate` that is assigned to a new instance of `StringNode` inside `DecodingNode`'s constructor:

```
public class DecodingNode implements Node...
   private Node delegate;

   public DecodingNode(StringBuffer textBuffer, int textBegin, int textEnd) {
      delegate = new StringNode(textBuffer, textBegin, textEnd);
   }
```

Given this code, I apply this refactoring as follows.

1. Since `delegate` is already assigned to a value within `DecodingNode`'s contructor, I can move to the next step.

2. I apply *Add Parameter* [F] and use a default value of new StringNode(text-Buffer, textBegin, textEnd). I then alter the assignment statement so that it assigns delegate to the parameter value, newDelegate:

```
public class DecodingNode implements Node...
    private Node delegate;

    public DecodingNode(StringBuffer textBuffer, int textBegin, int textEnd,
                        Node newDelegate) {
        delegate = newDelegate;
    }
```

This change involves updating the client, StringNode, to pass in the value for newDelegate:

```
public class StringNode...
    ...
    return new DecodingNode(...,
        new StringNode(textBuffer, textBegin, textEnd)
    );
```

I compile and test to confirm that everything still works just fine.

After completing this refactoring, I will apply *Remove Parameter* [F] several times, so that the constructor for DecodingNode becomes:

```
public class DecodingNode implements Node...
    private Node delegate;

    public DecodingNode(StringBuffer textBuffer, int textBegin, int textEnd,
                        Node newDelegate) {
        delegate = newDelegate;
    }
```

And that's it for this short and sweet refactoring.

Extract Parameter

Afterword

Let's go back to high school for a moment. In algebra class, the instructor began by teaching many different manipulations, such as "add the same value to both sides of the equation" or "the commutative property of addition allows us to swap its operands." This went on for several weeks, at which point the teacher switched gears and handed you a paragraph that started off, "A train leaves New York heading west. . . ." After the initial panic (the effects of which you may still feel as you read the previous sentence), you settled down and expressed the problem in terms of an algebraic equation. You then applied the rules of algebra to the equation to arrive at an answer.

Design patterns are the word problems of the programming world; refactoring is its algebra. After having read *Design Patterns* [DP], you reach a point where you say to yourself, "If I had only known this pattern, my system would be so much cleaner today." The book you are holding introduces you to several sample problems, with solutions expressed in the operations of refactoring.

Many people will read this book and try to memorize the steps to implement these patterns. Others will read this book and clamor for these larger refactorings to be added to existing programming tools. Both of these approaches are misguided. The true value of this book lies not in the actual steps to achieve a particular pattern but in understanding the thought processes that lead to those steps. By learning to think in the algebra of refactoring, you learn to solve design problems in behavior-preserving steps, and you are not bound by the small subset of actual problems that this book represents.

So take these exemplars that Josh has laid out for you. Study them. Find the underlying patterns of refactoring that are occurring. Seek the insights that led to the particular steps. Don't use this as a reference book, but as a primer.

—John Brant and Don Roberts
Cocreators of the world's first refactoring browser

References

[Alexander, PL]

Alexander, Christopher. *A Pattern Language*. New York: Oxford University Press, 1977.

[Alexander, TWB]

Alexander, Christopher. *A Timeless Way of Building*. New York: Oxford University Press, 1979.

[Anderson]

Anderson, Bruce. "Null Object." UIUC Patterns Discussion Mailing List (*patterns@cs.uiuc.edu*), January 1995.

[Astels]

Astels, David. *Test-Driven Development, a Practical Guide*. Upper Saddle River, NJ: Prentice Hall, 2003.

[Barzun]

Barzun, Jacques. *Simple and Direct*, 4th ed. New York: HarperCollins, 2001.

[Beck, SBPP]

Beck, Kent. *Smalltalk Best Practice Patterns*. Upper Saddle River, NJ: Prentice Hall, 1997.

[Beck, TDD]

Beck, Kent. *Test-Driven Development*. Boston, MA: Addison-Wesley, 2002.

[Beck, XP]

Beck, Kent. *Extreme Programming Explained*. Reading, MA: Addison-Wesley, 1999.

[Beck and Gamma]

Beck, Kent, and Erich Gamma. JUnit Testing Framework. Available online at *http://www.junit.org*. See also Erich Gamma and Kent Beck, "JUnit: A Cook's Tour," *Java Report*, May 1999.

[Bloch]

Bloch, Joshua. *Effective Java*. Boston, MA: Addison-Wesley, 2001.

[Cunningham]

Cunningham, Ward. "Checks: A Pattern Language of Information Integrity." In *Pattern Languages of Program Design*, eds. James O. Coplien and Douglas C. Schmidt. Reading, MA: Addison-Wesley, 1995.

[DP]

Gamma, Erich, Richard Helm, Ralph Johnson, and John Vlissides. *Design Patterns: Elements of Reusable Object-Oriented Software*. Reading, MA: Addison-Wesley, 1995.

[Evans]

Evans, Eric. *Domain-Driven Design*. Boston, MA: Addison-Wesley, 2003.

[Foote and Yoder]

Foote, Brian, and Joseph Yoder. "Big Ball of Mud." In *Pattern Languages of Program Design IV*, eds. Neil Harrison, Brian Foote, and Hans Rohnert. Boston, MA: Addison-Wesley, 2000.

[F]

Fowler, Martin. *Refactoring: Improving the Design of Existing Code*. Boston, MA: Addison-Wesley, 2000.

[Fowler, PEAA]

Fowler, Martin. *Patterns of Enterprise Application Architecture*. Boston, MA: Addison-Wesley, 2003.

[Fowler, UD]

Fowler, Martin. *UML Distilled*, 3rd ed. Boston, MA: Addison-Wesley, 2003.

[Gamma and Beck]

Gamma, Erich, and Kent Beck. *Contributing to Eclipse*. Boston, MA: Addison-Wesley, 2003.

[Kerievsky, PI]

Kerievsky, Joshua. "Pools of Insight: A Pattern Language for Study Groups." Available online at *http://industriallogic.com/papers/kh.html*.

[Kerievsky, PXP]

Kerievsky, Joshua. "Patterns & XP." In *Extreme Programming Examined*, eds. Giancarlo Succi and Michele Marchesi. Boston, MA: Addison-Wesley, 2001.

[Parnas]

Parnas, David. "On the Criteria to Be Used in Decomposing Systems into Modules." *Communications of the ACM*, 15(2), 1972.

[Roberts, Brant, and Johnson]

Roberts, Don, John Brant, and Ralph Johnson. "A Refactoring Tool for Smalltalk." Available online at *http://st-www.cs.uiuc.edu/~droberts/tapos/TAPOS.htm*.

[Solomon]

Solomon, Maynard. *Mozart*. New York: HarperCollins, 1995.

[Vlissides]

Vlissides, John. "C++ Report." April 1998. Available online at *http://www.research.ibm.com/designpatterns/pubs/ph-apr98.pdf*.

[Woolf]

Woolf, Bobby. "The Null Object Pattern." In *Pattern Languages of Program Design III*, eds. Robert C. Martin, Dirk Riehle, and Frank Buschmann. Reading, MA: Addison-Wesley, 1997.

Index

Other Addison-Wesley Titles of Interest

Design Patterns

Erich Gamma, Richard Helm, Ralph Johnson, John M. Vlissides
0-201-63361-2

This is the seminal book in the field of design patterns. Capturing a
wealth of experience about the design of object-oriented software,
four top-notch designers present a catalog of simple and succinct
solutions to commonly occurring design problems. Previously un-
documented, these twenty-three patterns allow designers to create
more flexible, elegant, and ultimately reusable designs without
having to rediscover the design solutions themselves.

Refactoring

Martin Fowler
0-201-48567-2

This is the seminal book in the field of refactoring. Renowned object technology mentor Martin Fowler breaks new ground, demysti-
fying the master practices of refactoring and demonstrating how
software practitioners can realize the significant benefits of this
process. In this book, the author shows you where opportunities for
refactoring typically can be found, and provides the proper training
that skilled system designers can use to rework a bad design into
well-designed, robust code.

For more information about these and other titles, please visit www.awprofessional.com

Code Smells

Smell	Refactoring
Alternative Classes with Different Interfaces (43) [F]	Unify Interfaces with Adapter (247)
Combinatorial Explosion (45)	Replace Implicit Language with Interpreter (269)
Conditional Complexity (41)	Replace Conditional Logic with Strategy (129) Move Embellishment to Decorator (144) Replace State-Altering Conditionals with State (166) Introduce Null Object (301)
Duplicated Code (39) [F]	Form Template Method (205) Introduce Polymorphic Creation with Factory Method (88) Chain Constructors (340) Replace One/Many Distinctions with Composite (224) Extract Composite (214) Unify Interfaces with Adapter (247) Introduce Null Object (301)
Indecent Exposure (42)	Encapsulate Classes with Factory (80)
Large Class (44) [F]	Replace Conditional Dispatcher with Command (191) Replace State-Altering Conditionals with State (166) Replace Implicit Language with Interpreter (269)
Lazy Class (43) [F]	Inline Singleton (114)
Long Method (40) [F]	Compose Method (123) Move Accumulation to Collecting Parameter (313) Replace Conditional Dispatcher with Command (191) Move Accumulation to Visitor (320) Replace Conditional Logic with Strategy (129)
Oddball Solution (45)	Unify Interfaces with Adapter (247)
Primitive Obsession (41) [F]	Replace Type Code with Class (286) Replace State-Altering Conditionals with State (166) Replace Conditional Logic with Strategy (129) Replace Implicit Tree with Composite (178) Replace Implicit Language with Interpreter (269) Move Embellishment to Decorator (144) Encapsulate Composite with Builder (96)
Solution Sprawl (43)	Move Creation Knowledge to Factory (68)
Switch Statements (44) [F]	Replace Conditional Dispatcher with Command (191) Move Accumulation to Visitor (320)